Breaking the War Habit

CHILDREN
YOUTH+WAR

Breaking the War Habit

THE DEBATE OVER MILITARISM IN AMERICAN EDUCATION

Seth Kershner

Scott Harding

Charles Howlett

The University of Georgia Press

ATHENS

© 2022 by the University of Georgia Press
Athens, Georgia 30602
www.ugapress.org
All rights reserved
Designed by Kaelin Chappell Broaddus
Set in 10.5/13.5 Garamond Premier Pro
by Kaelin Chappell Broaddus

Most University of Georgia Press titles are
available from popular e-book vendors.

Printed digitally

Library of Congress Cataloging-in-Publication Data
Names: Kershner, Seth, author. | Harding, Scott,
author. | Howlett, Charles F., author.
Title: Breaking the war habit : the debate over militarism in American
education / Seth Kershner, Scott Harding, Charles Howlett.
Description: Athens : The University of Georgia Press, [2022] |
Series: Children youth + war | Includes bibliographical references and index.
Identifiers: LCCN 2021060248 | ISBN 9780820362212 (hardback) |
ISBN 9780820362229 (paperback) | ISBN 9780820362236 (ebook)
Subjects: LCSH: United States. Army. Reserve Officers' Training Corps.
| United States. Army. Junior ROTC | Committee on Militarism in
Education (U.S.) | Military education—United States—History. |
War and education—United States—History. | Militarism—United
States—History. | Education and state—United States—History.
| Civil-military relations—United States—History. | United
States—Armed Forces—Recruiting, enlistment, etc.—History.
Classification: LCC U428.5 .K47 2022 | DDC
355.2/232071173—dc23/eng/20220119
LC record available at https://lccn.loc.gov/2021060248

CONTENTS

CONTENTS

ACKNOWLEDGMENTS

One of the rewards of completing a book is the opportunity to thank those who contributed to its realization. At the University of Georgia Press, James Marten, editor of the Children, Youth, and War series, and press editors Jon Davies, Mick Gusinde-Duffy, and Beth Snead have been patient in their work on the manuscript. Special thanks to copy editor Polly Kummel, who has seen us through the final stages of the project with insight, kindness, and patience.

We also are indebted to the many activists who discussed their lives and experiences while they were engaged in counter-recruitment. We are especially grateful to Rick Jahnkow for helping to arrange interviews with counter-recruiters in California and elsewhere, and for allowing us to consult materials from his personal archive.

During our research we relied on terrific librarians and staff at the Swarthmore College Peace Collection; Chicago History Museum; New York State Archives; City of Portland Archives; Seeley G. Mudd Manuscript Library at Princeton University; M. E. Grenander Department of Special Collections & Archives at the University at Albany; Thomas J. Dodd Research Center at the University of Connecticut; and Special Collections and University Archives at the University of Massachusetts, Amherst.

We also benefited enormously from the advice and guidance of colleagues, including Larry Wittner, Scott Bennett, Mike Clinton, Deborah Buffton, Heather Fryer, and Wendy Chmielewski. All have made valuable contributions to the flourishing field of peace history. Our intellectual debts to them and other members of the Peace History Society will, we trust, be obvious in the pages that follow.

Some parts of the book have drawn upon articles published earlier. All of the previously published material has been substantially rewritten and revised. The articles include the following: Seth Kershner, "'The New Beachhead Is in Secondary Education': Campaigns against Junior ROTC in Baltimore," *Peace & Change* 42, no. 3 (2017): 436–464; and Seth Kershner, "The Soldier as Super-Citizen: A Successful Activist-Scholar Collaboration to Challenge the JROTC," *Fellowship* (Winter 2011): 32–33.

ABBREVIATIONS

ACLU	American Civil Liberties Union
AFL	American Federation of Labor
AFSC	American Friends Service Committee
ASVAB	Armed Services Vocational Aptitude Battery
CCCO	Central Committee for Conscientious Objectors
CME	Committee on Militarism in Education
CPU	Church Peace Union
CUNY	City University of New York
JROTC	Junior Reserve Officers' Training Corps
NCDOS	National Campaign to Demilitarize Our Schools
NEA	National Education Association
ROTC	Reserve Officers' Training Corps
TFORM	Task Force on Recruitment and Militarism
WILPF	Women's International League for Peace and Freedom
WRL	War Resisters League

Breaking the War Habit

INTRODUCTION

In 1926 a striking editorial appeared in the *Army and Navy Register* establishing the battle lines between opponents of militarism in education and those strongly endorsing it. "You must admit," the essay began, "that the ROTC must keep pushing hard to keep the naturally pacific mind of America from becoming pacifist.... Young men of this country are naturally conservative and conventional, not radical in their opinions." Playing on such sentiment, defenders of the program noted self-righteously that only "if we had compulsory military training and a conscription system, we could park our spurs on our desks and let the citizens go hang.... But with a voluntary training system, we need the limelight. Our staid and unattractive work needs to be brought to popular attention, and, indeed, the best way to bring anything to the attention of the public is to start a fight about it."[1] It turned out to be quite a fight, one pitting the determination of advocates for peace and justice against a powerful, entrenched American military establishment.

The analysis that follows provides the first historical account of challenges raised to the military's influence in U.S. colleges and schools. It traces the history of opposition to the Reserve Officers' Training Corps (ROTC) and Junior Reserve Officers' Training Corps (JROTC); that history took on added weight after the First World War, as an emerging movement sought to curb the growing influence of military recruiters on high school campuses. It is a fascinating, hidden story of the prolonged, uphill struggle of peace activists trying to prevent establishment of a military mindset in a country whose Founders warned of such perils.

Historians have rarely addressed this topic, and little scholarship exists on the campaign against militarism in education. Yet the decades-long struggle to prevent the military from infiltrating and influencing public education has much to teach. Chronicling the way a diverse array of Americans—clergy, women, socialists, veterans, leaders of peace organizations (the spearhead of the campaign), and teachers—have debated ROTC over the years reveals much about Americans' changing attitudes toward the armed forces. The virtues of military training in high schools and colleges are now so widely accepted, it is easy to overlook just how controversial the subject was before World War II. When the military first introduced ROTC on a wide scale in the early 1920s, educators opposed it on the ground that it was incompatible with schooling in a democratic society. Far from fostering independent thinking, tolerance, and cooperation—key values for an emerging progressive public education—critics contended that ROTC would promote the militarization of American society.

But this is not just the story about challenging ROTC and JROTC, programs with a long-standing foothold in the U.S. educational system. It is also about the power the military exerts when seeking high school graduates, especially from poor and minority communities, to fulfill its recruitment quotas in the all-volunteer military. Peace activists and opponents of militarism in education have thus faced long odds in trying to convince the public of the virtue of their cause, and few readers know the full story.

What is apparent is that the U.S. military has an outsized role in a democratic society and strongly influences how Americans conduct their lives. Indeed, the military force is the largest and best equipped in the world, with about two million enlisted service members and an annual budget exceeding $700 billion. Typically depicted as preserving democracy, the U.S. military maintains a global network of bases that house thousands of U.S. troops.[2] But according to Cynthia Enloe, the well-known expert on militarism, this conventional picture of the U.S. military overlooks one essential fact. "Militaries," she observes, are "fragile and contingent" and "are not automatically raised or sustained, not easily mobilized or deployed."[3] "Fragile and contingent" is a description that does not normally come to mind in reference to the armed forces in late capitalist societies. But consider that the Pentagon currently spends about $1.4 billion per year on recruiting and hundreds of millions annually on other marketing initiatives intended to convince the public to enlist—costly efforts to ensure a steady stream of new soldiers each year.[4] The most important part of this effort is the Pentagon's decades-long drive to win over the teenage mind by establishing a beachhead in American high schools and colleges.

The military's integration into schools is of enormous importance to its goal of enlisting approximately two hundred thousand new volunteer recruits a year. The army's *Recruiter Handbook* notes that "no other segment of the community network has as much impact on recruiting as schools."[5] In fact, school militarism in the United States is a highly structured comprehensive system, a cornucopia of initiatives drawing on a mixture of local, state, and federal support. The most important aspect of this is military recruiters' physical access to students. Since 2002 federal law has required U.S. public high schools to allow recruiters direct access to campus and student contact information. Schools that do not comply risk losing valuable federal funding. Consequently, military recruiters make weekly visits at high schools across the United States to set up information tables, volunteer to coach sports, and deliver guest lectures to history classes—all in a bid to achieve what the U.S. Army refers to as "school ownership." Army Recruiting Command documents that we obtained under the Freedom of Information Act show that recruiters visit some high schools as often as a hundred times in a 180-day school year.[6]

ROTC has been a presence on U.S. college campuses since its creation in 1916, although the teaching of military tactics at public universities has a longer history. About seventeen hundred institutions of higher education across the country now offer the officer training program. In return for scholarship money and graduating college as commissioned officers, participating students practice military exercises and maneuvers (commonly referred to simply as "drill"), complete an annual summer training program, and learn about military history and other specialized subjects. The Pentagon prizes the ROTC program as a means of cultivating the next generation of military leadership. For the army, the largest branch of the U.S. military, ROTC represents the greatest single source of newly commissioned officers.[7]

Support for the program cuts across the political spectrum. Barack Obama praised ROTC when running for president in 2008. A report from the politically centrist Center for a New American Security cast ROTC as the "natural bridge" needed to overcome the "growing familiarity gap between society and the military." In 2011 the conservative American Enterprise Institute weighed in with its recommendation to bring more ROTC programs to New York City. The institute suggested that ROTC "plays an invaluable role as a source of competent military officers and leaders for the armed forces" and that the military could benefit from engaging with the Big Apple's diverse student population.[8]

The Pentagon commits nearly $400 million annually to sustain a high school version of the ROTCprogram. Since the early 1970s, more cadets have enrolled in JROTC than in the college-level program. JROTC currently has a presence in nearly thirty-three hundred high schools in the United States, enrolling more than 550,000 students (known as "cadets"), who are as young as fourteen. In addition to training in drill and taking courses in military science, some JROTC cadets also practice marksmanship with air rifles at on-campus firing ranges. While the military is forthright about seeing ROTC's value chiefly in terms of its ability to generate new officers, Pentagon planners strenuously deny that JROTC is geared toward making youth interested in military careers. Instead, as one U.S. Army commander recently claimed, the JROTC is designed as a "leadership and citizenship program." However, the Pentagon's own surveys show that nearly 40 percent of students who spend at least three years of high school in JROTC end up joining the military.[9]

Critics cite the disproportionately high number of youth of color enrolled in JROTC and the presence of military-training programs in cities—where one in four high schools has a JROTC unit—to suggest that JROTC and other forms of school militarism constitute a school-to-military pipeline for economically disadvantaged youth.[10] As Lesley Bartlett and Catherine Lutz observe, advocates of JROTC have long engaged in racially coded discourse, casting the military program as a way to control immigrant youth and other marginalized groups. Former Chicago mayor Richard Daley Jr. illustrated this tendency when he wrote that JROTC "provides students with the order and discipline that is too often lacking at home. It teaches them time management, responsibility, goal setting, and teamwork, and it builds leadership and self-confidence."[11] Supporters of the program have also argued that JROTC offers an antidote to a range of urban ills and a pathway to social mobility.

These sentiments suggest that schools and students both stand to profit from participation in military programming. Donald Downs of the University of Wisconsin, for example, claims that a "gulf between the military and the university is not healthy for American democracy." Downs specifically identifies ROTC as the medicine needed to restore universities to a healthier balance.[12] Indeed, tangible and intangible benefits are associated with ROTC: branches of the military gain a reliable stream of educated officers, and cadets get an assist on their way to completing college and entering the armed forces. Similarly, high school cadets value the camaraderie of participating in a physically active and fun group activity; they can also receive scholarship money if they wish to continue with ROTC in college. But a contrary view of school-based military programs is also deeply rooted in U.S. society.

Origins of Opposition before World War I

Opposition to militarism in schools dates to the 1830s, when the educational reformer Horace Mann insisted that schoolchildren learn that war is not heroic and demanded that history textbooks devote less attention to the subject. "What can save us, and our children after us, from eternal, implacable, universal war," Mann wondered, "but the greatest of all human powers—the power of impartial thought?" The issue of war, he strongly believed, "will never be settled, until we have a generation of men who are educated, from childhood, to seek for truth and to revere justice." In numerous lectures and essays, Mann, who later represented Massachusetts in Congress, condemned the art of war and questioned the need for huge military expenditures. He advocated that future generations be "educated to that strength of intellect which shall dispel the insane illusions of martial glory."[13]

The advent of the American Civil War in 1861, however, undermined Mann's views. By then the martial spirit had penetrated all aspects of society, in both North and South. In the South a strong military tradition was deeply rooted in civic virtue and preserving the peculiar institution of slavery. A military education, instantiated by such venerable institutions as the Virginia Military Institute and the Citadel, stood as a shining example of Southern valor and honor. The Southern aristocracy thus long considered obtaining a military education or serving in the army a rite of passage for its children.

In both the North and South the war profoundly influenced colleges and secondary schools. According to the educational historian Lawrence Cremin, the psychological effects were enormous. "For those who did not go off to war," he found, "there were drills, rallies, patriotic observances, and a curriculum considerably constricted, on the one hand by disloyalty (loyalty oaths were widely applied during the war years) and, on the other hand, by the general scattering of expertise." Even the "novel experience of conscription," he notes, "may have been the most significant and portentous educational development to be associated with the war; for it brought citizens into an educational relationship with government that was new and untried." In the second half of the nineteenth century, patriotic organizations and local community groups pushed for military drill in schools, an effort that emanated from the threat and subsequent reality of the Civil War because they considered drill a worthwhile educational mechanism for instilling loyalty: in the North for preserving and strengthening national unity; in the South to prove that its inhabitants were more patriotic than their Northern counterparts.[14]

Despite the lingering effects of the Civil War's martial enthusiasm, however, most public schools did not establish cadet corps for boys before World War I; those that did relied on regimentation, obedience, and loyalty. The most common argument deployed to sustain these programs was the need to create physically fit males and the importance of physical education classes for sound mind and sound body. Young boys also found it hard to resist the lure of wearing a uniform, marching in parades with a wooden rifle, and earning ribbons. School boards and parents who supported cadet corps did so out of a sense of duty and patriotism. Schoolteachers struggled to condemn these programs, especially if they could be used to address behavioral problems among recalcitrant boys; the disciplinary components of drill and taking orders also proved useful as urban school districts were swelling with immigrant youth in need of direction and purpose in their new homeland. Many young boys also found it hard to resist the call to duty and, if trained properly, a future military career with leadership perks. Boys who joined these cadet corps liked the physical training and wearing uniforms. Given that most school districts did not have established sports programs until the end of the nineteenth century, the cadet corps also served as a viable after-school activity. Patriotic organizations and military officials supporting drill in schools neatly camouflaged it as physical education, which appeased concerned parents.

Nevertheless, when the war ended in 1865 and reconstruction of the South began, Mann's vision persisted despite a lingering glorification of war as a patriotic endeavor. Keeping Mann's vision alive in the second half of the nineteenth century was Alfred Love. A Quaker woolens merchant from Philadelphia, Love became titular head of the newly formed Universal Peace Union (UPU), a radical pacifist organization that stood in stark contrast to the more established and conservative American Peace Society. Between 1866 and 1913, UPU actively promoted a wide variety of peace methods, including disarmament, arbitration, and calls for amending the U.S. Constitution to abolish the federal government's ability to wage war and to challenge the glorification of militarism in all aspects of society.[15]

Accompanying UPU's ambitious efforts was its ongoing campaign to confront military drill in the curriculum for high school boys. "Much attention was given in the publications of the Union to the goal of pacifist education," according to the historian Peter Brock. "No corporal punishment in home or school, no military drill in school or college, no warlike playthings for the young were to be permitted; the war spirit was to be expunged from school textbooks," he added. Adhering to these strict standards would further reinforce the Union's basic aim of remolding society "in a spirit of Christian love and human brotherhood . . . along with the achievement of social justice within the nation."[16]

Throughout numerous resolutions, annual reports, and its periodicals, including *Bond of Peace* and *Peacemaker*, the Universal Peace Union warned against the "'science of arms' among youth; the establishment of military academies; and the introduction of military professorships into public schools" because they "sowed the seeds of future wars, and contributed to make us a nation of warriors." A principle essential to the organization's mission was teaching children the importance of peace and justice; the UPU deemed training boys in military drill to be contrary to this goal. Throughout UPU's existence it continually battled against all forms of military training in schools. The group also circulated numerous petitions urging the federal government to shutter West Point or, at the very least, convert its curriculum to constructive ends in the name of social justice and community building.[17]

Mann's view and Love's actions held sway among supporters of peace throughout the latter half of the nineteenth century, especially when it came to opposing military drill in schools. Thus, during America's formative years, opponents of militarism and empire fought to maintain the integrity of an expanding public education system. Even events of the 1890s—marked by business expansion into overseas markets, imperialistic plans to expand the country's global reach, and patriotic organizations' promotion of military drill in schools—proved futile when trying to silence peace activists.

The leading female peace activist of the time, Hannah J. Bailey, and the Peace and Arbitration Department of her Woman's Christian Temperance Union (WCTU) undertook one of the more notable efforts to resist introduction of a military presence into the nation's schools. Bailey was motivated in part by a noticeable reactionary movement within America's rural communities. The rising tide of immigration from foreign shores and emergence of an urban-industrial society was greeted with suspicion that they threatened the long-cherished ideals of an agrarian way of life. Public schools were considered a necessary mechanism for Americanizing immigrant children and protecting native-born children from foreign and radical views that would undermine the republic. "Anxious Americans," the historian Robert Wiebe astutely notes, "looked to their schools as a bulwark of local defense, with increasing numbers insisting that public education infuse a new strength, a new cohesion, into the threatened community." By the mid-1890s patriotic organizations like the Grand Army of the Republic began to see the public schools as a way to amplify their glorification of war and military service. In such an environment, Wiebe continues, schools "would simply have to inculcate [their] youth with pure narrow truth." Promoting military drill in schools, Bailey argued, would become one of those unpleasant mechanisms for furthering "pure narrow truth." Thus a program of peace education in schools was desperately needed to offset this threat.[18]

This concern grew more urgent by the turn of the new century as the children of immigrants enrolled in public schools in growing numbers. The situation was especially acute in New York City, a major port of entry that saw tens of thousands of immigrants pour into the city. From 1899 to 1914 the school system experienced a 60 percent increase in student enrollment. Accompanying construction of new schools to ease overcrowded classes was a growing awareness that schools were necessary for integrating the immigrant child into American society. The push for Americanization accompanied a desire for social control. The principal of DeWitt Clinton High School in the Bronx, where teachers would lose their jobs during World War I for criticizing U.S. involvement in the conflict, summed up this sentiment. "The nation has a right to demand intelligence and virtue of every citizen," the principal wrote in 1902, "and to obtain these by force if necessary." Encouraging military drill in schools became a key means for achieving that goal.[19]

Bailey's peace advocacy coincided with what many historians have considered a golden age of internationalism that gave rise to new forms of global cooperation in communications, commerce, and law before the First World War. An international movement for peace evolved, one that welcomed the efforts of social reformers, industrialists, peace activists, workers, and political figures eager to participate in the creation of a humane and secure world order. Much of the attention devoted to peace in the 1890s and early 1900s emphasized the importance of arbitration and international conciliation. Bailey added to this discussion with her appeal that school militarism would hurt the cause of world peace.

Bailey's efforts laid a path for other reformers to address problems associated with military drill in schools. She took the lead in challenging the equation of patriotism with manliness and militarism. In 1893 the Grand Army of the Republic endorsed military instruction in public education as a means for improving national defense by developing a ready-made pool of qualified soldiers. Former president Benjamin Harrison spoke favorably of the plan: "The military taste and training acquired in the school will carry our best young men into the militia organizations, and make those organizations reliable conservators of public order, and ready and competent defenders of the national honor." Bailey and the WCTU promptly criticized Harrison, arguing that such "taste and training" would lead to a false impression among children about the benefits of military service. Her organization also insisted that the Grand Army of the Republic's endorsement of military drill represented a clear path toward the creation of a large standing army, which violated long-held American views regarding civil-military relations and threatened cherished democratic liberties.[20]

The Woman's Christian Temperance Union established musical ensembles, known as peace bands, for children and worked zealously "to convince mothers of the danger and inconsistence [*sic*] of placing military toys, pictures, etc., in the hands of children." In Bailey's view "the most important work which has been or is being accomplished by our department, is that bearing directly upon the training of children . . . [through] military drill in public schools." Most certainly, Bailey argued, it was time "to see the end of military education for children, and we

hope the time is not far distant when the war stories which now have a place in
the books which our children read and study will be expunged, and their places
occupied with stories and incidents written in the interests of peace and peaceful
pursuits."[21]

Almost Becoming Mainstream

There were other notable examples of opposition to military drill during this period. In 1895, during a decade of rising U.S. global expansionism, the New York
State Legislature approved a bill authorizing military training in public schools,
but the governor refused to sign it. A similar attempt also failed in Pennsylvania,
where organized labor joined hands with peace advocates to defeat the measure.
In Ohio, labor unions were equally outspoken in their condemnation of military
training in public schools. At its September 9, 1895, meeting in Cincinnati, Federal Labor Union No. 5335 passed a resolution stating: "We deem a military training in public schools and especially as it is in vogue in this City, dangerous to the
youth, and not in any sense a healthy physical training; but as creating dissention
and widening the gulf between classes."[22] The union resolved to protest any expen-
diture that would pay for military drill in the public schools.

Why were unions opposed to such militarizing practices in secondary education? As we describe in chapter 1, labor organizations and their allies on the Left
saw military drill as an effort to convert youth into future strikebreakers. The
post–Civil War period had seen periodic uprisings of labor militancy, such as
the 1877 national railroad strike. These rebellions often came in response to economic slumps, but employers usually had an easy time regaining control because
of the superior resources at their disposal—including the ability to turn militia
and police against strikers.[23] At the earliest stage of this militancy, employers' efforts were crude and often involved the use of brute force to intimidate strikers
and discourage workers from collective action. In 1894 labor unions and their allies were horrified when President Grover Cleveland dispatched twelve thousand
federal troops to end a strike by Pullman railroad car workers. Thus the actions by
labor federations in Ohio and Pennsylvania in 1895 were understandably driven
by fears that military drill in school would normalize this kind of violent response
by the state and turn youth into obedient tools of the capitalist class.

Other organizations voiced their opposition to school militarism as well. In
November 1895 the American Peace Society's journal, the *Advocate of Peace*, editorialized against "this military craze" and noted that the "American People are
opposed, as a whole, to the militarizing of the youth of the country." The editorial
concluded with an expression of hope that other states would follow the example

of New York and Pennsylvania "in refusing to listen to those who would foist in
upon us the war-institutions of the Old World."[24]

Such sentiment held sway in the early years of the new century, though that
would change with the outbreak of war in Europe in 1914. Public opposition to
military drill in schools and colleges shifted dramatically as preparedness advocates in the United States ramped up efforts for a broad program to instill the
martial spirit in American education. This effort intensified once the United
States entered the war in 1917. From that point forward, the military would begin its long march toward becoming an accepted part of the nation's educational
landscape.

Book Overview

In what follows we trace the history of opposition to the military's presence in
American schools and colleges. To tell this story we draw on oral history interviews; deep engagement with the periodicals published by the pacifist, socialist,
and labor press; and archival research at sites across the United States. In chapter 1
we chart the rise of military training in schools and colleges in the United States,
which was accompanied by growing concerns about militarism from clergy, labor, and other groups. Chapters 2 and 3 focus on a scrappy band of activists, the
Committee on Militarism in Education (CME), and highlight its outsize influence on elected officials and public opinion during the 1920s and 1930s. Although
World War II snuffed out the organization amid the national mobilization for
war, CME's legacy is visible today in the equally plucky movement of counter-
recruiters—the parents, veterans, and peace activists scattered across the United
States who are seeking to curb the military presence in schools.

Chapters 4 to 6 illustrate how a small but sophisticated movement to counter
the recruiters, beginning in the 1970s, raised awareness of the myriad ways that the
Pentagon has infiltrated all levels of public education—what we refer to as *school
militarism*. Whether resisting JROTC, establishing rules for military (aptitude)
testing in public high schools, or limiting military recruiters' visits to high schools,
the countermovement has been surprisingly successful. Working with limited
funds and personnel, the antimilitarists have helped delegitimize JROTC, publicly questioned the rosy narratives that military recruiters sell to teenagers, and secured state laws curbing military influence in high schools. Since the movement
arose in the early 1970s, its strategy and tactics for countering recruiters have remained similar to those used in the 1920s and 1930s by the CME: lobbying elected
officials; using the media to publicize the antimilitarists' aims and make visible an

issue that is too often ignored; and researching the issue of school militarism with the aid of sympathetic allies in education.

Throughout more than one hundred years of activism, those struggling against school militarism have also been consistent in the way they frame their efforts. CME organizers of the 1920s believed that by lessening the military's influence in education, they could help Americans break the ideological underpinnings of America's "war habit"; decades later, activists believed that countering recruiters was a way to challenge the social and institutional foundations for a nation constantly at war. Because educational values have been a central concern motivating anti-ROTC forces, we explore how they have understood and enacted different visions of education—particularly public education—in a democratic society, and we ground these understandings in the historical context of national politics at the time.

We start by illustrating how the idea of ROTC emerged after the Spanish-American War, which taught U.S. military leaders that they would need a continual supply of officers to lead imperial ventures. In chapter 1 we also unearth the early years of opposition to ROTC. The carnage of the First World War raised the awareness of teachers and students, citizens and clergy, and made them particularly sensitive to the way that school militarism had laid the foundation for war since the turn of the century. Americans opposing ROTC during the war years took particular umbrage at the widespread practice of compulsory enrollment of male students in ROTC at publicly funded, land-grant institutions.

Before 1916, when Congress created ROTC and Junior ROTC, high school militarism existed at a lower level, enabled by a patchwork of state laws concerning military drill and other forms of martial exercise for schoolboys. The preparedness movement that preceded U.S. entry into World War I encouraged Congress to create ROTC. Chapter 1 describes the first major protests against school militarism, which were led by Jewish and socialist-inspired students. By 1920 educators, socialists, and labor activists were carefully framing their arguments in an attempt to steer public opinion against school militarism. Writing in pacifist magazines and small-circulation church-based weeklies, they opposed ROTC on the ground that it was incompatible with schooling in a democratic society.

Chapter 2 depicts the establishment in the 1920s of what would become the leading advocacy group opposing school militarism, the Committee on Militarism in Education. Primary source materials pertaining to the committee's ideology and motivations to abolish compulsory military training in U.S. colleges and public high schools help illustrate CME's organizing efforts during the 1920s. Among the committee's most well-known advocates was John Dewey, the Columbia University philosopher recognized as the godfather of progressive education in America. Along with other leading educators, Dewey feared that military training in high schools would stimulate the growth of the martial values of obedience to authority, thus impeding teachers' efforts to encourage in youth a capacity for critical and creative thought. The chapter also notes other nationally recognized CME supporters, including the social worker Jane Addams, founder of the Settlement House movement; and Reinhold Niebuhr, one of the country's best-known Protestant pastors. In a context of widespread (and often hysterical) anti-communism, proponents of military drill sought to destabilize their critics with red-baiting, surveillance, and other controversial tactics.

Chapter 3 examines the CME's prominent national and local campaigns. The committee was active nationally in lobbying to pass federal legislation opposing compulsory ROTC and challenging mandatory drill in the courts on behalf of college students who were conscientious objectors. We also explore CME's propaganda efforts, including its newsletter, *Breaking the War Habit*, and other efforts aimed at shaping public opinion and supporting state and federal legislation to ban compulsory ROTC on college campuses. CME's research on school militarism proved influential; it included the first analysis of how various ROTC units carried out their mission and how Junior ROTC affected the educational curriculum for boys of high-school age. The chapter also describes successful demilitarization efforts at Ohio State University and other college campuses.

Amid growing conflict in Europe and gradual American preparations for war, CME eventually dissolved. Efforts by Quakers and others to oppose ROTC during the McCarthy era, an inauspicious time to be an antimilitarist, were mostly unsuccessful, and campaigns against ROTC were effectively dormant until the 1960s. Anti-ROTC organizing experienced a heyday during the Vietnam War, when campus activism erupted across the United States and contributed to a sharp decline in ROTC enrollment. Chapter 4 begins with an analysis of how ROTC became a focus of the anti–Vietnam War movement. Yet as activists aimed their anti-ROTC organizing at universities, few paid attention to the Pentagon's increasing attempts to strengthen the *high school* version of the program. We assess legislation in the 1960s that moved JROTC into the mainstream of American public education, noting how these efforts faced little opposition, even from most teachers. In response antimilitarists—following CME's organizing playbook—formed grassroots groups to educate the public and prevent JROTC from turning high school students into what *Ramparts* magazine called "teenie militarists."[25]

Although one of the country's oldest pacifist organizations, Fellowship of Reconciliation, undertook to revive the CME in the late 1970s, this effort proved futile. Instead, counter-recruitment and anti-JROTC activists created a more durable coalition, the Task Force on Recruitment and Militarism, which operated during the 1970s. Throughout the decade organizers successfully exploited the cultural upheaval generated by the Vietnam War to push for widespread acceptance of their antimilitarist agenda. By the end of the 1970s they had formed strategic alliances with the faith community, members of Congress, and the press and were on the cusp of delivering a decisive blow to school militarism. Along the way they broadened their work in response to ever-multiplying forms of school militarism. In chapter 4 we profile the unlikely collaboration between a Republican member of Congress and Quaker pacifists to rein in the Pentagon's high school "vocational testing" program.

Yet the expanding activist networks, clergy and congressional allies, and sympathetic media coverage were not enough to dampen the resurgent American patriotism that led to a major expansion of JROTC in the 1980s. Amid a renewed cultural embrace of militarism, anti-ROTC campaigns at colleges were rare during the Reagan era. Organizers instead focused on high school militarism. Yet shifting cultural norms also made it difficult for counter-recruiters and others to challenge the military presence in high schools, especially when JROTC was typically framed in positive terms. A case study of a years-long anti-JROTC campaign in Baltimore proves instructive. Chapter 5 draws from archives and the mainstream and alternative press to show how Baltimore-area activists ultimately failed to prevent establishment of the JROTC because their antimilitarist, ideological messages did not connect with pragmatic school board members and the local community. In other instances a weak economy and a changing public mood created challenges for those seeking to demilitarize public schools. Although the JROTC established a beachhead in Baltimore and other parts of the country, local organizing—led by the American Friends Service Committee—represents an important phase in the history of the post-Vietnam peace movement.

The 1990s witnessed the growing importance of national networks to those opposed to the military presence in high schools. The National Campaign to Demilitarize Our Schools (NCDOS) emerged after the Gulf War as the first truly national clearinghouse for efforts to counter militarism since the days of the CME. The 1990s were fertile times for this activism, after Congress in 1992 doubled the number of JROTC units allowed under federal law. Activists affiliated with NCDOS used their ties to the academy to produce a report that received national media coverage and led to revisions to the army's JROTC curriculum. Chapter 6 also explores how the 2003 Iraq War shaped public perceptions of school militarism as a problem, because the war increased interest and energy in countering recruitment.

In the conclusion we review the strategies that anti-ROTC campaigners used historically and analyze their influence. While acknowledging that ROTC can help deliver an affordable path to higher education and a military career for some, we consider the trade-offs involved in perpetuating the ROTC model. A contested topic for much of the twentieth century, school militarism today appears to be a largely forgotten issue. Indeed, with the seeming normalization and increased invisibility of U.S. "forever wars," the peace movement is relatively muted and anti-ROTC activism has become sporadic. As American society apparently makes peace with its militarized educational system, and as school and university stakeholders embrace their many pacts with the armed forces, we pose the inconvenient but necessary question: *At what cost?*

CHAPTER 1

Making Citizen Soldiers

As armed conflict raged in Europe, military officials and other prominent members of American society began beating the drums of war. War preparedness fell heavily upon the American educational system. By early 1917 Americans saw schools as particularly important to national defense and were quickly co-opted into this endeavor. U.S. participation in the Great War demanded conformity in all segments of the community. For that to succeed all teachers and students would have to fall in line and support President Woodrow Wilson's call for a war to end all wars and make the world safe for democracy. Generally, this was an easy sell as school districts throughout the nation willingly bought in.

The historian Stephan Brumberg has found that preparation for war had an immediate effect on New York City public schools, the nation's largest school system. Teachers and school facilities were swept up in the campaign to conduct a census of the city's draft-age men and register those aged twenty-one to thirty-one for the military draft. "Not a single school building could escape some level of involvement in war work," Brumberg concluded, after reviewing reams of reports filed by the board of education. A year before, in 1916, the New York State Legislature had passed a law, known as the Slater Bill, that mandated three hours of weekly extracurricular training for all males aged sixteen to nineteen who were enrolled in school.[1]

But some students in Brooklyn were having none of it. A majority of students at Eastern District High School, located in the borough's Williamsburg neighborhood, were Jewish, and many of their parents had immigrated from eastern Europe. When a reporter visited in January 1917, he found the walls of the school covered in placards opposed to military training. One "erudite youngster" who showed "signs of membership in the debating team" gave this reason for why he so firmly opposed military training: "War is hell. Preparedness is for war. Military training is for preparedness." Yet not all students at Eastern District High were pacifists. "If we want to train, we will join the army," another youth proposed, suggesting that he thought schools were simply not the appropriate place for learning military drill. When a reporter questioned students' loyalty to their country, one boy replied: "We're just as patriotic as the others are who are always shouting for war. . . . If there is danger of an attack, then we would join a regiment as quickly, if not more so, than the shouters."[2]

Of the school's roughly fifteen hundred students, only a few dozen showed up for military training exercises that winter. This level of resistance, which came despite the urging of the principal and physical education director, was far from unusual in New York City schools at the time. Because the Slater Bill contained no penalties for noncompliance, implementation was spotty. While average student attendance at military training was between 40 and 50 percent, as the board of education reported in March 1918, it fell as low as 2 percent in some of the city's high schools. Even with a report noting that the training was "admittedly unpopular," board members felt a "moral obligation" to find some way to force student compliance with any law related to military activities. Thus they passed a new policy, effective in April 1918, to make participation in military training a graduation requirement. Before this took effect, however, a further wave of protests—led, once again, by Jewish students—roiled city schools during the 1917–18 school year. Although these demonstrations often targeted other issues—notably, a disruptive school reorganization plan—students also criticized the military training regimen.[3]

While these youthful protesters were probably not aware of it at the time, their rejection of school militarism was part of a long American tradition of opposition to military meddling in civil affairs. Indeed, concerns about civil-military relations in the United States date to the American Revolution. A significant legacy of that revolt was the mutual suspicion of civilians and the military. According to the historian Arthur A. Ekirch Jr., new state constitutions customarily contained language expressing the perspectives of the Founders. These included the fear of standing armies in time of peace; a belief in the superiority of civil, not military, authority; and the right to be free from the housing of troops in private dwellings. When the Articles of Confederation proved ineffective in uniting the thirteen independent colonies, the Constitution that replaced it embodied such antimilitaristic principles.[4]

The Constitution sought to limit the possibility of military domination of U.S. society by enforcing a separation of powers in all questions of peace and war. Only Congress would have the power to declare war, troops were not to be housed with citizens in time of peace, and the civilian arm of the government was to control the army. The president, a civilian, was to be its commander in chief, and Congress was to renew military appropriations each year. Thus the Declaration of Independence established the basis for a subsequent body of laws that affirmed the belief that military rule was at odds with the ideals of a democratic society. Individual freedom, representative government, and limits on the powers of the national state and executive were seen as principles that would be endangered if military authority were to take precedence in civil affairs. Many key figures—James Madison regarded a standing army as "one of the greatest mischiefs that can possibly happen"—embraced these ideals, as legislated in the Constitution and codified in the Bill of Rights.[5]

Military Training in Schools and Colleges before World War I

Although an indigenous strain of antimilitarism flowed through the new nation, prominent Americans also worried about the perceived dangers of a military establishment that they regarded as remote and alienated from civilian affairs. In part, the military's construction and financing of its own schools to train officers fostered this concern. As Donald Downs and Ilia Murtazashvili observe, the idea for military training in higher education grew out of this uneasiness and spurred the formation of civilian military colleges in the early nineteenth century. The need to supply the Union Army with officers during the Civil War led to a milestone in the history of military education, the Land-Grant College Act of 1862, better known as the Morrill Act. It provided subsidies and federal land to states for the purpose of creating colleges but required that these "land-grant" institutions also establish military training programs for male students. At first, instruction in military tactics was limited in scale, and many students did not take it seriously. Most trainees simply went through the motions with little or no desire for a military career. Usually a faculty member who had once served in the military was responsible for teaching courses, but few uniforms were available, equipment was inferior, and the syllabus was meager.[6]

In 1866, at the start of Reconstruction, Congress passed legislation instructing the War Department to deploy regular army officers to land-grant colleges that had an enrollment of at least 150 male students. Conscious of the politics governing civil-military relations, Congress capped the number of army officers assigned to this duty at twenty; they were distributed across the United States based on population. In 1876, as enrollments at land-grant colleges increased, Congress expanded the number of army officers assigned to this duty. Further legislation was approved in September 1888, with a decided twist. It authorized the president to order military officers to serve as professors of military science at civil institutions that were not land-grant colleges. This was a crucial development: the War Department seemed determined to participate in the civilian educational life of the country. Five years later, in 1893, seventy-nine U.S. colleges and universities offered military instruction, varying by state and institution as to whether it was mandatory or voluntary for male students.[7]

While federal funding for high school military programs had to wait until World War I, the programs themselves date to the Civil War. In 1863 a petition reached the Boston school committee asking that it introduce a program of "military gymnastics" for young men. The committee agreed, apparently persuaded by the petitioners' claim that such instruction would fortify both young bodies and the nation's defenses. Although school-based military drill was not popular at the time, Boston was one of several cities to provide this instruction to some of its students.

In the late nineteenth century, Civil War veterans often supervised military drill programs for high schoolers. Cities like Gloucester, Massachusetts; Hartford, Connecticut; and Washington, D.C., used municipal funds to purchase the equipment needed for so-called cadet corps. Military programs for high school students were informal and generally confined to after-school hours, and the number of youth involved was relatively small. By the turn of the century, fewer than 5 percent of American high schools gave students an opportunity to partake in military drill.[8]

A Major Leap Forward: The National Defense Act of 1916

Military training in schools and colleges took a major leap forward in the second decade of the twentieth century. The emergence of the United States as a world power, and the difficulty of raising a sufficient number of officers during the Spanish-American War, encouraged business leaders, military officials, and college presidents to support a program for commissioning reserve officers from the general populace. The World War I preparedness movement helped promote the arguments for military training of high school and college students. As it became apparent that war in Europe was inevitable, supporters of American military readiness became more vocal. The preparedness movement received an additional boost with the release in 1915 of such sensationalist texts as Bernard Walker's *America Fallen* and Hudson Maxim's *Defenseless America*. Maxim, whose brother invented the modern machine gun, painted a dark picture of how American men would have to surrender their wives and daughters to a voracious, conquering Imperial German Army. Such scare tactics made it easier for preparedness advocates to gain backing for their ideas, including the Reserve Officers' Training Corps.

Led by Major General Leonard Wood, the army chief of staff, the campaign for military training in schools portrayed the practice as a panacea, capable of cultivating patriotism, developing a sense of civic virtue, and improving the physical conditioning of male youth. Proponents argued that at a time of increasing immigration, society needed military training to tame social tensions, assimilate newcomers from foreign lands, and instill discipline and the "moral qualities of 'good citizenship'" in youth. In a 1916 speech to the National Education Association, Wood made clear why a leadership class that looked warily at the nation's growing immigrant population had embraced military training:

> What is needed is some kind of training which will put all classes which go to make up the mass which is bubbling in the American melting pot, shoulder to shoulder, living under exactly the same conditions, wearing the same uniform, and animated by a common purpose.... With this training will come a better physique, a greater degree of self-control, habits of regularity, promptness and thorones [sic], respect for law and the rights of others, and a sense of individual responsibility and obligation for service to the nation.

As well, supporters claimed that military drill in schools could teach the male immigrant the fine art of being a man. After all, as an editorial in *School Review* noted, American citizenship implied a "manly readiness to participate, if need be, in the defense of the nation." Secretary of War Newton D. Baker, writing in 1916, was even more emphatic, describing military training for youth as "the process by which boy-material is fashioned into manhood." But behind this rationale lay the core of the issue: school militarism would strengthen the nation's warfighting ability. "The solution of the problem of future military preparedness for our country," the head of the California National Guard declared, "is contained in the nation-wide adoption of the high-school cadet movement."[9]

In the wake of German military aggression, preparedness advocates such as former president Theodore Roosevelt and the banker J. P. Morgan, along with such patriotic organizations as the Navy League, persuaded Wilson to present his preparedness program to Congress. This led to passage of the 1916 National Defense Act and the subsequent 1920 National Defense Act, which together established what would become the Reserve Officers' Training Corps (ROTC), allowing Congress to fund the program on college and high school campuses. ROTC would include courses in military subjects, with weekly military drill instruction and a summer training component. Graduates of the college program would automatically receive a commission in the U.S. Army. An enticement for students was that some candidates would be eligible to apply for scholarships to their college or university, along with living expenses and additional stipends provided by the army when students enrolled in the advanced course. Such financial inducements doubtless motivated many young men to participate in ROTC.

Military officials and preparedness advocates also envisioned other ways of creating future officers. A year before the outbreak of World War I, Major General Wood established summer military training camps for college students. This initiative received support from college presidents, including H. S. Drinker of Lehigh University, who viewed the system of "students' military instruction camps" as a means of stimulating interest in and respect for military policy. After war broke out in Europe, these camps became the blueprint for the so-called Plattsburgh model of summer military training camps, established first at Plattsburgh, New York, before spreading to other parts of the country. Nearly thirteen thousand business and professional men participated in these camps. Lobbying by Wood, Teddy Roosevelt, and former secretary of war Elihu Root helped secure federal funding for the camps for the purpose of commissioning graduates in the army's newly established Officers' Reserve Corps.[10]

ROTC had little time to become established before the United States entered the war in 1917, and the army secured only half of the two hundred thousand officers it needed to lead its 3.5 million soldiers who fought in Europe. While ROTC may not have met the expectations of its proponents during this period, it contributed to the future militarization of U.S. society. The historian Charles Thwing observed that by 1918, with an ROTC curriculum prescribed by the War Department and patterned after that taken by junior officers in the regular army, civilian colleges had become "essentially military institutions," with students pursuing a "course of study which was either military or colored by military considerations."[11]

Though the high school component of ROTC could never compete with its college counterpart in terms of producing future officers, it served yet another role. Writing in *Infantry Journal*, Major William Edwards explained that the 1916 National Defense Act had two separate but equally important functions. "The first," Edwards noted, "is so obvious as to need no comment, that of training officers and men for the reserve forces; its second function, while no less important, is less apparent, and therefore sometimes overlooked entirely, that of training the popular public mind to the necessity and needs of defense." Edwards acknowledged that the Junior ROTC was able to work only indirectly toward the fulfillment of the first mission. If, however, one paused to consider its ability to "train the public mind," one would find "no greater or better agency at our command."[12] The message was clear to those who had a stake in the continuation of the JROTC: the high school program's chief utility was its ability to sway public opinion and portray the military as having a constructive and positive role to play in society.

Many Americans were, like Edwards, inclined to view military training in either high school or college as an essential step in the development of civic responsibility in young men. Putting ROTC on a more permanent footing, its supporters reasoned, would strengthen the country by instilling patriotism in its youth. "A serious defect in our national life in America," one ardent supporter of ROTC wrote during the war years, "is the lack of loyalty for or sense of duty toward the Government." Thus putting men through military training during their teenage years was important since "patriotism kindled at the most susceptible age" will "abide with them all their lives thereafter." Democracy was hard work but critical to maintain, as witnessed by the battles raging in Europe at the time. Military training, then, was seen as uniquely capable of teaching youth to "make cheerfully the thousand smaller sacrifices of good citizenship."[13] This message resonated with future generations of military men, policy planners, and educators, who would go on to emphasize the ability of ROTC to churn out patriotic young men.

Opposing the Rising Wave of School Militarism

This creeping school militarism, however, would soon bring socialists, teachers, clergy, and pacifists in the United States to lead a sustained campaign against ROTC. But opposition to military training in schools had emerged decades earlier in England. As the British military historian Michael Howard found, "one of the explicit criteria of national education after 1870 in most Western European countries was to produce generations physically fit for and psychologically attuned to war. It was a necessary part of citizenship." During the latter part of the nineteenth century and into the early twentieth century, many state-run British schools provided instruction in marksmanship and military drill. In a widely publicized speech in 1906, the former commander in chief of the British army called for compulsory military training of children—a practice that led Quakers and others on a decades-long quest to oppose militarization of British schools.[14]

Initially, local communities, either through churches or the labor movement and in some cases both, undertook the campaign opposing school-based military training. British clergy were in the forefront, warning their parishioners of the dangers and pitfalls of military training for schoolchildren; the clergy argued that these activities were counterproductive and would lead to intolerance of other peoples of the world while instilling in impressionable young minds a distinctly chauvinistic attitude. The labor leader and peace activist William Randall Cremer, for instance, was a prominent public figure leading the charge against militarism in education.

Cremer, a tireless critic of military training in schools, was the founder and permanent secretary of the Workmen's Peace Association (1871–1908) and recipient of the 1903 Nobel Peace Prize. In his many speeches he insisted that education was designed to encourage internationalism rather than a complacent workforce that would blindly accept industrial oppression and imperial conquest. In response to high-profile calls for compulsory military training of youth, a local chapter of the Socialist Party condemned "the desire to cultivate a martial spirit amongst the populace" and viewed school militarism as a method used by the upper classes to "repress any attempt to undermine its privileges."[15]

In the 1890s British military officials urged adoption of military drill as part of the physical education program for all schoolchildren. In response opponents called for a curriculum in the public schools that would emphasize cultural achievement and training in citizenship instead of glamorizing war and military conquest. Pacifists and peace leaders also encouraged the educational establishment to reject jingoistic school history texts. The head of the British Peace Society, Joseph Pease, carefully monitored all attempts to introduce militarism in Britain's educational system until the outbreak of World War I. Backing Pease's efforts was one of the leading British critics of military training, the Quaker Edward Grubb.

At the conclusion of the Boer War (1899–1902), when military officials lobbied for a military component to physical education instruction in schools, Grubb regularly criticized British imperialism and militarism. As editor of the *British Friend*, Grubb was outspoken regarding the establishment of a primary physical education course adapted from the Royal Army drill book. Calls for training youth in marksmanship at schools led Grubb and other peace leaders to expand their publicity campaign to oppose all forms of school militarism. Through his writing and advocacy, Grubb insisted that militarization of education ran counter to the principles of nineteenth-century liberal rationalism—the view that reason alone was the best guide to human affairs. Peace activists widely endorsed his position until war broke out in 1914.[16]

As in England, some of the earliest and most vociferous opposition to military training in schools and colleges in the United States emerged from the labor- and socialist-aligned Left. Socialists viewed school militarism through the lens of power and exploitation, predicting that military training for youth could be used to grease the wheels of empire, crush working-class dissent, and break up the organized power of the masses. According to Frances Fox Piven and Richard Coward, a major reason for the failure of the American labor movement before the Great Depression was the "legal and military power of the state." Indeed, between 1892 and 1914 Democratic and Republican governors alike used the National Guard, state militia, or state police to break some of the largest strikes in the history of organized labor. Writing in 1895, a year after federal troops repressed the massive Pullman strike, a reporter for *Appeal to Reason*—a Kansas-based socialist newspaper with a national circulation in the hundreds of thousands—had ample reason to fear that schoolboys in New York State were then being "drilled in the manner of arms by the officers of the American Guards." "Plutocracy is thoroughly organized," he wrote, so it should therefore be no surprise to see schoolboys trained by "the present capitalist government" to prepare "for any outburst or riot on the part of the oppressed people."[17]

Decades later the U.S. campaign for preparedness led to a renewed push for military drill and fresh criticism from socialists. At the time of protests against military training, one student at Eastern District High School in New York City told a reporter: "I am a Socialist. I'm against everything that belongs to war and fighting." According to the historian Ryan Shafto, at the time socialists viewed all aspects of preparedness, including the pursuit of military drill, as a means to "furnish capitalists with the weapons and manpower necessary not only to protect and expand its investments abroad, but to control or even eliminate the domestic labor movement." In March 1914 an article in the Kansas-based *Shawnee County Socialist* observed that those who advocate military drill in colleges "don't care a fig for your boy. What they want is to so train the American youth that when they wish to kill a lot of working men on a strike, or want to steal the lands or markets of some other peoples, or wish to create a demand for the manufacture of war materials for profit, that they will then have an army of boys who have been trained to obey orders and who will shoot the life out of his fellow-man if ordered to do so by his captain."[18] Military training, socialists argued, would thus weaken the social supports necessary for working-class struggle.

Other segments of American society also lent their support to these efforts. Then as now, the critics of school militarism regarded as most credible were those who had some connection to the world of education and could call upon their own firsthand experience with youth. Concurrent with the growth of school militarism at the start of the twentieth century was a strong peace sentiment among many teachers in U.S. public schools. Concerned about the promotion of military drill, some educators began pushing for the introduction of a standardized peace curriculum in public education. One of the leading proponents for teaching peace and internationalism among schoolchildren was the Massachusetts educator Fannie Fern Andrews. In 1908 Andrews founded the American School Peace League, conceived as a network of frontline decision makers in American education—superintendents, principals, and school board members. The league apparently enjoyed mainstream recognition, as it soon began holding its annual meetings in conjunction with the National Education Association, which had the largest teacher membership in the United States. State branches of both organizations encouraged participation with regional teachers' associations, and the league also distributed literature, supplied speakers for schools on the subject of peace, and developed curriculum materials.[19]

One of the league's most notable contributions to peace education was its four-hundred-page curriculum guide, *A Course in Citizenship* (1914). Andrews initiated the project in 1910, joined by a group of other peace-minded educators: the primary author of this guide, Ella Lyman Cabot; Mabel Hill, coauthor of *The Study of History in the Elementary Schools* and dean of the Mitchell Military Boys' School in Massachusetts; Fannie Coe, a children's book author; and Mary McSkimmon, a Massachusetts grade school principal. Written for elementary and junior high school educators, *A Course in Citizenship* contained comprehensive monthly lesson plans for grades one through eight. This text was a landmark in the emerging field of peace education and sought to shift the focus of "citizenship education . . . from a national to an international perspective."[20]

Andrews's organization also formed study groups for teachers and held essay contests on peace issues for high school students. Through these and other activities, the American School Peace League became "perhaps the most influential of all the juvenile propagandist bodies in the world."[21] Considering that the publication of *A Course in Citizenship* coincided with the outbreak of World War I, any attempt to introduce military training into the public school curriculum would be met with deep skepticism among peace organizations and opponents of war. Despite calls for preparedness in the run up to American involvement in the war, educators warned the public that military drill for young students was both threatening to their well-being and antithetical to the progressive view that schools should foster mutual understanding and cooperation.

With the outbreak of world war, more and more teachers then began lending their support to new peace organizations such as the Woman's Peace Party. Founded in 1915, the New York branch of the party was particularly outspoken about military drill in schools. During the winter of 1916 it held meetings and sponsored a dinner addressing a bill then before the state legislature that sought to establish compulsory military training in public high schools. More dramatically, the party conducted a large demonstration down Broadway led by two horse-drawn carriages adorned with large signs condemning military drill in schools and asking, "Shall schools be saved for democracy?" Branch members scoffed at the preparedness movement's efforts to introduce militarism in New York's public high schools "because it is the wrong kind of physical training, because it is bad education, because it is a waste of money ... because modern warfare has made it useless and because the greatest American educators are against it."[22]

In addition to strong support from rank-and-file teachers and newly formed peace organizations, opponents of military training in schools had prominent intellectuals on their side. One of the leading critics from the field of education was David Starr Jordan, president of Stanford University, a relatively new institution that was rapidly becoming known as a hub of academic innovation. In February 1917, at a time when fears of the Prussian empire's military prowess dominated newspaper headlines, Jordan wrote that the United States would have to hold firm against any attempt to insert militarism into public education. Voluntary military drill in schools, he suggested, was "a misuse of time that might generally be better employed," while compulsory drill was "thoroughly evil" and "an entering wedge of a movement subversive of democratic freedom." In an allusion to geopolitics that his readers would have surely understood, Jordan asserted that "even militarized Prussia," with its system of universal conscription for military-age males, "has not placed military training in any school." Comparisons of U.S. school militarism and the Prussian regime would become an even more common rhetorical strategy in the future, when memories of the Great War's tremendous loss of life remained sharp and efforts to militarize schools increased.[23]

While Jordan's status as one of the country's leading educators lent credibility to those who opposed military training, he rarely used antimilitarist imagery, choosing instead to frame his arguments in terms of effective pedagogy. In contrast, the noted Columbia University philosopher and educator John Dewey refused to mince words in his critique of school militarism. Although he was careful to distance himself from what he called "professional pacifists" and initially supported President Wilson's war aims, Dewey's philosophical commitments impelled him to staunchly oppose military training in schools. In his view the mind of the individual pupil was an instrument shaped by the school. Dewey, who is considered the founder of progressive education in America, believed that the educational process was the most influential force in changing society and in redirecting it toward more democratic ends.

The key to understanding Dewey's opposition to ROTC was his belief that education was capable of empowering people to learn to live together peacefully and cooperatively. Perhaps the earliest hint of why he would forcefully argue against military training in schools appears in his *Moral Principles in Education*, which he penned five years before the outbreak of world war. In this work he condemns the

American educational system for its inflexible and dogmatic pedagogy. This view became more entrenched during the preparedness campaign in the United States, when Dewey wrote in *Schools of Tomorrow* (1915): "The conventional type of education which trains children to docility and obedience . . . is suited to an autocratic society."[24]

Military training in schools, Dewey argued, fosters acquisition of information at the expense of encouraging responsiveness and participation in common and enjoyable tasks, which should be the true goal of learning. By relying on an educational method that emphasizes discipline and adherence to a rigid set of doctrines, he suggested, students would be forced to fit into a pattern of accepted social and political attitudes as determined by those in positions of power. Conformity at all costs, Dewey observed, removes the child's ability to become a conscious agent in criticizing and reconstructing social and political life. Establishing military training in schools and colleges would therefore encourage a military mindset while blunting efforts to teach social cooperation and appreciation of other cultures.[25]

Many educators echoed Dewey's position and were never sympathetic to the idea of military training in school. The director of physical education for the San Francisco public schools proclaimed that once America entered the war, it was crucial for military leaders to keep their distance from secondary pupils: "In the name of Jehovah and the little red schoolhouse on the hill, keep your hands off the American boy until he is at least nineteen years of age."[26] Even the U.S. Bureau of Education, referring to views expressed by European educators, considered military training "as an anomaly in the school system justified only by the exigencies of national defense."[27] Thus, for America's most influential voices in education, separating the military from schools was seen as a logical and fitting arrangement.

Nonetheless, a vocal segment of American education showed that opposition to military training in schools did not necessarily imply antimilitarism. In 1915 Dudley A. Sargent, director of Harvard University's state-of-the-art Hemenway Gymnasium, told the *Boston Transcript* that military training had no place in public schools, in part because schoolboys were not yet ready to learn the "real art of war." Military training for youth was not in itself a bad thing, he insisted, but was simply more appropriate at a later age. Two years later Charles Eliot, president emeritus of Harvard and an influential public intellectual, agreed with Sargent. Eliot reasoned that while training with bayonets and other weaponry "should not be begun before the twentieth year," certain parts of military drill were valuable forms of calisthenic exercise and therefore had earned their place in the public schools.[28]

Student Dissent on College Campuses

Although much discussion by educators centered on military drill in public high schools, opposition also emerged at the university level. Dissent came mostly from students who objected to the mandatory component of ROTC. What led to this growing opposition was the widespread fear of war and the new demands that would be placed upon student cadets to conform to additional military requirements. In 1915, before armed intervention by the United States, the Students' Anti-Drill Society at Washington State College published a pamphlet calling compulsory military drill the "great college menace." These student activists took the common refrain of drill advocates—that military training strengthens moral fiber—and reversed it. It would be absurd, the pamphlet said, "to say that military drill, with all its suggestions of murder, of rifles, of strict obedience, of might makes right, of superiority of the military to everything else," would not have a corrosive effect on students' morals. Included in the pamphlet was a plea to the board of regents and faculty decrying the "militaristic spirit" of military training and urging them to at least consider abolishing the compulsory component of drill at the college.[29]

The Ivy League also had its share of dissenters. At Princeton University, student leaders, including the captain of the football team, penned a strong anti-ROTC letter to the student newspaper. "We are opposed to the military propaganda now being carried on in American colleges," the letter read, adding that universities were "not the place for drilling or for instruction in military matters." As the United States inched closer to war, many college students agreed, expressing reservations about how ROTC would affect their academic studies and how its campus presence would foster a war mentality. Although the 1916 National Defense Act authorized the formation of only sixteen new ROTC programs at college and universities, their creation signaled a more formal alliance between officer training programs and the established military system. Once the United States entered the war, demands for total loyalty swept through the entire American education system.[30]

Schools at Arms

While educators and parts of the general public vocally opposed military training, this resistance melted away once the United States entered World War I. School districts then attempted to outdo each other when demonstrating their allegiance to the flag. According to H. C. Peterson and Gilbert Fite, as well as the historian

David M. Kennedy, federal and state governments made every effort to convert schools into "seminaries of patriotism" and receptive instruments of war propaganda. The National Education Association (NEA) in 1915 had firmly opposed military training in schools in a resolution passed at its annual convention declaring that compulsory military training in schools was "reactionary and inconsistent with American ideals and standards." A year later, on the eve of American intervention in the war and facing pressure from Major General Wood, the NEA passed a weaker statement recognizing the need for such training but urging caution lest "military ends . . . be permitted to pervert the educational purposes and practices of the schools."[31]

During the war the NEA—which a few years earlier had enjoyed close relations with the American School Peace League—adopted a less tolerant view and joined the Committee on Patriotism through Education to promote a ban on teaching German. The two organizations also demanded loyalty oaths. Education officials at the highest levels fully endorsed the campaign to root out antiwar teachers. "What a travesty it would be," the New York State commissioner of education told a gathering of educators in November 1917, "if beneath the national flag there skulked a disloyal teacher accepting his salary from the country while openly or insidiously weakening its defenses." In the years immediately following the war, this same commissioner oversaw a purge of allegedly disloyal and politically deviant teachers so extreme that the editors of the nation's leading education journal termed the expulsion an "intellectual reign of terror."[32]

Perhaps the commissioner's comments were a by-product of the views expressed by one member of the New York City Board of Education, the retired general Thomas Wingate. Swept up in his own chauvinistic proclivities, he held nothing back when he boldly proclaimed: "It is time to read the riot act to some of these teachers. . . . The teacher who teaches pacifism and that this country should not defend itself is a thousand more times dangerous than the teacher who gets drunk and lies in the gutter." His remarks led to numerous casualties. For instance, Jessie Wallace Hughan, an Eastern District High School teacher, fervent Socialist, and founder of an organization—the Anti-Enlistment League—that collected individual pledges of war resistance, came under intense pressure during student protests against military training. Hughan, who taught English at the school, had sterling credentials that included a doctoral degree from Columbia University and numerous publications. Although she told a reporter that her politics never entered the classroom, Hughan was pilloried in the press. An editorial in the *Brooklyn Eagle* urged that she be removed from her position. Having an antienlistment teacher in the classroom, the paper warned, would "undermine the very life of the Republic by corrupting its walls of defense with moral dry rot." Once the United

States entered the war, many states imposed loyalty oaths on school personnel, directly challenging those who stood behind the banner of academic freedom.[33]

Other efforts were soon introduced to ensure loyalty among American educators. Nationally, more than eight hundred thousand high school teachers and students were subjected to the National Board for Historical Service's war study plan prepared by Samuel B. Harding, a history professor at Indiana University. The board enthusiastically encouraged districts to adopt Harding's curriculum as a means for stimulating patriotism in the schools. "Such teaching," it argued, "will not merely stimulate the patriotism of the child and the various war services imposed upon the schools" but also carry over into the community. "Our public schools are the most important agency we have in advancing the cause of democracy."[34]

Harding's study plan, published by the U.S. Committee on Public Information, Woodrow Wilson's main font of propaganda, consisted of historical examples of America's military might and questions for discussion; its narrative blamed World War I on German militarism and cast the Allied Powers as peace-loving peoples. Originally developed to educate troops in training, the curriculum eventually found its way into the civics classrooms of the nation's secondary schools. It provided a guide for introducing specific topics in order to help students understand why the United States was fighting a war for democracy and against autocracy. Emboldened by the National Board for Historical Service and Harding's efforts, moreover, the New York State Legislature created a commission to hear and examine complaints about supposedly seditious textbooks in subjects like civics, history, economics, and English literature. And school district leaders asked teachers in the nation's elementary schools to instruct on the themes of patriotism, heroism, and sacrifice, as well as the differences between German autocracy and the American democratic way of life.[35]

Conclusion

Military drill for high school and college students went through three phases of development. After the Civil War and throughout the late nineteenth century, military drill for schoolchildren was an informal, community-organized activity. Later, some parts of the country, such as California and New York State, codified these practices in state law and/or made them beneficiaries of state funding. Finally, with the National Defense Acts of 1916 and 1920, military training in schools and colleges received the blessing (and the largesse) of the federal government.[36] After the passage of the National Defense Act of 1916, and amid growing patriotism and intolerance of antiwar dissent, military drill continued to expand in the education system. By June 1919, 19 colleges and 128 high schools had created ROTC units enrolling more than 90,000 students. Six years later postwar ROTC enrollment peaked at 111,558 students, with 42,190 students enrolled at high schools.[37] Some school districts made the practice mandatory for all boys, whereas other states—such as California—operated sophisticated high school cadet programs without federal support, relying entirely on the state's national guard for equipment and instructors.

The growth of school militarism was the result in part of the continued use of propaganda that tapped into Americans' fears and insecurities in a rapidly changing world. In 1917 a reader could look through the *New York Times* opinion pages and learn, as one headline suggested, that "military training would make us a new race." Despite the War Department's intention to promote military training across the country, opponents continued to insist that such practices would produce a generation of American youth prepared to kill on command, promote rigid conformity, and encourage intolerance of other cultures. Shortly before the passage of the National Defense Act of 1916, *Appeal to Reason* criticized the proposed creation of the JROTC in American high schools, warning of its potential to "poison young minds": "Let them once control the moulding [*sic*] of the minds of the young, and militarism will grow by leaps and bounds." Yet, despite the rapid growth of school militarism, the 1920s would prove to be a dynamic time for those opposing high school and college ROTC. By honing rhetorical skills; building a public relations apparatus fit to compete with the War Department's; forming a national coalition of allies in education, faith communities, and government; and developing the Committee on Militarism and Education, a national movement emerged in opposition to ROTC and other forms of school militarism. Challenging the role of militarism in education was now in full swing.[38]

CHAPTER 2

Postwar Peace Activism and the Committee on Militarism in Education

World War I was one of the deadliest conflicts in human history, resulting in an estimated 22 million deaths of civilians and combatants. Another 20 million soldiers were wounded. The belligerents contributed about 65 million troops to fight in the war and introduced a range of modern weaponry: airplanes, submarines, tanks, and poison gas. A mood of disillusionment that accompanied the destructiveness gave a significant boost to the postwar peace movement. In fact, historians have credited this period as marking the birth of the modern American peace movement, defined by the late historian Charles DeBenedetti as committed to both domestic reform and world peace. In this context activists now understood peace as both the absence of conflict on the international scene as well as the abolition of unjust social structures on the home front.

One of the most active of the postwar peace groups was the War Resisters League (WRL), which grew out of the radical educator Jessie Wallace Hughan's Anti-Enlistment League. The ever-changing leadership, composition, and levels of participation in the burgeoning peace movement make it difficult to sketch a profile of the typical peace activist of this period. However, as in the 1910s, the movement continued to consist of international lawyers, ministers and preachers, businessmen, social workers, and pacifist educators like Hughan, as well as those from the historic peace churches (Mennonites, Quakers, Church of the Brethren). But in the 1920s a much larger group of socialists, communists, working-class unionists, and lower-income citizens, including women and minorities, combined with those from more privileged positions to give the modern movement a more democratic and diverse outlook.[1]

These new peacemakers diligently connected their actions to broader social and political domestic concerns, including civil rights, support for labor unions, and equality for women. In the aftermath of World War I, they argued that war was an integral aspect of an unjust social order. As Linda Kay Schott points out in her study of the Women's International League for Peace and Freedom (WILPF), those involved in this radical group during the interwar years embraced what today would be considered an intersectional view of war and militarism. The women of WILPF considered "the eradication of violence" just as important as "getting rid of racism, sexism, class inequality, and the exploitation of human and natural resources."[2] Activists who developed their political consciousness in other movements, such as organized labor, would also play key roles in the struggle for peace during the 1920s. In this chapter we show how a new organization, the Committee on Militarism in Education (CME), stood out in this milieu by being solely concerned with eliminating the influence of the military in American schools. Composed of a small cadre of committed individuals—pacifists, educators, socialists, and clergy—those involved with the founding of CME believed that by opposing the militarization of education, they could prevent the formation of the military mindset capable of tipping the nation into another world war.

Notable Opposition before CME

The steady growth of school militarism after the war spurred the demand for an organization committed to separating militarism from education. "Although originally billed as a training program," the historian Charles Chatfield notes, the end of wartime conscription meant that ROTC "soon served principally as a recruitment and public relations device."[3] In 1920 Congress passed another National Defense Act, which dramatically expanded ROTC by giving it more resources and greater publicity. By 1925, 124 colleges in the United States were offering ROTC courses, and eighty-three of these institutions made the program compulsory for at least some students (usually first-year males). In 1925 the War Department's budget for the program was about $4 million ($60 million adjusted for inflation) with 768 officers and 1,064 enlisted men in charge of running these programs on campus. By 1927, after approximately fifteen years of continuous growth in school militarism, the federal budget for military training in schools and colleges had increased exponentially. Annual spending rose in this period from $725,168 to more than $10 million (roughly $150 million a year today), while the number of students enrolled in ROTC quadrupled during the same period.[4]

Although signs of growing militarism in American education were clear, those who would eventually found the CME also saw historic possibilities for reducing the military presence on high school and college campuses. Notable campus protests demonstrated that educators and others would not quietly accept the War Department's ROTC plans. In some cases the growth of ROTC led to increasing friction as the army's subject matter ran afoul of faculty expectations as to what constituted legitimate educational programs. Usually, however, the opposition in the early part of the decade sprang from students themselves. In nonbinding referenda, students at Cornell University and Ohio State voted against mandatory military training. Of the many land-grant universities that held similar votes, by 1926 the majority of students at only one university had voted in favor of compulsory ROTC. At the University of Wisconsin student protests against mandatory military training compelled the state legislature to act: in 1923 it passed a bill allowing students to choose between ROTC or physical education. The legislation was controversial because of its interpretation of the Morrill Act of 1862. Until then the War Department had led college officials to believe that the law required land-grant universities to make ROTC a graduation requirement for male students. Despite challenges to the Wisconsin law, U.S. attorney general William D. Mitchell later decided that making ROTC optional at their universities was a right reserved to the states.[5]

Wisconsin was among several sites of postwar opposition to ROTC. At North Dakota Agricultural College, a land-grant school in Fargo, the campus newspaper published a letter from two students condemning compulsory military drill. In the ensuing months of controversy, the college president lashed out at anti-ROTC faculty members, leading two to resign, while the student letter writers felt compelled to withdraw from school. While the situation in Fargo demonstrated the cost paid by some students and faculty who dared question military drill, another campus controversy—in Washington, D.C.—gave anti-ROTC forces reason for optimism. At historically black Howard University, in May 1925 nearly four hundred students conducted a strike protesting the university administration's decision to expel students who failed to comply with the school's mandatory military training policy. Student protesters, whose picket signs asked, "What is this going to be—an army or a university?" captured the attention of the national press, leading the school to agree to offer ROTC as an elective and to reinstate any dismissed students.

The protests made Howard something of an outlier among historically Black colleges and universities (HBCUs). During the interwar years many Black educational leaders viewed military officer training programs not as a means of militarizing the nation's youth but rather as an opportunity for Black advancement. Institutional racism ensured that Black participation rates in ROTC remained low until World War II, with units at only four HBCUs (Wilberforce, Hampton Institute, Howard, and Tuskegee).[6] Although the situation improved after the war, with the number of HBCUs offering ROTC rising to fourteen, even as late as the mid-1950s the southern states of Arkansas, Georgia, and Mississippi failed to offer this program to Black college youth. Many leaders in Black education used the language of civil rights to frame their requests for ROTC units, complaining of the "unjust and inequitable" way that "qualified Negro college student[s]" were "specifically penalized by this discrimination." Given the understanding of ROTC access as a civil rights issue, anti-ROTC protests were rarely seen at HBCUs during a time when such demonstrations were becoming more visible across the country.[7]

In the first half of the 1920s, resistance to ROTC suffered from lack of coordination among peace advocates. However, starting in 1925, formerly isolated activists joined together to raise awareness of ROTC nationwide through a series of publications that ultimately led to the creation of the Committee on Militarism in Education.[8]

Working toward a National Strategy

By the middle of the 1920s nearly two-thirds of all universities hosting ROTC had made the program mandatory for at least some of its male students. However, events in Wisconsin demonstrated that the army had little legal support for its "compulsory or nothing" stance. In 1925 the army suffered another setback with the publication of a well-researched report by the Philadelphia Friends Peace and Service Committee, *Regarding Military Training at Universities*. Walter C. Longstreth, a Quaker attorney, described the shortcomings of the Morrill Act and offered a road map for how colleges might legally sever their contracts with the War Department. Making the report difficult to dismiss were two key pieces of evidence. The first was a letter from Secretary of War John W. Weeks, in which he acknowledged that under the National Defense Act, college officials could elect to make military training either compulsory or elective. Longstreth also cited a revealing section from the application form universities used to request an ROTC unit on campus that seemed to indicate a choice between elective and compulsory ROTC. The report soon became a valuable resource for those opposed to military training in schools and colleges. Still, Longstreth reminded readers that although colleges could freely choose between offering compulsory or elective ROTC, the War Department's preference was to have all universities present it to students as a mandatory program.[9]

One peace activist who found the Longstreth report particularly intriguing was John Nevin Sayre, a devout pacifist minister and leading figure in the newly established Fellowship of Reconciliation (FOR). After receiving his education at Princeton and the Episcopal Theological Seminary, Sayre traveled to China and Germany before serving during the war years as an Episcopal priest in Rockland County, New York. His involvement with the Fellowship of Reconciliation, beginning with its founding in 1915, marked the beginning of a lifelong commitment to peace advocacy. Like many who were associated with FOR, Sayre considered himself a religious pacifist. According to the organization's "Statement of Purpose," FOR sought a classless society free of racism, war, and militarism. Sayre later told an interviewer that he considered militarism to be inseparably linked to concerns about war and peace; the most damaging effect of militarism in his view was the "element of compulsion," as when young men were forced to serve in the armed forces or in a military training program. According to Sayre, it was abhorrent that "any government should be able to dictate to the consciences of men what they should do" about such a vital matter as killing another person.[10]

These worries about the effects of militarism found an outlet shortly after the Longstreth report appeared, when in May 1925 members of FOR met in New York City to discuss the formation of a committee to curb military training in American schools. They agreed to appoint Sayre as head, and he immediately joined Edward Hachtel of the FOR-aligned Fellowship of Youth for Peace and Tucker P. Smith of the Young Men's Christian Association to produce a report that would further publicize the ROTC issue. Published in July, their paper was rich with data compiled from War Department documents, excerpts from military officials' own public statements, and secondary sources. Hoping to stimulate discussion about what the trio considered "the dangers of military training for American and high school college students," they included in the report enrollment statistics for high school and college military training programs, highlighted the curriculum used for junior and senior programs, and shared legal strategies that schools could use to eliminate military training programs. In a particularly affecting section, Sayre and his colleagues presented critical views of former ROTC cadets. "As an exsoldier, who was also trained in a university ROTC," said one, "I am convinced that the blight of military intrusion in the colleges is so serious as to challenge the opposition of any student with an open mind and a stout heart."[11]

Sayre sensed that enough people were interested in the topic of military training in schools to justify a follow-up report with wider distribution. In a July letter Sayre asked Winthrop Lane—a journalist who had written previously on prison reform and Progressive Era social work—if he was interested in the job. Lane had initially come to Sayre's attention with his 1919 article for *Survey* magazine reporting on the abusive treatment of conscientious objectors at the army's prison at

Fort Leavenworth. The nascent "Committee on Military Training," as it was then known, sought funding to provide payment to Lane and support national distribution of the ensuing publication. Once Sayre had secured more than $5,000 from the liberal millionaire Charles Garland's American Fund for Public Service, Lane began his research, which was to include scouring more than one hundred university course catalogs to examine ROTC requirements on each campus. The Lane report's reliance on official sources—his footnotes include references to the *Army and Navy Register*, reports from the War Department, and congressional hearing transcripts—would become a hallmark of future CME publications and help insulate the group from public attacks intended to cast doubt on their analysis.

Lane's report, *Military Training in Schools and Colleges in the United States*, was the result of impeccable research and would have an enormous influence on the ROTC debate. It was particularly critical of the War Department's push to expand the program in such a rapid and underhanded manner that "the general public has hardly known what was going on." While the War Department sought to deceive a war-weary public by dressing up the program in the pleasant-sounding language of "citizenship training," Lane reminded readers of the true purpose of ROTC: "To make soldiers." The report also highlighted plans by the War Department to expand the high school ROTC program, noting the secretary of war's public statement that his department desired that ROTC eventually expand into as many as twelve hundred American high schools. Another issue the publication addressed was the element of compulsion. Lane's investigation revealed that even though the Morrill Act did not ask colleges to make ROTC compulsory, a large majority of the more than one hundred universities offering the program did require it. Although the public had consistently rejected postwar plans for universal military training, Lane noted, with compulsory ROTC the War Department was getting a "near-substitute." When ROTC was not compulsory, Lane found, instructors offered inducements to encourage college men to participate—fancy uniforms, smartly adorned cavalry troops, parades, cash subsidies, and even comely women students serving as honorary regimental officers.[12]

Throughout the history of the Reserve Officers' Training Corps, some educators have looked favorably on military training. Some regarded the program as an effective means of instilling discipline in young men, while others viewed it as a way for colleges to provide the equivalent of physical education courses without paying for civilian instructors. Lane's report was effective at demonstrating the range of opposition to ROTC among educators, noting one common concern that still exists: loss of curriculum control. "When an institution contracts with the War Department for the establishment of an ROTC unit," Lane wrote, "it hands over to the Government control of this military instruction." In other words, the military would provide instructors, textbooks, salaries—and in return the college administration ceded control of the education of its students in this area of the curriculum.

There were numerous other objections to ROTC on educational grounds. Lane provided a sampling with a list of quotes from prominent educators like Samuel T. Dutton, professor emeritus of school administration at Columbia's Teachers College, who saw in school militarism a violation of what America represented. "Were the United States to become committed to military training for boys," Dutton warned, "it would . . . present to the world the lamentable spectacle of the most democratic nation on earth doing what not one of the great military nations of Europe has done."[13] Although Lane's report described patriotic reasons for opposing military training in schools and colleges, it still drew the inevitable charges of subversion from such organizations as the American Legion.

In his discussion of the psychological effects of military training, Lane anticipated concerns that would dominate later CME publications and appealed directly to readers attuned to the international dimensions of the peace issue. As several scholars have shown, peace advocates of the 1920s placed their hopes in the League of Nations, trusting that establishment of an international mechanism of arbitration would greatly reduce the chances of global conflict. But Lane argued that ROTC, with its "educational tendency towards a psychology for war," stood in the way of efforts toward disarmament and mediation of conflict. By creating a mindset in young men that "automatically thinks of war as the ultimate 'sanction' to be used by patriotism," the growth of ROTC across the United States represented a major obstacle to the peace movement's goals. Thus Lane's report quoted a petition against compulsory military training by students at the University of Washington that summed up this argument: "War should be outlawed. So long as thousands of schoolboys are forced, hoaxed or bribed into military service it will be impossible to abolish the institution."[14]

Beyond educating an ill-informed public, Lane's report suggested concrete measures that readers could take to oppose ROTC. He called for parents, educators, and average citizens to take their complaints to their local school boards, conduct forums, and lead discussions among community groups; for students to adopt resolutions opposed to military training; and for all concerned about the issue to petition Congress on the ground that taxpayer dollars were being wasted on military training.[15]

Striking a balance between carefully constructed argument and passionate commentary, the report elicited considerable public support. Sayre and his colleagues drew on their grant from the Garland fund to ensure the report received wide distribution. They mailed more than 150,000 copies of the first edition to clergy, civic clubs, peace groups, and newspapers (both large and small), not to mention every governor in the country and each member of Congress. Some newspapers, like *Kansas Labor Weekly*, reprinted large sections on their front page, while others—including mass-circulation magazines like the *Nation* and *Survey*, as well as church publications—published editorials in favor of the report. Part of the reason for its positive reception was, no doubt, the impressive roster of famous people who endorsed the report. Among them were W. E. B. Du Bois, cofounder the National Association for the Advancement of Colored People; Henry Sloane Coffin, noted author and Yale University chaplain; and Carrie Chapman Catt, a prominent figure in the struggle for women's suffrage. Sayre later recalled that the report made quite a splash, which underlined the need for a more permanent organization that would organize against ROTC.[16]

A Committee Is Formed

Modern historians have difficulty tracing exactly when the Committee on Militarism in Education formed. Neither the organization's records, held at Swarthmore College, nor other documents provide any clues. The historian who spent the most time in the CME's archives, Daniel Barthell, wrote that one explanation for the lack of documentation may have been that "most of the people involved worked very near to each other in the same building" in New York City "and did most of their communicating by word of mouth." Despite this omission in the historical record, it appears that a group of pacifists led by Sayre formed what would become the Committee on Militarism in Education sometime in 1925. So confident was Sayre of Lane's ability to spur debate and create the conditions for a national organization that by October 1925—months before the Lane report appeared in print—Sayre was telling colleagues of working to form a permanent organization dedicated to the ROTC question. When the Lane report came out the following year, it appeared under the temporary name of the "Committee on Military Training," which would soon be changed to the Committee on Militarism in Education. Unlike the War Resisters League and other peace organizations of the time, the newly minted CME would have no dues-paying members. "In its structure," Barthell notes, "the CME was similar to a head without a body." To pursue its goals the committee would rely on the Fellowship of Reconciliation, without which, Sayre later said, the CME "would not have been born," nor would it have been able to continue as long as it did. Sayre could also count on FOR's youth wing, Fellowship of Youth for Peace, to mobilize its members in support of the CME's aims.[17]

What were those objectives? In a white paper outlining its tentative program, the CME identified a number of goals. The most important was abolishing compulsory ROTC at the college level and eliminating any form of military training—even voluntary—in high schools. In an interview he gave toward the end of his life, Sayre reported that the ultimate goal of CME was to abolish *all* forms of military training from civilian colleges and schools. However, he correctly judged that this would have been politically impossible at the time, so the committee settled on focusing its campaign against compulsory college-level ROTC and any form of high school ROTC.[18] Secondary objectives included opposing War Department attempts to sell the military to the public, and researching and publicizing the actual content of ROTC courses.

Organizationally, the CME was composed of national and executive committees. The former served as the group's public face and included many of the same luminaries who had endorsed the Lane report, including representatives from labor, peace, political, and religious organizations. National committee members were not expected to do much more than lend their names to the CME letterhead and occasionally respond to the organization's fund-raising appeals. Members of the executive committee were far more active, functioning as a board of directors and meeting regularly to discuss the group's goals and assess its financial health.[19]

In these times and throughout CME's history, organizations were led by a secretary who was responsible for handling everyday duties for the establishment.[20] Two CME secretaries who served during the 1920s merit mention. E. Raymond Wilson, who served from 1925 to 1926, was the first. An Iowa farm boy, Wilson received his master's degree in religious education from Columbia University Teachers College, where he studied under George Albert Coe, who would later serve as CME's national chair. Wilson joined the CME from the Fellowship of Youth for Peace, where he had named the organization and argued successfully that it should be known as a fellowship *for* peace, not an organization against war. Wilson was succeeded at the CME by another man of faith. Roswell P. Barnes had studied at Union Theological Seminary and brought to the CME experience as a schoolteacher. While serving as secretary, Barnes helped the committee begin its operations and publicized its goals through college speaking tours. Frequently red-baited by the American Legion and barred from speaking on college property, Barnes often decamped to nearby churches whose enthusiastic pacifist ministers opened their doors to him. He was so uplifted by these encounters that in 1928, after just two years as executive secretary, he resigned to commit his life to the ministry full time.[21]

Within months of the committee's founding in 1925, a string of surprising victories encouraged Sayre and other activists. The board of education in Cleveland,

Ohio, voted unanimously to eliminate military training in that city's high schools. This was remarkable because the board voted amid fervent pro-ROTC organizing by veterans' groups and Newton Baker, a former secretary of war. During this period, as noted earlier, students at the Buckeye State's largest public university took their nonbinding vote against compulsory ROTC. And at the City College of New York, students opposed to compulsory military training singled out a section of the ROTC *Manual of Military Training*, "The Spirit of the Bayonet," that used gruesome language in instructing how to kill an enemy combatant. With support from the CME and City College faculty members like the philosopher Morris Cohen, students voted against mandatory drill in a January 1926 referendum. Later that year students and their allies in the CME were pleased to learn of the War Department's decision to eliminate bayonet drill from ROTC training. In their public statements and articles, committee members had singled out bayonet drill as reflecting the true nature of ROTC—to churn out trained killers. Understandably, they took some credit for its sudden disappearance from the curriculum.[22]

Legislative Efforts

The positive reception of Lane's publication, as well as the string of wins by opponents of ROTC, made it appear that the fight against school militarism would be an easy one. In its optimism the committee decided to take its campaign to Congress. U.S. Representative George A. Welsh, a Philadelphia Republican who was working with Longstreth, sponsored legislation prohibiting compulsory military training in any U.S. educational setting other than a military school. With Senator Lynn J. Frazier, Republican of North Dakota, as cosponsor, church and peace groups, such as the National Council for the Prevention of War and the Women's International League for Peace and Freedom, urged members to write their congressional representatives in support of the bill. Assistance also came from the American Federation of Labor, which issued a statement saying that the United States would soon become a "militaristic nation . . . unless something is done at once to curb the activities of the War Department and the propaganda of the military saber rattlers from making goose-steppers out of the schoolboys in America."[23] More congressional testimony in favor of the bill came from representatives of church bodies and academia.

The CME also received a boost when it learned that President Calvin Coolidge had told a newspaper of his opposition to compulsory military training. Although "Silent Cal" did not specifically mention the Welsh-Frazier proposal, he made his remarks on the same day that Sayre was to testify in favor of it, which struck the editors of the *Army and Navy Register* as more than "a mere coincidence." "It must have been a studied effort to aid the proponents of the Welsh bill," they opined. With his statement against compulsory ROTC, the editors charged that Coolidge was giving "aid and comfort to those who seek to minimize if not entirely prevent the effort to place the Government in a position to take care of its increasing responsibilities as a world power."[24] The editorial thus linked the global ambitions of an expanding U.S. empire to the necessity of mandatory military training for youth.

Unsurprisingly, officials at the War Department declared their opposition to the legislation, noting that whether to make ROTC compulsory should be the decision of states and municipalities. Despite support for the bill from the president, opposition from the War Department likely doomed the measure, which never made it out of committee for a vote. Although this early initiative failed, the campaign was not without achievements. Committee members learned valuable lessons about how to lobby Congress that they would refine and deploy in subsequent years. More important, lobbying for the Welsh-Frazier legislation taught the CME about the great need to educate the public about school militarism. While some members of Congress, including those opposed to the compulsory component, felt that the matter should be left up to the states and colleges, far more were simply ignorant of the issues surrounding military training. The committee would soon regroup and consolidate its efforts in the arena of public relations, making its case through pamphlets and newsletters to counteract the military's influence on the public mind.[25]

Confronting the War Mindset

Contrary to the notion—popular then as now—that the tendency toward war is inherent to human nature, the CME was founded on the idea that the use of military force, armaments, and power politics was the product of particular states of mind. The group claimed that, by promoting the idea that war was justified, military training in schools and colleges helped create an ideological predisposition to war. The threat to democracy represented by ROTC, the prominent Protestant theologian Reinhold Niebuhr wrote in 1926, was that it inclined young men to the "conviction that war is natural and inevitable." CME members often discussed their work as a way to oppose a predisposition to see war as a solution, one that the military sought to inculcate in the public. "I think it is clearer than ever," Sayre wrote to a correspondent, "that we shall not get disarmament of battleships and armies until we have more disarmament of the mind." This view also appears in the Lane report, which states that "it is hardly to be questioned" that military training in schools and colleges produces "a mind-set which automatically thinks of war as the ultimate 'sanction' to be used by patriotism."[26] Although the Progressive Era in America had ended by the time the committee formed, the idea that educational reform and better access to information could prevent wars reflected the progressive orientation of its members. After all, the progressive movement in America was distinguished by an abiding faith that "with proper information, social improvement could be achieved."[27]

It fell to a Columbia colleague of John Dewey's to articulate one of the clearest expressions of this mindset theory. George Albert Coe, who had a doctoral degree in theology but taught in the university's Teacher's College, was well versed in psychology and considered by many to be the father of the religious education movement. In a 1924 article for the journal *Religious Education*, Coe argued:

> War is, of course, a state of mind.... Habits of thought and sentiment, which I shall here call the national mind-set, may and do make war while there is yet peace. They make it, not by hating other nations, not by desiring war, but by adjusting the whole mental mechanism so that, in certain situations, war-favoring reactions will occur as a matter of course. War seems to break upon us like an electric storm or an earthquake; it seems to happen to us. But, in reality it happens in us, as a long, inter-connected series of events, the last of which—the call to arms and actual fighting—merely carries out the nature of the series.

In Coe's telling, schools were the obvious solution. "If the educators of today were given a commission thus to shift the mental mind-set of the whole nation," he continued, "and if they were granted a free hand," then "we could prevent war altogether, we could make it as obsolete as cannibalism."[28]

At the time Coe was writing, schools in the United States simply reinforced the military mindset by teaching what he deemed "militant nationalism" and "pseudo history." Coe expressed hope that school and college administrators might resist the view—then becoming dominant in the discourse about public education—that public schools should serve to reproduce the status quo. Coe condemned the "mechanizing influence" of this type of education and hoped educators would instead teach students to question and resist unjust social relations.[29] However, one could not expect public schools—embedded as they were in nationalist ideology—to reform themselves overnight. Thus in the interim Coe saw an important role for religious educators whose church schools, by operating outside the constraints of the state, could uphold a "tradition... that squarely contradicts the whole war-philosophy" and "point the way for the public schools" in teaching peace.[30]

Coe's sterling academic credentials, as well as his outspoken support for opponents of compulsory military training, brought him to the attention of Sayre, who quickly realized he had the perfect figurehead for the committee: someone from academia who was not directly tied to any pacifist organization. Coe, who like Sayre was an ordained minister, would serve as CME's national chair from the time he retired from Columbia in 1927 until the committee folded in 1940. Shortly before assuming this post, Coe would further refine his thinking about the military mindset. Writing in the pages of *World Tomorrow* in 1926, he condemned the War Department's tendency to mask the true purpose of military drill by draping it in the language of "citizenship training." "Within the velvet glove of this kind of 'citizenship training' are militarism's steely fingers," Coe declared. "They are long fingers. They reach quietly into our homes, our churches, our industries, the press, the cinema, our entire educational system."[31] Teachers and preachers, he suggested, had a moral obligation to present the true facts about the perils of any attempt to introduce military training into civilian life. Most important, Coe urged readers to consider that schools were not the only arena in which militarists sought to promote their agenda; the public should be alert to other forms of promilitary propaganda within the larger culture.

In the mindset theory lies the common bond linking CME to both pre- and postwar peace movements. Central to peace advocacy in both eras was the belief that the elimination of war was simply a matter of improved education. But the idea that education was crucial to achieving world peace grew stronger in the aftermath of World War I, when educators and peace advocates pushed for school curriculums that would include in classroom instruction the idea of internationalism. For example, in 1926, after the Association for Peace Education published a content analysis of typical school history textbooks in the United States, Paul Klapper—dean of the School of Education at City College of New York—published *The Teaching of History*, a text that would soon be in wide circulation among students preparing to become social studies teachers.

In a striking section discussing history and world peace, Klapper advised future teachers to "picture vividly the human cost of war" and to remember that "war persists only because some of the leading nations are not ready to maintain justice in international affairs on as high a plane as in individual matters." Before war can be eliminated, he maintained, schools must promote elimination of "bigoted nationalism and martial propaganda from history." Similarly, the CME believed that abolishing war could occur by eliminating military elements from public education and promoting peace in the schools. Following the failure of the proposed Welsh-Frazier legislation, CME members were ready to apply mindset theory in the public arena by undertaking a major campaign to educate Congress and the public about the pernicious effects of school militarism.[32]

Getting Started: A Propaganda Strategy

Despite a meager budget that rarely exceeded $10,000 during its fifteen-year existence, CME published a number of notable pamphlets maintaining that military training was incompatible with a progressive philosophy of education—one that sought to promote and cultivate the potential of every student's well-being. For a brief period the committee also produced a newsletter, alternately titled *CME News Bulletin* or *News Letter*. The number of copies distributed and amount of content in each issue largely depended on how much money the committee could raise. The six published issues included regular fund-raising appeals, news about military training in foreign countries, and information about anti- and pro-ROTC campaigns. A typical issue was the one dated February 7, 1927, which contained a lead editorial discussing a kerfuffle about an ROTC unit at the University of Oklahoma; an excerpt from the *Congregationalist* about the "youth movement for peace"; an Associated Press dispatch about a U.S. Army general's call for the dismissal of a high school teacher who was in favor of socialism; and coverage of a CME-sponsored talk at the Town Hall Club in New York City.[33] Following a period of inactivity, in 1932 the committee decided to revive its news bulletin, rechristening it *Breaking the War Habit*. Against the backdrop of overseas events, particularly the rise of Hitler in Germany and Mussolini's fascist rule in Italy, *Breaking the War Habit* generated a larger mailing list than earlier CME newsletters and remained in circulation until near the end of the group's existence.

While the committee's newsletters kept the public informed of ROTC-related developments, its well-documented pamphlets probably had the most lasting effect. Specifically, these publications were designed to use facts and statistics, not hyperbole, to inform the public; to convince readers of its position CME took an objective look at the national situation in its brochures. The tone was educational and, in many cases, relied on news accounts and congressional testimony to make its points. Certainly, that was the message in one of the committee's most noted publications, *Militarizing Our Youth: The Significance of the Reserve Officers' Training Corps in Our Schools and Colleges*, written by Roswell Barnes, the CME secretary.

Barnes began by asking readers to examine a selection of quotations about war, peace, and democracy. Until they flipped the page to find an answer key, they would not know which quotes were from the famous Prussian general Friedrich von Bernhardi's 1912 work, *Germany and the Next War*, and which were from the U.S. War Department's ROTC textbook. Through this clever exercise, CME challenged readers to discern any noticeable difference between the two texts. More than a few readers no doubt were surprised that some quotes—so redolent of Prussian militarism—were actually from the ROTC text.[34]

While Barnes essentially addressed many of the same themes as the Lane report, he provided more current statistical information about ROTC enrollment and new angles of inquiry. One fresh focus that Barnes offered was an extended discussion of how ROTC often was at the center of controversies about academic freedom. "Abridgement of free speech on political issues and interference with academic freedom," he wrote, "were essential features of the regimes of Napoleon, of Metternich, of Bismarck, and other autocracies." To demonstrate how such interference is "so close to the heart of the ROTC system," Barnes also provided brief descriptions of ten "typical cases" such as that involving a University of Georgia staff member who had been driven from office after opposing compulsory drill.[35]

The committee produced eighty-five pamphlets between 1925 and 1940. Some had catchy titles such as *Brass Buttons and Education* or *Expel the Trojan Horse*, whereas others struck a more academic tone. A number were reprinted from congressional testimony, military reports, and speeches that had appeared in the *Congressional Record*. Others were drawn from articles that had appeared in metropolitan newspapers, left-wing and religious journals, as well as pacifist periodicals like *World Tomorrow* and *World Outlook*. The consistent message of each concerned attempts by the War Department to militarize the national mindset. As Barnes noted in one pamphlet: "One of the postulates to the development of a mindset that will facilitate war responses is the belief that war is 'inevitable.' Perhaps the greatest obstacle to social progress is the acceptance of any evil of society as inevitable."[36] Such views persisted, nurtured by a powerful educational, political, and cultural apparatus. Through their withering critiques of ROTC, the committee's publications sought to undermine support for one of the key elements of that system.

In another pamphlet, *So This Is War: A Study of Popularized Military Training* (1929), Tucker Smith regretted how "the mass is still led to believe that war is inevitable and that preparedness is the only way to peace." Of the dozens of pamphlets published by CME, Smith's stands out for its satirical tone, ridiculing ROTC commanders' lavish spending on recruitment. Some of the most outrageous practices he cited were turning military horses into polo ponies; staging mock battles; sponsoring their own fraternity, Scabbard and Blade; establishing a dancing school for one unit in Maine and, in Alabama, a horseback-riding class for young women. In fact, such efforts recruited few reserve officers. But U.S. Representative Ross Collins, a Mississippi Democrat who was a key CME ally and member of the House Subcommittee on Appropriations, regularly cited these examples during annual budget appropriations debates. Collins took particular exception to "playing at war" in high schools, noting that teenagers enrolled in JROTC could become "easy victims of war psychology." In a statement reprinted in Smith's pamphlet, Collins said of high school cadets: "Being too young for serious military work, they are simply turned into boosters for the National Defense Act and the military machine."[37] By the end of the 1920s, the committee had garnered the support of a key member of Congress and was attracting media attention to its steady stream of publications. Additional support for the CME at this time came from another key constituency: women peace activists.

Support from Women Peace Activists

The issue of militarism in American life was important to women peace activists, particularly in the aftermath of World War I. Professional women—doctors, social workers, and journalists—constituted a large percentage of the peace movement between the wars. In their public statements these activists emphasized that their peace advocacy was an outgrowth of their traditional maternal roles in society. They argued that as women they were in a unique position to uphold the preservation of life, which male political leaders chose to ignore when leading nations to war. Although men dominated CME's leadership ranks, some notable women, including Jane Addams, endorsed its efforts. Best known for her pioneering efforts in the field of social work, Addams also played a key role in the postwar women's peace movement. In addition to working with the Women's Peace Party—which she cofounded in 1915—and serving as the first president of Women's International League for Peace and Freedom, Addams enhanced her peace credentials in 1926 when she signed her name to the Lane report.[38]

As education director of the National Council for the Prevention of War (NCPW), Florence Boeckel worked closely with CME to support its work in schools. Founded in 1921 as the National Council for the Limitation of Armaments, during the twenties the group changed its name and urged formation of a progressive world organization, worldwide reduction of armaments through international treaties, and promotion of education for peace. As education director, Boeckel distributed peace pamphlets in elementary schools and sought to curb superficial, patriotic indoctrination in secondary school textbooks. She frequently pointed out that school systems largely rejected for classroom use works critical of American political and social institutions and those sympathetic to peace efforts. In addition to being an active suffragist, Boeckel worked tirelessly for more than twenty years to establish local and regional chapters of the NCPW and to publicize its work. She also critiqued school military training in her 1928 book, *Between*

War and Peace: A Handbook for Peace Workers, which drew upon statements from leading educators to support the CME's views on military training in education settings.[39]

The establishment of the CME also closely coincided with the publication of Maud C. Stockwell's *Some Facts Concerning Military Training at State Universities* (1926). This publication, prepared for the Minnesota branch of WILPF, was a carefully researched case study comparing three large public universities: University of Minnesota, University of Wisconsin, and the University of Michigan. In her report Stockwell sought to demonstrate that legislative pressure and public support were necessary to eliminate the compulsory feature of military drill. She noted how in February 1925 WILPF's Minnesota branch sponsored legislation to eliminate compulsory military training at the state university. When the bill was defeated later that year, a student group quickly formed the Anti-Compulsory Military Drill League at the University of Minnesota. Perhaps as a portent of what the creation of CME would bring, Stockwell warned: "From now on, the university authorities may look for organized opposition to the compulsion.... Should the authorities continue to refuse the petitions of the students for an opportunity to exercise the free choice which they employ toward other studies in the curriculum, recourse to the state legislature may be made, following the example of Wisconsin." It was a clear warning from one local branch, yet one intended to speak for all members of WILPF.[40]

Perhaps no woman did more to advance the cause of CME's work than Zona Gale, the noted author and playwright who in 1921 became the first woman to win the Pulitzer Prize. Writing in the *Nation* at the end of the decade, Gale observed that in its original form, the Morrill Act did not contain any provision for teaching military tactics—crucially, that phrase was added during the Civil War. "For a period of sixty-seven years," she continued, "the interpretation was modified and its parts magnified, until 'and including military tactics' came to mean 'and compelling military tactics.'" Eventually, she said, the phrase evolved to mean "laying an obligation upon every freshman of a land-grant college." She concluded that "it seems loose procedure that the training of thousands of college boys should hang upon a phrase so casually included in the text of a law otherwise not literally interpreted."[41]

Support from the Clergy

Besides women, by the late 1920s the CME's strongest supporters were members of the clergy. In the first quarter of the twentieth century, before the expansion of higher education after World War II, religious leaders in the United States outnumbered college presidents and professors by about seven to one. Because of their high levels of education, their vast numbers, and the respect they enjoyed in their communities, clergy exercised an outsize influence on American public opinion. Thus their endorsement was critical to bolstering the CME's credibility.[42]

Members of the clergy signed petitions, lent their pulpits to antimilitarist speakers, endorsed CME publications, and critiqued ROTC from the pages of their periodicals. By 1927 clergy leadership on the issue had led dozens of religious bodies, including the Northern Baptist Convention and the National Council of the Congregational Church, to publicly oppose compulsory military training. Yet none had as much influence as the Federal Council of Churches, an ecumenical association of more than thirty Christian denominations. Its 1926 resolution called for the complete abolition of ROTC in high school, cautioned against compulsory ROTC in college, and recommended that churches give the issue careful study. As Reinhold Niebuhr wrote in 1926: "The churches have been more unanimous in their opposition to military training in colleges than in any other stand taken on the various national and international issues involving the war question."[43]

This antimilitarist spirit represented a significant shift from just a few years earlier, when nearly all houses of worship had flags waving in their pulpits and preachers across the nation lined up to support U.S. entry in World War I. Yet in a postwar period marked by disillusionment, greater numbers of clergy were publicly supporting the peace movement. Liberal Protestant ministers such as Sayre, Coe, and Niebuhr embraced nonviolence as an expression of their Christian faith. "The motivating spirit behind this dedication to pacifism," one historian of the period noted, "was the belief that war represented a collective sin of mankind which need not be tolerated." Once CME was fully operational, religious bodies quickly aligned themselves behind its goals and objectives. Faith-based opposition to school militarism took many forms, but the most common was the idea that military training planted the seeds of violent conflict in youth, leading the nation to reap an inevitable harvest of future wars.[44]

To emphasize their arguments, writers for religious audiences made frequent references to the horrors of World War I. In a December 1925 editorial responding to the Lane report, a denominational journal, the *Herald of Gospel Liberty*, noted: "The supreme evil of the thing is that through the student body it scatters here and there and everywhere throughout our nation a host of embryo army officers, young chaps with the army viewpoint and the army attitude towards the whole question of huge military equipment, and through them impregnates this whole nation with the same pagan military conception and atmosphere that has led to such terrible consequences in the nations of Europe."[45]

Besides increasing the prospect of future wars, the spread of ROTC was alarming to clergy and editors of church periodicals because it signaled their loss of control of the nation's youth. The clergy and the editors perceived the military presence in schools as encroaching on a traditional church domain—the formation of ethical values among the young. As the *Herald of Gospel Liberty* editorialized in February 1926: "Nothing could go farther to counteract the peace teachings and peace efforts of the churches than to have our future citizenship impregnated with the military viewpoint during the formative years of student life. Hence it is of tremendous importance that Christian people everywhere be aroused to the insidious danger of military training in our schools and colleges." To emphasize this point, the editors applauded recent statements from a large national gathering of Christian student activists in support of CME policy (complete abolition of JROTC; no compulsory ROTC in college) and called for the end of all military training in church schools. "Surely the abolition of such student training," the editorial continued, "ought to be considered as one of the first and primary steps in the process of Christian education against war."[46]

Notable clergy who supported CME's goals included Francis J. McConnell, Episcopal bishop of Pittsburgh, representing a denomination not known for peace sentiment; Charles Clayton Morrison, the irascible editor of the weekly *Christian Century*, house organ of liberal Protestantism; and Stephen Samuel Wise, the noted rabbi and member of the executive committee of the World Jewish Congress. All three signed their names to the first edition of Lane's groundbreaking report. But by far the two most prominent Protestant preachers supporting CME's efforts were Harry Emerson Fosdick and Reinhold Niebuhr.

Fosdick served in what has long been considered the nation's most prestigious pulpit, Riverside Church on the Upper West Side of Manhattan. After defending just war doctrine and Wilsonian interventionism in his book *Challenge of the Present Crisis* (1918), Fosdick became a fervent promoter of world peace. His support for peace initiatives inevitably led him to support the Committee on Militarism in Education. According to his biographer, Fosdick fully supported the committee "and in manifold and other ways labored to achieve its goals, believing as he did that the greatest hope for a world without war rested with the youth of the world."[47]

Perhaps the most notable clergyman to speak out against ROTC was Niebuhr. Although he served a relatively obscure, working-class church in Detroit during the 1920s, his writings and frequent public lectures had an enormous influence on public opinion. By the 1940s Niebuhr had risen to a prestigious academic post at Union Theological Seminary, the nation's leading divinity school, and was on his way to becoming the preeminent midcentury theologian. Like Fosdick, Niebuhr had supported Wilson's aims in World War I and was greatly disheartened by its

outcome. By the 1920s Niebuhr was developing his own brand of Christian social-
ism, which he often articulated in Sayre's journal, *World Tomorrow*. In one article,
"The Threat of ROTC," Niebuhr wrote that military training in schools instilled in
students the "conviction that war is natural and inevitable" and "thrusts a type of
training and an attitude of mind into the college atmosphere which is thoroughly
incompatible with the spirit of democracy and science." In one passage Niebuhr
even characterized school militarism as the litmus test capable of distinguishing
the authentic "lover of peace" from the mere dilettante: "The attitude of a citizen
toward this issue is at the present the most telling criterion of the genuineness of
his peace enthusiasm and the quality of his imagination. If we cannot see the war
system in militarized schools we are blind to the real issues which face a war weary
world."[48] That both Niebuhr and Fosdick endorsed the Lane report and supported
the CME in other ways lent considerable legitimacy to CME's efforts.

Challenging the Committee's Work

Although the committee's tactics were nonviolent, emphasizing persuasive writing, and despite having some of the nation's most respected religious and academic
figures on its letterhead, some critics were not deterred from charging the CME
with subversion. "Nothing will be as fatal to the success of the militaristic attempt
as knowledge of the facts," Dewey had written in his introduction to the Barnes
pamphlet. Alongside this expression of faith in the power of reason to prevent future wars, the eminent philosopher made this ominous prediction: "To suppress
dissemination of this knowledge is the logical course for the militaristic interest to
pursue." What Dewey had in mind was the War Department's "zeal in discredit-
ing those who make the facts known." The military's efforts to suppress knowledge
about ROTC would come encrusted with words familiar to the professional red-
baiter—"paid agitators," "Communist dupes," and the like—all designed to keep
the ship of militarism afloat.

This slanderous campaign began shortly after the Lane report appeared, when
Assistant Secretary of War Hanford MacNider derided the committee at a gathering of the Women's National Republican Club. After labeling all pacifists as "paid
agitators, sentimental sob-sisters, and Reds," MacNider turned his ire specifically
on those who had written and signed the report. MacNider did not understand
how anyone could honestly argue that there was a "pernicious attempt through
military training in our schools to incite the next generation to aggressive warfare." Thus the only reasonable conclusion could be that those behind the Lane
pamphlet were "professional agitators."[49]

The Lane report also placed the CME in the crosshairs of the American Legion.[50] In an editorial for its weekly publication, the patriotic organization urged its readers to counteract the CME's "silly and wrong-headed" campaign by forming ROTC support committees at the local level. As with the legion's attempt to discredit the CME as silly, a decidedly unmanly trait, many critics of the committee's work often used gendered language to disparage opponents of ROTC. In a news bulletin mailed to its members, Scabbard and Blade—the ROTC commanders' national fraternity—charged that the CME was made up of "dupes ... being used to further the aims of Communists in reducing our country to a helpless state." One army officer used the pages of *Infantry Journal* to lament how pacifists were trying to "render the country helpless by abolishing military training in our educational institutions."[51] If ROTC meant manly strength and vigor, critics of ROTC were weakening national defense. At a time when patriotic organizations urged the populace to gird for battle, advocates of military training cast ROTC as the only thing preventing penetration by a foreign enemy.

Even after the initial criticism of CME subsided, officials and their enablers in the private-sector surveillance industry—which was booming by the late 1920s—kept a close watch on CME leadership.[52] During the New Year's holiday in 1927, George Coe and Kirby Page, then editor of *World Tomorrow* and an influential figure in the interwar peace movement, traveled to Milwaukee to lead a two-day gathering at the National Student Conference. Unbeknown to both men, a spy from the Chicago-based Military Intelligence Association, a private organization staffed by retired army intelligence agents, was there to record their every move. (The agent described Coe as "mighty clever" but "insidiously subversive and disloyal to the United States.") In 1928 another private surveillance outfit, the Industrial Defense Association, displayed keen interest in Mary Ellen Wooley, president of Mount Holyoke College, partly because her liberal reformist pedigree included membership in the newly formed Massachusetts chapter of the CME. As late as 1936, Reinhold Niebuhr ended up on a list of "radical professors and teachers" maintained by yet another private snoop—in this case, the former head of army intelligence—because Niebuhr's name appeared on an anti-ROTC petition.[53]

Conclusion

Concerns about school militarism had pricked the conscience of Americans well before the formation of the CME. What prompted John Nevin Sayre and his colleagues to organize their efforts during the second half of the 1920s was increased federal support for military training, including the creation of high school and college ROTC. In their view ROTC at the college and high school level fostered a militaristic mindset and prepared the public to accept war and organized violence as normal functions of the state.

Lacking resources and recognizing their limited political capital, the leaders of CME had to be strategic in choosing which aspects of the issue to address. While not opposed to established military schools and academies, the CME focused on making the public aware of how the War Department was using ROTC as an instrument to establish a culture of militarism within civilian schools. The committee sought to address a number of objectives during its first five years of existence, including lobbying legislatures to abolish the compulsory feature of military training in colleges. This failed effort taught the CME the importance of educating the public about the pitfalls of school-based military training. Through its many publications the committee drew on official government documents and expert testimony to show the devious ways military officials persuaded colleges to offer ROTC and revealed how ROTC textbooks promoted an ideology that closely resembled Prussian militarism. Despite military officials' repeated claims that drill benefited youth, the CME demonstrated that ROTC existed primarily to serve the needs of the expanding postwar military establishment.

Naturally, the American Legion and others did not take kindly to the committee's work. But it was difficult for opponents to paint CME as a radical rabble-rousing organization: the committee's well-researched reports drew on the military's own documentation, and the CME's supporters were often prominent women and clergy. That the CME caused such consternation among military personnel and patriotic groups reveals something important about this spirited organization: it was surprisingly effective. The committee's organizing efforts aided successful demilitarization campaigns in Cleveland and New York City, while CME publications amplified the antimilitarist message and generated support from such key members of Congress as Ross Collins of Mississippi. The committee could even claim some credit for the War Department's decision to eliminate bayonet drill from ROTC training. But the most passionate period of organizing was yet to come, spurred by the social and economic upheavals of the 1930s.

CHAPTER 3

Successful Organizing Confronts the Rising Tide of War

As she was growing up in a Mennonite household in rural Indiana, Rachel Weaver Kreider learned early the value of peace activism. When World War I began, she was seven years old, a time of heightened jingoism and persecution for those who belonged to historic peace churches like hers. Wartime pressures on pacifists contributed to her father's decision to abandon his career as a school administrator. When the United States entered the war, Kreider saw her family home become a destination for young Amish and Mennonite men seeking advice from her father—a former pastor—about how to become conscientious objectors. While some Mennonites in their community later took a conservative turn, her family refused to abide by a strict dress code for women. Years later Kreider told an interviewer that she held in low regard those Mennonites who place "bonnet-wearing and pacifism ... on the same level."[1]

Kreider spent her undergraduate years at Mennonite-run Goshen College, where she met her future husband. Once married, they moved close to the campus of Ohio State University in Columbus, where her husband earned a doctoral degree in chemistry while she worked on a master's degree in philosophy. In January 1934, while Rachel Kreider was writing a term paper on "my people, the pacifist Anabaptists," the university's president made the fateful decision to suspend seven male students who had sought—in vain—to be considered conscientious objectors and thus exempted from compulsory ROTC. The largest-ever mass suspension of college student peaceniks set her on the path to become one of the first Mennonite women peace activists.[2]

At the time of the suspensions Ohio State's administration and board of trustees were seeded with distinguished military men. One was General Edward Orton Jr., dean of the College of Engineering, who led the initial campaign to establish military training on college campuses; in the 1920s he also served on an advisory committee for a patriotic organization that pressured public officials to keep ROTC compulsory at land-grant universities. During the 1930s Ohio State's board also included former secretary of war Newton Baker. Still, Ohio State had long been the site of anti-ROTC ferment. As early as 1926 the campus newspaper captured student sentiment by noting that "compulsory drill has no educational value." By spring 1931 a faculty committee studying the issue recommended that ROTC be made an elective course. But objections from the university administration, along with red-baiting from the campus ROTC commander, combined to stifle debate. In response to opposition to compulsory military training, the university decided to allow student members of historic peace churches to apply for conscientious objector status and thus be excused from the ROTC requirement. By the 1933–34 academic year, after the university extended this exemption to those judged to be sincere in their beliefs, the number of students refusing military training reached forty.[3] While this was a fraction of the overall enrollment, it was significant enough to cause consternation among the powerful at Ohio State. The suspension of the seven students in January 1934 can thus be seen as a desire by the university president to appease those promilitary elements.

The plight of the seven suspended students caught the attention of the Committee on Militarism in Education (CME), which sent its inexperienced secretary, Edwin Johnson, to Columbus for a meeting with church leaders about how to offer support. Johnson was raised in small-town Indiana and had taken four years of military drill in high school. Although he enjoyed that experience at the time, he later came to see how military training in schools and colleges provided the psychological groundwork for war. When then-CME secretary Tucker Smith resigned in the summer of 1931, Johnson—who had been working part time for the committee—took over and served the CME in that capacity until 1940. As secretary, he was responsible for most of the committee's organizational and public relations work.[4]

While Ohio church leaders resisted Johnson's push to file a lawsuit on behalf of the suspended students, some clergy did support legislation calling for voluntary ROTC in the state's land-grant universities. Rachel Weaver Kreider could not resist the urge to get involved. "No matter how much I aim to stay quiet and irresponsible," she wrote in her journal, "I always get myself into some situation eventually where I'm exceedingly busy.... The latest thing is this matter of compulsory military training." She sent letters to Ohio Mennonite pastors urging them to support the legislation, and she attended a hearing held by the Ohio legislature's Military Affairs Committee. A local Methodist pastor who had been counseling Ohio State students to resist ROTC spoke in favor of the bill to make ROTC elective. These efforts were not enough to counter the testimony of the American Legion, whose representatives characterized the ROTC proposal as "Communist propaganda" put forth by "pseudo conscientious objectors." Although the legislation was not brought to a vote, this did not deter Kreider from further peace activism at Ohio State. In fact, it seemed to only strengthen her resolve. Like other student peace activists, she took part in the nationwide "Strike Against War" on April 12, 1934, a symbol of the growing antiwar sentiment on college campuses across the country. Campus activists also organized a large demonstration in University Hall on May 29, 1935. Although she had oral exams for her master's degree later that day, Kreider was a key part of the proceedings, as one of several students selected to appear on stage. For this young Mennonite woman, the anti-ROTC effort at Ohio State instigated a decades-long career of peace activism that would culminate in protests against the Iraq War decades later, when she was ninety-three.[5]

Climate of Activism in the 1930s

While pamphlets and public education formed the bulk of the CME's work during the 1920s, the following decade saw the committee engage in more explicit political activity: petition drives, lobbying, and campaigns to support local activists engaged in anti-ROTC work throughout the United States. The CME found that audiences were increasingly receptive to its message in the 1930s, the peak of the American peace movement.[6]

The new decade brought fresh voices into the debate about military training in schools and was a time when college students formed a powerful new base for political activism. Before the 1930s students were not known for radical politics. During the previous decade the student Left had just a single national organization with two thousand members—a fraction of the overall college enrollment of more than one million. But as economic upheavals triggered an era of unprecedented activism in America, college students began to mobilize.

During the roughly ten years of the Great Depression (1929–39), the United States suffered its longest and most severe economic crisis in history. Between 1930 and 1934 nearly one-third of all U.S. banks collapsed and the gross domestic product shrunk by nearly 25 percent. At its nadir one in four Americans was out of work; in some parts of the country unemployment rates rose as high as 50 percent. Economic crisis quickly led to social fracture, sparking food riots, labor disputes, homelessness, and a widespread sense of despair. "Many collegians seeking to comprehend the economic crisis," the historian Robert Cohen notes, "found that the Left alone was able to explain the Depression and offer alternatives to the faltering capitalist system." Students and their organizations campaigned for Socialist political candidates, supported the cause of organized labor, and advocated for a jobs program for unemployed youth. Until the 1960s the student movements of the Great Depression represented the most compelling political mobilization by America's youth.[7]

After the Japanese invasion of Manchuria in 1931 and Hitler's rise to power in 1933, the student Left pivoted toward peace activism. Students on many college campuses called for an end to compulsory ROTC. In a national 1932 survey of more than twenty-five thousand students, 81 percent "disapproved of compulsory ROTC," while 38 percent urged colleges to abandon voluntary military training. The next year a national poll showed that nearly a third of American college students said they would fight in a war only if the United States were invaded.[8]

Fearing the outbreak of another world war, the era's two major student organizations—the Student League for Industrial Democracy and the National Student League—organized a series of nationwide student strikes against war that grew exponentially throughout the decade. The first took place on April 13, 1934, and involved approximately twenty-five thousand students, most from colleges and universities in New York City. A year later more than 150,000 undergraduates participated in a similar action on more than 130 college campuses across the country. While the 1935 strike was centered in New York, its effect was also felt at Ivy League schools like the University of Pennsylvania, where three thousand activists cheered the Socialist leader Norman Thomas as he urged them to stay out of war. Even at less selective institutions like Los Angeles Junior College, another three thousand observed the strike, despite severe repression against student activists.[9] These demonstrations were a precursor to the largest nationwide strike against war, on April 22, 1936, involving an estimated half-million students. One of the specific targets of the striking students was the Reserve Officers' Training Corps. "Military drill is being used to prepare us to fight for the profits of big business," read one handbill passed out by Harvard's Anti-war Strike Committee, while thousands of students at the University of California's most elite campuses, Los Angeles and Berkeley, passed resolutions urging abolition of ROTC.[10]

As students were agitating against ROTC, support for their cause came from a surprising place: former military officers. In 1930 an education journal published an article by Richard Welling, a Harvard graduate and former naval officer. As the former head of a committee calling for the revitalization of civics education, Welling was steeped in Progressive Era educational values. His article, "Defend the Public Schools against Militarism," offered a version of the "mindset theory" that the CME had widely embraced. "I welcome proficiency in marksmanship, horsemanship, flying, chemistry, seamanship, ballistics, whatever you will," he wrote, "but when the public-school children are ordered out to march, the psychology is 'war' and it has no proper place in the public schools." Welling's status as a former military officer lent legitimacy to the growing anti-ROTC cause. Several others with equally impressive credentials also cast doubt on the wisdom of compulsory military training programs in schools. Men like Major Enoch Garcy—formerly the ROTC commander at Johns Hopkins—and Major F. M. DeRohan, Garcy's counterpart at the University of Washington, publicly stated that ROTC units were easier to maintain when cadets could *freely* choose to participate. "I'd like to give every student who does not like drill an excuse," DeRohan once said, "and tell him to get out." The only reason he did not, he suggested, was that he was bound by his university's policy of compulsory participation.[11]

Still, the peace movement's driving force continued to be members of the clergy. In 1931 *World Tomorrow* revealed that 54 percent of the more than nineteen thousand clergy in its survey were against war.[12] Throughout the decade the annual conventions of regional and national church bodies proved quite willing to swat away what CME's national chair, George Coe, had called the "steely fingers of militarism." In 1931 the Methodists of New England passed resolutions opposing high school courses in military science or military drill. The following year the Methodist Episcopal Church used its national convention to petition Congress to cease its financial support for military training in schools and colleges. In 1934 the Federal Council of Churches passed a resolution urging state legislatures to eliminate compulsory ROTC. Opposition to school militarism even came from more conservative corners of American Protestantism.[13] At their 1934 annual assembly in Cleveland, delegates from the Presbyterian Church rejected military training in educational institutions and offered a sweeping denunciation of war and militarism, emphasizing that "Christians cannot give their support to war," the *New York Times* reported. "The Presbyterians are not, in general, an excitable people," the editors of *Christian Century* had wryly noted six months earlier. "They are little given to being stampeded into ill considered and precipitate action." Such explicit antimilitarist statements from a normally conservative church body made it apparent to the editors that "there is in this country a large number of those who . . . 'break with the whole war system.'"[14]

These persistent efforts to oppose ROTC frustrated preparedness-minded members of nationalistic organizations. At a meeting of the Women's Patriotic Conference on National Defense in 1932, Lieutenant Colonel Orvel Johnson, executive secretary of the Reserve Officers' Training Corps Association, declared that "pacifist preachers" were "the greatest menace" to the ROTC. Johnson saved his harshest rhetoric for the Federal Council of Churches, which he charged with pushing youth toward "the road to communism." As they had during the first years of the CME's existence, these organizations maintained their advocacy for compulsory ROTC, which they saw as essential to national defense. At its state convention in 1935, the Indiana chapter of the American Legion passed a resolution condemning DePauw University president G. Bromley Oxnam. A former adviser to the pacifist intellectual Sherwood Eddy, Oxnam was a CME board member in 1929 when he became president of the prestigious private university in Indiana. In 1934 his campus leadership on the issue brought an end to compulsory ROTC at DePauw. Oxnam was acting not only in accord with his own values but in support of a years-long student-led campaign against compulsory military training. Yet in the eyes of the American Legion, Oxnam's "constant efforts" to commit his university "to a program of radicalism and communistic activities" merited censure.[15]

The previous decade had given the CME experience in managing the red-baiting tactics of some of its adversaries. But it was unprepared to handle the War Department's newer, more sophisticated methods of promoting ROTC. Perhaps the most notable instance came in 1932 with the publication of a major survey of men who had graduated ROTC between 1920 and 1930. Of the more than ten thousand respondents, 93.6 percent denied that the program instilled belligerent or prowar attitudes in cadets. But critics seized on the demographics of the study: it had hardly sought the opinions of an unbiased group. After all, it was widely known that ROTC graduates were former or current army officers who tended to strongly favor the military training and education they had received through the program. The editors of the *New York World-Telegram* were also unimpressed, and in a critique reprinted in Scripps-Howard newspapers across the country, they characterized the War Department report as a "symposium for a selected group, whose favorable opinion of military training could have been known in advance," making it "of doubtful value even as propaganda."[16] Despite the clear bias, the survey, conducted by Major Ralph Chesney Bishop with the support of the U.S. Office of Education, became a mainstay of War Department propaganda in the coming years, as it sought to reassure a worried public that ROTC was not producing militaristic young men.

Resistance to the CME's activities did not deter it from carrying out its mission. At the start of the new decade, sixty-five high schools and colleges had dropped military training completely and nearly a dozen others had chosen to make it elective rather than mandatory. But while the CME could rightly take credit for much of that progress, the committee could not afford to become complacent. The reality was that the War Department—with an assist from scores of college presidents—was able to replace these losses with new ROTC programs nationwide.[17]

For years America's university leaders had complained of shabbily dressed cadets and other signs that the ROTC program did not receive sufficient funding. Finally, in the 1930s the War Department persuaded Congress to allocate more money to the program, including for new equipment. By the middle of the decade, more than forty colleges and universities were reporting growth in their ROTC enrollment of 15 to 20 percent compared to the previous year. Press accounts attributed some of this increase to the appeal of those snazzy new government-supplied uniforms. As a result of the "generous appropriations of Congress," CME secretary Edwin Johnson later wrote, the number of units and cadets soared during the first half of the decade. There were various ways to chart this growth. In 1913 the War Department had assigned only 85 officers to ROTC duty. By 1933 that number had increased to 1,658. And between the 1930–31 and 1938–39 school years, ROTC registered an increase of more than 70,000 enrolled students.[18]

For all the hard work the CME put into its campaign against military drill, it was unable to overcome the enormous financial resources, influence, congressional goodwill, and local patriotic sentiment that the military establishment enjoyed. Despite widespread support for peace from religious bodies and prominent educational and military figures, the American public favored greater military spending. This sentiment, along with pushback from the War Department and veterans' organizations, highlights how difficult it was for the CME to oppose militarism in schools. Yet the committee's work during the 1930s represents an important countercurrent in American culture, especially at the end of the decade as debates raged about whether the nation should intervene or remain neutral in the emerging global conflict.[19]

Appeals to the Courts

By the early 1930s the growing student peace movement and continuing pressure by the War Department to maintain compulsory ROTC led the CME to believe that it was time to test the constitutionality of mandatory drill. Also catching the committee's attention, in fall 1932, were the more than one hundred students who had sought the CME's help to avoid mandatory training at their colleges and universities. Seizing the moment, the committee decided to establish its own campaign to directly recruit and advise student conscientious objectors. As the historian James Hawkes notes, "The conscientious objector afforded a peg on which to hang the legal test" of compulsory ROTC. CME officials predicted that student conscientious objectors could attract press coverage and stand as compelling public symbols of all that was wrong with mandatory military training.[20]

The CME first targeted students at state-supported institutions with literature discussing how to seek an exemption from compulsory military drill. One pamphlet suggested that students should always conduct themselves in an "earnest and dignified" manner when ROTC officers pressured them to remain in ROTC classes. Another pamphlet, *Steps to Take in Refusing Compulsory Military Training*, recommended that prospective conscientious objectors seek assistance from religious and other organizations critical of compulsory drill, and emphasized that these students should make clear that their appeal for exemption was directed at the civilian authorities responsible for permitting military compulsion on campus, not War Department officials. Most important, this brochure noted that students at tax-supported institutions would have good legal standing to insist on having a college education free from military indoctrination and promised that the CME would provide legal aid to prospective conscientious objectors.[21]

The committee's campaign crystallized in 1932, when the president of the University of Maryland expelled two students for refusing to attend a compulsory ROTC course. The students appealed to the Maryland Board of Regents, which upheld the president's decision. Relying on financial and legal support from the Methodist Episcopal Church and the CME, one of the students, Ennes H. Coale, took his case to court. At the time of his protest Coale was a first-year student from Bel Air, Maryland, and a member of the Methodist Church. "The course in military training is a preparation for war, which is contrary to my religious convictions," he noted. "I cannot take a part in it and be true to my understanding of the teachings of Jesus." Coale's lawyers argued that Maryland's university charter permitted exemption for conscientious objectors to Quakers and other members of historic peace churches. When the Superior Court judge compared Methodist Episcopal doctrine on war with that of the Quakers', he found that they were virtually indistinguishable. The judge therefore ruled in Coale's favor, noting that if the University of Maryland had historically relieved Quaker students of their ROTC duties, the school should also do the same for those in Coale's church.[22]

Pro-ROTC forces were quick to react. In the *Baltimore Sun*, Orvel Johnson of the Reserve Officers' Training Corps Association portrayed Coale as a pawn in a communist campaign to propagandize American youth. In an editorial the *Army and Navy Register* warned of a domino effect stemming from the court ruling. "If a youth may evade a military service because he claims to be a conscientious objector as a member of the Methodist Church," the editorial intoned, "he may claim such an exemption because he is a member of any other denomination, and we will find the slackers and evaders claiming such exemptions when their services are needed in an emergency. That cannot be, and the churches would not have it so."[23] The noted *Baltimore Sun* journalist J. F. Essary viewed the Coale case in much the same way. If allowed to stand, he wrote, the ruling could lead to the total breakdown of the compulsory ROTC system at the nation's land-grant colleges and universities. After the University of Maryland appealed, an appellate court judge reversed the earlier ruling. Without citing evidence, the judge decided that Coale's real motive was "a disposition to join the society mentioned (the committee on militarism in education) to defeat the government in an attempt to be ready for war if forced upon the country." Then, in November 1933, the U.S. Supreme Court dismissed his appeal on the ground that the matter was for the states to decide.[24]

That same year two Methodist students at the University of California, Albert Hamilton and Alonzo Reynolds, were also suspended on similar grounds. Adopting a unique legal strategy, they claimed that the university's action denied them their equal rights under the U.S. Constitution. The basis for their claim was the U.S. Senate's ratification of the 1928 Kellogg-Briand Pact renouncing war as an instrument of national policy, which they claimed superseded state law. In this instance the California courts ruled in favor of the university. The case then went to the U.S. Supreme Court, which held that the university's compulsory military training did not violate conscience or the First Amendment's free exercise of religion, and said that the right to exemption from military service on conscientious grounds was not a constitutional privilege or immunity of U.S. citizens.[25]

The Supreme Court's actions in both *Coale* and *Hamilton* rested on two critical issues. The court first established as law that conscientious objectors had no right under the U.S. Constitution to exemption from military service. Second, it ruled in favor of military education, declaring that the privilege of attending a university was granted by the state, not the federal government. Although the CME failed in its quest to have compulsory ROTC declared unconstitutional, the committee was pleased to see these legal cases generate favorable publicity for the cause. Shortly after the Supreme Court's *Hamilton* decision, the Federal Council of Churches passed a resolution suggesting that Congress had the power to act to ensure that conscientious objectors could be exempted from ROTC at colleges and universities. The *Hamilton* case also prompted an editorial against compulsory ROTC in the *New York World-Telegram* that ran in numerous other dailies owned by the Scripps-Howard national newspaper chain. The editorial explained why compulsory military training was "unfair, illiberal and unwise" before saying that the "battle against compulsory militarizing of the students of state universities should go on. But the fight will have to be made in Congress, which controls appropriations for the Army and the Reserve Officers Training Corps, on which the state compulsory military education system rests in practice." The CME agreed. In a confidential bulletin the committee advised members that the unfavorable court rulings were a clear signal that they could more fruitfully campaign against compulsory ROTC by lobbying for state and federal legislation.[26]

Heading to the Halls of Congress

By the mid-1930s CME leaders were seasoned lobbyists. Between 1926 and 1930 CME members regularly appeared before congressional committees to express their opposition to ROTC. The committee had also spent enormous sums mailing thousands of letters and pieces of literature that urged supporters to ask their representatives in Congress to vote against further War Department appropriations for ROTC. Typical of the committee's lobbying efforts was a 1933 petition submitted to Congress by George Coe and signed by 340 educators from across the country, including many from leading schools of teacher education.

Strategically, the committee sought to muster as many educators as possible to convince Congress that education for military training was "unfair, illiberal, and unwise." Congressional lobbying campaigns by the CME typically consisted of three arguments: that military training in schools and colleges had no educational value; it was without legal basis in the National Defense Act; and it contradicted established American policy of leaving educational decisions to the states. Inspired by the wave of student antiwar activism, in the summer of 1935 CME leaders sought congressional support to outlaw compulsory military training. The committee was counting on the isolationist mood of the nation, which had been growing as global conflict loomed.[27]

By 1935 European fascism was on the march, underlined by Italy's invasion of Ethiopia in October. Initially CME's intention was to promote a bill eliminating ROTC, but geopolitical tensions and rising militarism forced it to take a more realistic approach. The committee decided instead to support legislation to amend the National Defense Acts of 1916 and 1920 by eliminating the words "or compulsory" and adding a provision stipulating that no ROTC unit would be established or maintained until the secretary of war could verify that student enrollment was voluntary. In the summer of 1935 this bill found sponsors in Senator Gerald P. Nye, Republican of North Dakota, who had chaired the well-publicized Senate committee investigation of the munitions industry during World War I, and Paul J. Kvale, a Farmer-Labor representative from Minnesota.

Opposition to the Nye-Kvale Amendment was fierce, if not predictable. Secretary of War George H. Dern argued that a federal mandate for voluntary ROTC infringed on states' rights and weakened the national defense. In his department's 1934–35 annual report, Dern explicitly challenged the CME, characterizing anti-

ROTC campaigners as misguided purveyors of "seditious propaganda" who "despise our form of government and desire its overthrow." The secretary of war considered compulsory ROTC such a critical element of military manpower strategy that opposing it was tantamount to "seeking to undermine the Nation's ability to defend itself." Undeterred, proponents led by Coe and the CME sent a letter to President Franklin Roosevelt, insisting "that the change in the ROTC from a compulsory to a voluntary basis would actually strengthen the national defense by permitting the army to concentrate its efforts upon those students who were not indifferent or hostile to a military-type training." The letter also used Dern's words, especially his use of the loaded term "seditious propaganda," to bolster the committee's argument. "If insinuations of this nature are to be directed against those who have reason or inclination to oppose compulsory military training," the letter read, "that fact, it seems to us, will constitute further ground upon which to rest objection to the war department's present activities in our civil schools and colleges."[28]

Seeking to consolidate support, the committee organized a nationwide editorial-writing contest for college students on the subject of why Congress should pass the Nye-Kvale Amendment. At Senate hearings on the legislation, one of the country's most prominent educators, Guy Stanton Ford of the University of Minnesota, stated that after witnessing about thirty years of student drill he was not convinced of the military's claim that it assisted in individual student improvement, nor was he moved by the argument that it contributed to national preparedness. Despite the large number of educators and religious leaders who supported this federal legislation, the bill was defeated the following year.[29]

Demilitarization through Referendum: The Oregon Campaign

Seeing that its work in Washington was yielding diminishing returns, the CME began to consider other strategies. By 1936 the committee had decided to support a growing student-led campaign in Oregon, one of several states that allowed citizens to initiate legislation through the petition process. Students at the state's land-grant colleges had been trying to abolish compulsory ROTC since the early 1930s. Although reactionary university presidents and unsympathetic state legislators had nixed those efforts, by 1936 student leaders had support from the Oregon Federation of Labor and the Oregon Grange and had gathered enough signatures to place the issue on the ballot for November's statewide election.[30]

Ballot questions normally did not generate national publicity, but the Oregon initiative was deemed to be history-in-the-making by some of the country's leading newspapers. A *New York Times* article noted that it marked "the first time in history the question of compulsory military training in American public schools and colleges is to come to popular vote." Richard Neuberger, a prominent Oregon resident and newspaper columnist, wrote that the referendum marked "an entirely new departure in the prolonged opposition to mandatory participation in military courses." The editors of the *Oregonian*, one of the state's high-circulation daily newspapers, also supported the initiative. Calling the national defense arguments for compulsory ROTC "utterly fallacious," an editorial declared that between the state's National Guard and citizens' military training camps, the paper saw no apparent lack of men trained and willing to fight. To vote yes on the referendum, the paper advised readers, would end the "wholly unnecessary injustice of making college students the one class among all our young men who are compelled to take military training in peacetime." For its part the *Baltimore Sun* editorial board also questioned the logic of compelling only college students to complete military training: "They are not a class apart. If it is their 'duty' to be trained as soldiers, then it is the 'duty' of every citizen to be so trained." Compulsory ROTC, the editorial warned, led inexorably to universal peacetime military training—a system "not only un-American and undemocratic but positively dangerous to our democratic institutions."[31]

Contrary to the expectations of Neuberger and other political observers, the ballot measure failed. The CME's 1936 annual report attributed the loss to a lack of financial support from other groups in the peace movement, as well as a vicious red-baiting campaign by the conservative daily *Oregon Journal*. While this outcome was disappointing to members of the CME, Edwin Johnson, the secretary, found reason for optimism: of multiple measures on the ballot, no question received as many yes votes—more than 130,000—as the issue of ending compulsory ROTC. In a postmortem analysis of the failed measure, the editors of the weekly *Christian Century* commented that the campaign was hobbled from the start by lack of funds. In a letter to the magazine's editors, Johnson agreed that finances were a problem but suggested that churches were also partly to blame for the defeat.

That churches had declined to more fully support the measure illustrated what Johnson saw as a troubling disjunction between resolutions passed at churches' annual assemblies and parish-level leadership. "The churches have passed good resolutions—yes; but beyond that comparatively little has been done," he wrote. "If each preacher in Oregon had carried his own congregation on the military drill question, the outcome of the vote might have been different. On this issue, as on so many others, church leaders have mastered a resolution-adopting technique, but as yet comparatively few of them have learned that social ideals cannot be translated into political realities without hard and costly struggle." Although the CME had initially pledged financial aid to the referendum campaign, the committee had grossly underestimated the cost of radio advertising and other expenses. Thus one observer noted that the Oregon campaign was a "costly failure" for CME and would place the committee in a financially compromised position as it entered the fraught years of the late 1930s.[32]

The Split in the Peace Movement

After the defeat of the Nye-Kvale bill, and the failure of the Oregon referendum, much of the CME's energy was depleted by events outside its control. The world stage offered little solace as the rise of military dictatorships in Europe and Asia eroded popular support for peace. Roosevelt's policies favoring neutrality, combined with the rise of Japanese militarism in the Far East and the rapid spread of fascism in Italy and Germany, sparked divisions that would ultimately wreck the peace movement in the second half of the 1930s. Historians such as Charles DeBenedetti, Charles Chatfield, and Lawrence Wittner have described how peace advocacy organizations underwent a disastrous split in 1935 when the collapse of the League of Nations and heightened European militarism spurred fears of another world war. The National Council for the Prevention of War, the Women's International League for Peace and Freedom, and other organizations recognized their inability to prevent war in Europe and began to focus on isolating America through neutrality agreements. Meanwhile, conservative groups like the Carnegie Endowment for International Peace and the Church Peace Union, urged "collective security," by which they meant curbing "aggressor nations" and aiding America's allies.[33]

Throughout the mid- to late 1930s, peace coalitions struggled to make the goal of neutrality a workable reality. One such effort was the Emergency Peace Campaign, an outlet for liberals and conservatives who were in favor of neutrality and against communism. In 1937 CME's Edwin Johnson arranged for the committee to join the peace campaign without consulting the executive board. Although the vice chair, John Sayre, and the national chair, George Coe, criticized Johnson's lack of transparency, more serious was the effect it would have on the committee's fund-raising ability. By this time Johnson was struggling to keep the organization afloat. Continued financial woes had reduced the number of CME staff to only two people in 1935. By the end of 1936 the organization had fallen behind on payments to staff. According to Oswald Garrison Villard, a board member and the CME's chief financial backer, Johnson's controversial decision to tie the committee to a group favoring neutrality so angered the director of the Church Peace Union (CPU), one of the CME's key donors, that Villard doubted the committee could count on the CPU's future financial support. The imbroglio about the

CME's alliance with the peace campaign highlights the divide that emerged between radical pacifists and the more conservative sector of the American peace movement.[34]

Neither wing of the antiwar movement, the neutralists and collective security advocates, formed a unified political whole. While each wing advocated some of the same policies, they remained two distinct and frequently conflicting political and ideological camps. At the core of their divide was the troubling issue of whether America's commitment was to a wider world community or instead to a narrow nationalism. The only peace group that remained intact until the end of the decade was the CME.[35] The committee's longevity was largely the result of its focus on a single issue: militarism in education. Toward the end of the 1930s, however, the CME's emphasis started to shift.

Notable Campaigns of the Late 1930s

The historian Ronald Schaffer finds that there were no major anti-ROTC campaigns after 1936. Although it is true that the CME's traditional focus on universities began to wane in the late 1930s, Daniel Barthell suggests that this reflected Johnson's strategic judgment that the War Department had reached a "saturation point" in the number of ROTC units and cadets at land-grant universities. In the CME secretary's view, the War Department was thus beginning to focus on establishing its presence within a larger target: the nation's high schools. Under Johnson's guidance the CME therefore began its belated campaign of opposition to Junior ROTC (JROTC).[36]

As it had with university campaigns, the CME acted in a supportive role in the resistance to high school militarism by providing local anti-JROTC activists with guidance, organizational support, literature, and sometimes financial aid. This pattern played out in the fall of 1935, when the War Department sought to penetrate the New York City public schools.[37] With little public discussion the city's school board approved a plan to install Junior ROTC at two high schools, one in Brooklyn and another in the Bronx. Military personnel would teach the program during school hours, and students would be permitted to take JROTC to satisfy their graduation requirement in physical education. "Immediately a storm of opposition criticism broke loose," the CME's Johnson later wrote.[38]

The backlash coalesced under the banner of the United Committee Against Militarism in New York City Schools, which consisted of representatives from the city's teachers' union, the forty-thousand-member United Parents Association of Greater New York, the CME, and other peace organizations. While many of these groups had mobilized in 1929 in an earlier, unsuccessful campaign against a proposed JROTC unit at a Queens high school, this time the coalition avoided alienating potential supporters with ideological appeals.[39] Instead of relying on antimilitarist rhetoric, as activists had done in 1929, the United Committee Against Militarism stressed how the proposed JROTC units would violate existing city and state educational codes. To what extent this legalistic approach was a deliberate strategy to avoid having to take a stand for or against JROTC is not known. What is certain, however, is that it worked. On March 23, 1936, after weeks of contentious debate, the school board withdrew its proposal.[40]

The CME also poured resources into another local battle in 1936, after the school board of Carbondale, Illinois, voted 4–1 to set up a JROTC unit. While local veterans supported the board's decision, other sectors of the farming community vocally opposed the plan. The town's Ministerial Association and the League of Women Voters also condemned it. When the school board responded by organizing a community referendum on the question, the CME used its literature to educate local residents and solidify opposition to high school military training. The committee also scored a major public relations coup by converting Roscoe Pulliam, the president of the local state teachers' college (later christened Southern Illinois University), into a fierce opponent of JROTC.[41]

Pulliam had impeccable credentials to speak on the issue, as he was both an educator and a veteran of the Great War who had spent nine months fighting on the western front. In a statement about the controversy, Pulliam declared: "Military training and sound, modern education are altogether incompatible." While contemporary schools tried to produce an informed citizen capable of independent thought, he observed, the military sought to manufacture only "an obedient automaton." Military training for fourteen-year-olds may have made sense for countries under fascist control, like Germany and Italy, but had absolutely no place "in any of our free democratic American schools." In a testament to the power of Pulliam's rhetoric, the final tally of the referendum vote was 442 to 347 against the high school military units, which led the school board to abandon its JROTC plans.[42]

But the argument about a military presence in U.S. high schools had just begun. By the late 1930s the War Department appeared to be making a major push to enter the country's largest urban school districts. In the span of just two years, Chicago schools added more than a dozen JROTC units. By 1937 more than ten thousand Chicago high school students were enrolled in the program. The president of the city's school board endorsed the JROTC expansion, declaring that it "strengthen[ed] pupils' loyalty, both to their country and their school" and thus inoculated them from "communistic influences." The school board largely ignored organized opposition to the militarization of Chicago's youth.[43]

Even as the CME's focus shifted to support grassroots campaigns against

JROTC, the committee still sought opportunities to oppose a military presence in colleges. In January 1936, after months of protests led by the student newspaper, the *Daily Texan*, faculty at the University of Texas, Austin, voted overwhelmingly to reject the proposed establishment of ROTC on campus. The committee was in constant touch with Texas activists, offering advice and literature. The next year CME became involved in opposing California legislation that would have made graduation from state teachers' colleges contingent on completion of ROTC. As national chair of the CME, Coe—who had recently moved to Claremont, California, where he had family—was in an excellent position to lobby against the bill. He sent letters to the state superintendent of public instruction, who happened to be a Quaker, and appealed to him on the basis of those beliefs; talked with several friends on the faculty at the Claremont Graduate School of Education; and sent a letter to the nephew of (Coe's) late wife, state senator William Knowland, who was then serving on the state senate's education committee. Joining the CME in opposition to the proposal were local members of the Women's International League for Peace and Freedom, as well as a Methodist pastor who publicly condemned efforts to "militarize our citizenship." When the bill—which had strong backing from the state's American Legion—later underwent significant revision to soften its most militaristic aspects, the CME's Johnson considered it a "partial defensive victory of great importance."[44]

The Committee's Last Hurrah

Confronted by the rising tide of war and a peace movement split by how best to confront the world crisis, the CME struggled to remain relevant. In a 1937 article for the *Clearing House*, an educational journal, Johnson linked the argument about school militarism at home to the battle against fascism abroad. Writing that "the militarizing of our public schools constitutes a certain drift in the direction of fascist regimentation," the CME secretary considered it self-evident that military training in high schools "cultivates a fascist mentality in those who are subjected to it."[45] Though financial difficulties limited the committee's ability to produce and distribute new literature, one of its final pamphlets contained a compelling new slogan: "The fight against war and fascism is lost—unless it's won in our schools and colleges."[46]

Despite its best efforts, by the end of the decade the CME faced an uphill battle. In 1938 the committee managed an optimistic tone with one of its last pieces of literature, a pamphlet highlighting seventeen cases since 1923 in which organizers had secured the elimination of compulsory ROTC. Despite these victories, ROTC's appeal seemed only to increase as calls for U.S. military preparedness grew louder in a war-torn world. By 1940 ROTC had commissioned more than one hundred thousand officers, providing an easy way for universities to demonstrate their patriotism. "Within twenty-four years of its creation," according to one scholar, "220 colleges and universities had successfully acquired a unit, and many more sat anxiously on waiting lists."[47]

In the mid-1930s the CME hoped to gain a fresh perspective by adding to its executive board the peace historian Merle Curti. In 1936 Curti had published his magnum opus, *Peace or War: The American Struggle, 1636–1936*, in which he had signaled his respect for the committee's work. While tracing the history of America's struggle against war, Curti marveled at how the CME had "conducted a vigorous campaign against compulsory military training in schools and colleges, and in spite of an extremely meager budget has made its influence felt all over the land." Curti's pioneering history of pacifist ideals and peace movements demonstrated that analysis of peace movements could be as exciting and rewarding as the study of major wars, and it made clear to former Columbia faculty like Coe and Dewey that Curti could contribute to one of the CME's newest projects: peace education.[48]

The emphasis on peace education marked another shift in CME's evolution from purely oppositional campaigns based on what education should *not* be and toward a more positive vision of what education *could* be. Shortly before Curti joined the board in late 1936, the CME began to prepare for what the committee's secretary called a "constructive proposal" in the area of peace education. The curriculum Johnson envisioned would serve as an elective course of study for students at colleges and universities that had compulsory ROTC. It was yet another accommodation to the reality that courts and state legislatures had consistently upheld forced military training in schools and colleges; unable to eradicate compulsory ROTC, the committee would use peace education as a salve for students stuck in the maw of militarism.

In CME's annual report for 1936, Johnson noted that a special committee had been established to coordinate the peace education campaign. In 1937 the CME took its first important step, a survey to determine which colleges and universities were already offering "formal courses in problems of war and peace." Among the nine schools where professors were teaching on this topic, several had seen student- and clergy-led opposition to compulsory ROTC during the previous decade. Although little is known about the CME's peace education program, the committee's reports suggest that one of the next steps would have been to use the survey to identify a model curriculum, after which the CME would commit to "lending every possible aid" to encourage the development of similar courses at other colleges.[49]

But there was a slight problem: money. Financial difficulties bedeviled the organization throughout the 1930s, probably beginning with the decision by Tucker Smith, the secretary at the time, to run up an enormous debt printing CME literature. When Smith was replaced as secretary in the summer of 1931, the committee was $5,000 in arrears (the equivalent of $88,000 today), a large portion of the committee's $12,000 annual budget. CME's debt gradually declined over the years, but by early 1938 the committee still carried a deficit of more than $1,000 from the previous year. In December 1938 Sayre painted a dire picture of the committee's finances before asking a supporter to consider advancing the date of her annual contribution. "He has a wife and three children," Sayre wrote of Edwin Johnson, "and must depend entirely on the thirty-two hundred dollar salary which our Committee tries to provide, but which is now four hundred dollars in arrears."[50]

For years Johnson had tolerated late payments of his salary. But by the spring of 1939, the long-suffering CME secretary was sounding desperate. "The situation, as I see it, has become most hopeless," he wrote to Coe. "During the last three or four weeks we have received one discouraging blow after another," as major donors ceased their annual giving. Johnson was forced to admit that two groups in particular—the Church Peace Union and the Christian Social Justice Fund—had stopped supporting the CME because of his decision to place the committee in the camp that advocated neutrality. "As you can imagine," Johnson wrote, "the net effect of the above losses has been to knock the bottom right out from under our budget." As Johnson explained to the CME's national chair, only two solutions were available. Either the committee should seriously consider revisiting the idea of merging with another peace organization or it could reduce the size of the CME to "a minimum skeletal form" that would cost $5,000 annually to run. As to the latter possibility, Johnson referenced his earlier economic sacrifices on behalf of the CME: "What my own personal status will be in the event such a decision is made, I cannot say. While I would be willing to suffer much in order to postpone or avoid the break-up of our work, it is a fact that I have responsibilities toward my family that I must meet."[51]

In a confidential report dated May 4, 1939, Sayre sounded another pessimistic tone. "The fear of imminent war appears to be an important factor," he observed, "in reducing the income of the Committee on Militarism in Education to a threatening starvation point." Still, he added, the executive board had unanimously approved a resolution testifying to the continuing need for the CME and affirming its belief that the organization was "carrying on a unique and very valuable service not only for the peace movement, but also for the future of American education and democracy."[52]

But by 1940 the CME was a spent force. Heavily in debt, the committee could barely afford to pay its few remaining staff members. More important, it was losing the battle for public opinion, as many of its long-time allies began to view war as the only path to eliminate the threat of fascism. The CME gradually lost its traditional base of support: pacifist Protestant clergy and progressive educators. Pacifism in American churches began to decline after 1939, and even Reinhold Niebuhr—who had once served on the CME's board and advocated against ROTC—had by 1941 become so disillusioned with Christian pacifism that he started his own magazine, *Christianity & Crisis*, to help blunt its appeal. By the end of the decade teachers too were becoming less receptive to the peace message and more willing to do whatever was necessary to support national defense. This tension had emerged at the 1936 convention of the National Education Association, when delegates supported a resolution against compulsory military training in schools and colleges but overwhelmingly rejected a separate committee report that would have offered a far more sweeping denunciation of ROTC, criticizing its "tendency to militarize the schools."[53]

Given the climate of public opinion, and the increasingly dire world situation, peacetime conscription was all but inevitable. Despite a last-minute scramble by the CME, including a petition drive resulting in the signatures of more than four hundred prominent Americans, on September 16, 1940, with strong congressional approval, President Roosevelt signed the Burke-Wadsworth Act into law. Establishment of the first peacetime conscription in U.S. history sounded the death knell of the CME. One month later, in a letter addressed to "Friends of the CME," Sayre acknowledged that the end had come. "Once this bill was passed, putting the full weight of the government behind the compulsory principle," he wrote, "it was evident that the lines along which much of our former work had been conducted would be hopelessly out of date." In October, at the committee's final executive board meeting, the majority of the board voted to disband the organization and surrender its archives to Swarthmore College.[54]

Conclusion

During 1935–40, as nationalism slowly gripped the nation and "finally choked the life out of the committee," the CME fell victim to events largely beyond its control. Perhaps a stronger, more financially sound organization might have survived the rising tide of militarism in the run-up to World War II, but the Burke-Wadsworth Act applied the coup de grace.[55]

Despite its demise, the CME deserves recognition for focusing attention on the issue of militarism in public education. For the first time in American history, an organization had alerted the public to the dangers of a military influence in civilian education. The committee also tried to expose how and why the War Department attempted to popularize ROTC. By the mid-1930s the CME was responsible for encouraging dozens of colleges and universities to abolish compulsory military instruction. The development and expansion of Junior ROTC was also largely restrained as the CME effectively persuaded teachers, parents, and other members of the public that militarism had no place in the high school curriculum. Through its political activity at the federal, state, and local levels, moreover, the group promoted legislation to bar compulsory military training in colleges. Last, the CME sought to use the judicial process to exempt student conscientious objectors from mandatory military drill.

Although the organization did not achieve its main goal of eliminating compulsory military training at public colleges and universities, the CME did win modest victories at the state and local level, as well as in Congress, which sometimes denied funds for a major expansion of ROTC units. Despite vicious red-baiting campaigns and limited budgets, the CME persevered to become one of the more influential peace organizations of the interwar period. Perhaps the committee's most important contribution was nurturing the antiwar sentiment that grew out of the disillusionment from World War I. It did so by generating awareness of military training in education, questioning military control of public schools, and defending an individual's right to conscientiously object to compulsory drill. In so doing, the CME set the stage for the debate that would convulse American society throughout the 1960s and 1970s: how to balance the foundations of a democratic education based on openness and tolerance with the established military principles of obedience and conformity.

Abolish the ROTC. Poster produced by the Rebel Artists Group in 1934 and used in the 1934–35 Strike Against War by students on college campuses across the country. Box 30, Joseph Lash Papers. Courtesy of the Franklin D. Roosevelt Presidential Library and Museum, Hyde Park, New York.

Vietnam War protest, 1969, Washington, D.C. Papers of Clergy and Laity Concerned about Vietnam. Courtesy of Swarthmore College Peace Collection.

John Nevin Sayre, secretary of the Fellowship of Reconciliation for many years, was instrumental in founding the Committee on Militarism in Education. John Nevin Sayre Papers. Courtesy of Swarthmore College Peace Collection.

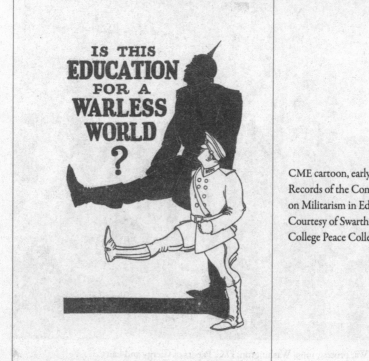

CME cartoon, early 1930s. Records of the Committee on Militarism in Education. Courtesy of Swarthmore College Peace Collection.

STUDENTS PLAYING AT WAR

Acme Photo

NO MUD—NO BLOOD—
NO SUFFERING—NO SACRIFICE

Read

SO THIS IS WAR!

A Study of Sugar-coated Militarism

by

TUCKER P. SMITH

Forty-eight pages of illustrations and copy, showing how pretty girl officers, polo ponies, sham battles, snappy uniforms and parades are used to prettify war for high school and college students. Fifteen cents postpaid.

George A. Coe, Chairman

COMMITTEE ON MILITARISM IN EDUCATION

2929 Broadway, New York City

So This Is War! poster publicizing pamphlet published by the Committee on Militarism in Education in 1929. Records of the Committee on Militarism in Education. Courtesy of Swarthmore College Peace Collection.

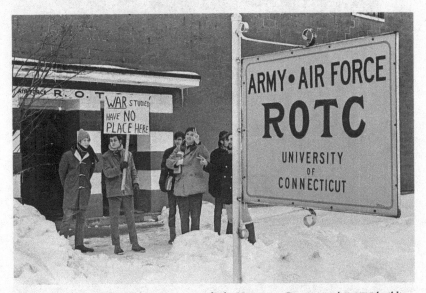

Students brave the winter cold to protest outside the University Connecticut's ROTC building, February 26, 1969. Howard Goldbaum Collection of Connecticut Daily Campus Negatives. Courtesy of the Archives & Special Collections, University of Connecticut Library, Storrs.

Mike Konopacki cartoon that originally appeared in the February–March 1986 issue of *The Veteran*, published by the Vietnam Veterans Against the War. Courtesy of Mike Konopacki.

Women's Peace Party parade in Manhattan opposing military drill in public schools, ca. 1916. WILPF Records, DG 43. Courtesy of Swarthmore College Peace Collection.

CHAPTER 4

The Decade They Almost Stopped School Militarism

The end of World War II failed to produce a lasting peace. Rising tensions with the Soviet Union spawned a U.S. national security state of unprecedented size and scope, and creation of a permanent war economy. "The new militarism in post-war America was most apparent," the historians Charles F. Howlett and Robbie Lieberman note, "in the large percentage of the national budget devoted to war preparation and in the close connection between the armed forces and American industry."[1] The postwar emergence of the United States as the sole global superpower and rising Cold War fears fueled the largest peacetime military establishment in U.S. history. The rise of what Harold Lasswell called "a garrison state," combined with state surveillance of the Left during the new red scare, took an enormous toll on the American peace movement. The embrace of Cold War logic by former left-wing activists like Reinhold Niebuhr illustrated the distance between peace activists and their former supporters.[2]

Without an organized campaign to pick up where the Committee on Militarism in Education had left off in 1940, the ROTC issue went cold until the Vietnam War.[3] In this chapter we explore how opposition to school militarism re-emerged during the 1960s and 1970s. Spurred by widespread opposition to U.S. military involvement in Southeast Asia, students and faculty protested the most visible symbols of militarism on college campuses: military recruiters and ROTC. As a result college ROTC enrollment dropped dramatically, leading some to predict its complete demise. The story of the Vietnam era antiwar movement is by now so familiar that we emphasize a different story: what happened *after* the war, which is too often ignored. Outrage at the Pentagon's ramping up of high school recruiting programs to compensate for the end of the draft led to an eruption of anti-JROTC activism during the mid- to late 1970s.

The post-Vietnam period is often portrayed as "the lost years" for the peace movement in America, a time when conservatives gained power as the Left withdrew from public life. "While studies of conservatism in the 1970s have flourished," one historian notes, "scholarship on the American left in this same period has languished."[4] Indeed, historians have largely overlooked the widespread opposition to militarism that emerged in this period.[5] Drawing on oral history interviews, archival documents, and the era's voluminous alternative press, we illustrate how, by the late 1970s, opposition to military involvement in education—particularly JROTC—was in fact widely shared in American culture.

Braying for JROTC

Few historians have studied how mobilization during World War II shaped the lives of youth on the U.S. home front. Most have focused their attention on children of elementary school age, neglecting the ways in which the war effort led to a reexamination of the military's partnerships with secondary and postsecondary public education.[6] To military planners U.S. involvement in the war demonstrated the value of ROTC. The college training program was especially valuable for churning out officers. By the middle of 1941 fifty-six thousand reserve officers—most of them ROTC graduates—had been called to serve in the armed forces. The military later suspended the ROTC program to make way for faster and more specialized training—such as the navy's V-12 College Training Program—that lasted throughout the war and enabled many colleges to turn civilians into military officers. By the end of the war, more than one hundred thousand ROTC graduates had served, leading General George C. Marshall to announce that the program needed to be expanded. "Just what we would have done in the first phases of our mobilization without these men I do not know," he wrote. "I do know that our plans would have had to be greatly curtailed and the cessation of hostilities on the European front would have been delayed accordingly."[7]

After the war ended, the repressive Cold War atmosphere constrained peace activism throughout the 1950s. Although no national peace organization campaigned against ROTC, scattered and numerically small actions during the late 1950s nonetheless set the stage for further protests. In October 1959 eighteen-year-old Frederick Moore, a student at UC Berkeley, fasted for seven days as part of a lonely vigil to protest compulsory ROTC. In an accompanying statement Moore wrote: "I will neither participate in nor support any action whose purpose is killing. The purpose of military training is to train men for war—train men to kill. I therefore cannot comply with the ROTC requirement." In 1962 the board of regents voted to end the University of California's compulsory ROTC requirement. The following spring Arizona State University students and faculty rallied to support students expelled for protesting mandatory ROTC. Although the university retained its military training requirement for several more years, the first major campus protest in a generation resulted in the immediate reinstatement of the expelled students.[8]

World War II had seemed to demonstrate the value of college-level ROTC, but defense officials were far less enthusiastic about its high school counterpart. In 1948 a commission led by Gordon Gray, assistant secretary of the army, concluded that the army should scale back its participation in Junior ROTC and transfer control of the programs to local schools. This recommendation led to a moratorium on new JROTC units. Between 1947 and 1963 more than five hundred high schools applied for JROTC units and were rejected. During this period the military consolidated its view of JROTC as both an unnecessary expense and an ineffective way to achieve its stated purpose—developing a corps of reserve officers. In fact, Defense Secretary Robert McNamara felt that the Pentagon should divest itself of the high school program and shift responsibility for funding it to local school districts.

According to the official history of the Army ROTC Command, McNamara's tenure (1961–68) was marked by "intense scrutiny" of Junior ROTC.[9] However, few in Congress shared his views. On the contrary, lawmakers sought to expand the program and framed JROTC as a means of instilling patriotism in youth while addressing the problem of juvenile delinquency. Congressional proponents of JROTC were also willing to use red-baiting tactics—a familiar ploy—to get their way. But what made these attacks different was that they spared no one—not even the Department of Defense. In lobbying for a bill to expand JROTC units nationwide, U.S. Representative William Bray, an Indiana Republican, made various insinuations about why the Pentagon might oppose federal funding for high school military training. Perhaps, he suggested, it was because McNamara and his minions had fallen under the influence of those "fellow travelers" and "pinko students" who had long fought school militarism. To the American Legion, McNamara's even considering elimination of high school military training meant that "the Department of Defense has subscribed to what the leftists and so-called pacifists have been trying to accomplish for years and is playing into the hands of our deadly and implacable enemies."[10]

This rhetoric, however, provoked a backlash. The editors of the *Hartford Courant* were disappointed that the pro-JROTC members of Congress were gaining traction. Noting that the military value of the high school program was question-able, a March 1963 editorial suggested that it made little sense to have the Penta-gon fund JROTC if it produced only such nonmilitary benefits as youth fitness and leadership education.[11]

Where were America's educators in this debate? At congressional hearings in 1964, one observer noted how representatives of educational associations were "conspicuous by their absence." In response to the proposed demise of JROTC, the Kansas City, Missouri, superintendent of schools said that if the army dropped the program, then present in seven city high schools, his district would have to make the costly decision to replace the military's instructors with civilian teach-ers. Sensing defeat, and seeking to avoid a protracted battle with Congress, Mc-Namara scrapped the plan to defund JROTC less than two months after propos-ing it.[12]

As a result Congress passed the ROTC Vitalization Act, which permitted a nearly fivefold increase in the number of JROTC units in American high schools, raising the nationwide limit on JROTC programs to twelve hundred. Although JROTC's congressional champions, led by representatives Bray and Edward He-bert, the Louisiana Democrat, had created the conditions for the first large-scale expansion of JROTC, Congress would not release full funding until the 1970s. For the remainder of the 1960s, the Pentagon had far more on its mind than strength-ening its high school "citizenship education" program.

Vietnam-Era Opposition to Militarism

In March 1965 President Lyndon Johnson took several critical steps toward esca-lating the war in Vietnam. By agreeing to deploy tens of thousands of additional U.S. ground troops, Johnson foreclosed any hope of a quick resolution to the con-flict. "It will be a long war," McNamara told reporters later that year. A commit-ment to increasing combat troops also meant that growing numbers of draft-eligible working-class men would fight the war. The strategy of relying on the draft at this stage, as the historians Maurice Isserman and Michael Kazin note, allowed Johnson to "avoid calling up either National Guard or military reserve units, po-tentially controversial steps that could raise further questions about the necessity of the war." Reliance on the draft helped make it the primary focus of the antiwar movement and turned college campuses into hotbeds of organizing. Although high school students also protested the war, and some activism focused on high school ROTC, these actions were overshadowed by the much larger and more dramatic eruptions on the nation's college and university campuses.[13]

Most campus activism was directed at the visible symbols of militarism:

defense-related recruiters and ROTC buildings. However, these activities were typically not a part of the first phase of the antiwar movement, marked by the far more restrained teach-ins of spring 1965. This would change by 1967, when Johnson initiated a massive bombing campaign that in turn led to high casualty rates and an accompanying need for additional U.S. personnel. Johnson's decision to move nineteen-year-olds to the top of the draft list that summer catalyzed the antiwar movement and sparked a wave of protest against on-campus military recruiting. That year an article published in the house journal of Students for a Democratic Society (SDS) urged readers to organize against campus recruiters as part of broader "effort[s] to impede and disrupt the functioning of the military . . . machine wherever it is local and vulnerable." By that time SDS had become "the touchstone of American radicalism" and a major node in the antiwar organizing network—and for that reason it attracted the attention of federal and state surveillance agencies. Students responded to the SDS's calls to action: during the 1966–67 academic year, nearly one-quarter of U.S. universities experienced protests against recruiting by the military, CIA, or defense industries.[14]

Protests of recruiting soon intensified. In October 1967 Stop the Draft Week, a series of nationwide actions against conscription, was also the occasion for major demonstrations against private-sector military-related recruitment on college campuses. At the University of Connecticut students protested the presence of recruiters for Dow Chemical, the manufacturer of napalm. In response the board of trustees instituted a policy that reserved "the most severe of institutional penalties" for any member of the university who was involved in protesting recruitment. The next year several hundred students and faculty flouted that policy and again protested military-related recruiters on campus, leading to scores of arrests and the indiscriminate clubbing of demonstrators by the state police that hospitalized five students.[15]

In the popular imagination the years of protest during the Vietnam War boil down to a tidy, if deeply misleading, binary—working-class hawks and antiwar doves. It is certainly true, as the historian Christian Appy has documented, that the great majority of those who served in Vietnam came from working-class backgrounds. However, the divide between those who supported and those who opposed the war was never as simple as "hard hats and hippies," to borrow the title of Penny Lewis's work debunking this myth.[16] Instead, a vibrant antiwar movement existed even at nonselective schools and colleges with an overwhelming majority of working-class students. For example, a Stop the Draft Week protest against marine recruiters was the occasion for the first recorded demonstration at Dutchess Community College in New York's Hudson Valley. By 1968 antimilitary protests had become far more common at these schools. At the nearby State University of

New York at New Paltz, in spring 1968 New York State Police investigators closely monitored the formation of the Ad Hoc Committee on Military Recruiting. Co-sponsored by the campus chapter of SDS and a community peace group, the committee's manifesto made clear what was at stake. "The Marines, the shock troops of American foreign policy, are engaged in the subjugation of Vietnam, and recruiting is essential to that operation," the document gravely declared. "This is the context in which the problem of military recruiting on campus must be discussed.... There is a war on; something must be done."[17]

While campus military recruiters attracted the ire of student protesters, the activists more clearly viewed ROTC as an illustration of complicity in the war. The U.S. war in Vietnam, an Association of American Universities report noted, "has generated widespread disaffection and protest against the military establishment, and ROTC happens to be the most exposed symbol of the military on campus." Despite massive U.S. military involvement in Vietnam, the incidence of anti-ROTC protests ebbed and flowed. The army recorded 165 anti-ROTC incidents in May 1969. The following school year saw few such protests until President Richard Nixon's televised announcement, on April 30, 1970, that U.S. troops had invaded Cambodia. Within days antiwar protests were reported on 80 percent of the nation's college campuses, and dozens of those demonstrations targeted campus ROTC buildings.[18]

While most of the May 1970 demonstrations ended peacefully, on May 4 at Kent State University a detachment of the Ohio National Guard fired on a group of student protesters, killing four and seriously wounding several others. Ten days later the Mississippi State Highway Patrol opened fire on a group of unarmed Black youth on the campus of Jackson State College, killing two and wounding twelve more. These two events triggered further campus turmoil, as nearly two million students skipped classes to protest both government repression and the continued carnage in Southeast Asia: a fifth of all campuses completely closed for anywhere from one day to the rest of the semester. The nation's ROTC programs, one officer at the Pentagon said in June, "caught hell this spring." An Associated Press report summed up the damage done: "Classrooms were stormed, offices were sacked and buildings were firebombed. Uniforms were destroyed, equipment was stolen and trucks were overturned. Parades were cancelled. Cadets were booed. A commander took three shotgun blasts into the front of his house." Even in the conservative, military-friendly South, student protests sometimes involved damage to ROTC buildings and equipment.[19]

Rocked by student dissent against an unpopular war, many college campuses closed their programs or ended compulsory ROTC. As a result enrollment in the program fell dramatically, from 260,000 in 1966–67 to 87,000 in 1971–72.

JROTC Expands: Enrollment in ROTC and Junior ROTC, 1967–76

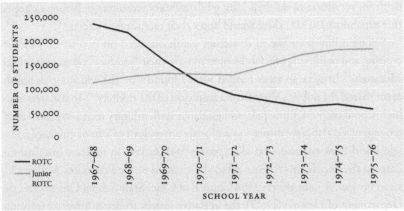

SOURCES: U.S. Department of Defense, *Selected Manpower Statistics, FY71* (Washington, D.C.: U.S. Department of Defense, 1972); U.S. Department of Defense, *Selected Manpower Statistics, FY 1976* (Washington, D.C.: U.S. Department of Defense, 1977).

College-level ROTC would eventually rebound, with military analysts later noting that the embattled program emerged leaner and stronger as a result of the Vietnam era unrest. Yet throughout the period of ROTC's decline, the military was also preparing for a volunteer force by quietly increasing its presence in U.S. high schools.[20]

The All-Volunteer Era

The nation's transition to an all-volunteer military force after the Vietnam War was not an easy one. The Department of Defense immediately struggled to maintain a sizable standing army without the aid of conscription. Despite offering increased financial inducements to entice enlistees, all branches of the armed forces (particularly the army) experienced "shortfalls in the enlistment of higher ability, high school graduates," according to a 1974 analysis by the Congressional Budget Office. To recruiters like U.S. Army Sergeant Charles Funari, who worked the New York City suburbs, there was simply no question about it: the draft would have to be reinstated. "It has to come back," he told a reporter in 1974.[21]

In the early 1970s, as the Pentagon transitioned from a reliance on the draft to the use of marketing and advertising, military involvement in public schools increased exponentially. In the struggle to enlist new service members, military officials were often quick to blame schools for not giving them a freer hand in recruiting students. Military recruiters across the country complained about the level of access to their area's high schools. The mayor of Hartford, Connecticut, pledged to form a committee to investigate why local school boards were making it difficult for recruiters to do their jobs, while military recruiters in Nebraska hoped that expanding JROTC there would boost their recruitment efforts.[22]

Selling military service to American youth operated on two levels. First, recruiting and marketing officials labored to have their "product" taken seriously by educators.[23] In 1972 an army-funded survey found that the education establishment shared the public's Vietnam era suspicion of the military.[24] To win over wary high school teachers, principals, and guidance staff, military recruiting services often organized elaborate displays at national conventions of school guidance counselors and took educators on all-expenses-paid junkets to military installations. Later in the decade this scheme led to the creation of the Education/Military Liaison Project. A joint effort of the Council of Chief State School Officers and the Department of Defense (DoD), the initiative sought to better integrate information on military careers into a school's guidance department and bring guidance counselors to military installations. By the end of the decade this was common practice. During fiscal year 1979 the army organized ninety-four educator tours across the United States, bringing approximately thirty-five hundred educators to tour army bases.[25]

In addition, recruiters directly targeted high school students. As early as 1971 the Pentagon was concerned about how it might persuade students and hired a contractor to research how the coming all-volunteer military could more effectively penetrate the teenage mind. With the spigot of federal funding wide open, new infusions of money for advertising and recruiting allowed blanket coverage of local high schools. Army recruiters in the Midwest, for example, drove thousands of miles a month to visit rural high schools, while the marines (acting on the advice of a consultant) moved all their recruiting stations out of federal buildings and into rented quarters near schools. The new marketing strategy was flourishing, according to plans laid out by the services' recruiting commands, which reminded their troops in the field of the importance of targeting high schools.[26]

Testing and Training in High School

One of the more important, though overlooked, aspects of the military-educational complex that arose during the 1970s is the expanded use of military testing in high schools. The military has long administered aptitude tests as a way to match the skills of potential recruits with the occupational specialties of each service branch. The idea of using military testing as a recruiting tool dates to 1958, when the U.S. Air Force began administering its Airman Qualifying Examination in secondary schools. After observing the air force's subsequent success at enlisting

Hidden Uses of School Testing: Number of High School Students
Taking the Military Aptitude Test (ASVAB), 1968–75

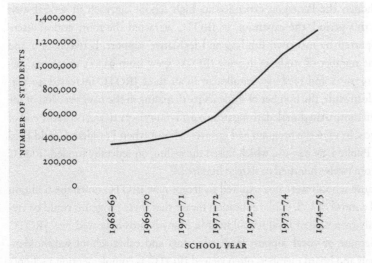

SCHOOL YEAR

SOURCE: Gus C. Lee, *Evaluation of the DoD High School Testing Program* (Alexandria, Va., 1979), 7.

high school graduates, the other service branches soon developed their own testing programs. Unforeseen, however, was that this would soon create confusion as
multiple service branches competed for the attention of high school administrators. Thus in 1968 the Department of Defense began a cooperative venture, the
Armed Services Vocational Aptitude Battery (ASVAB), a new test that each service could use to gather its own unique aptitude ratings.[27]

Until 1976, when congressional inquiries (aided by activists) forced changes to
the aptitude test, most students taking the hours-long exam were unaware that the
military would use the results. In fact, the ASVAB was a boon to recruiters: on
the basis of test results, they could learn what a student's future plans were and
whether a student was skilled in math, mechanical engineering, or other fields—
which was all they needed to create a customized recruiting proposal. According
to a retrospective assessment of the aptitude testing program, one Pentagon analyst concluded that recruiting concerns were the "driving force" behind use of
the test in high schools and that Pentagon planners saw it as a way to compensate for the loss of the draft. In another internal history, a DoD contract researcher
wrote: "During the transition to the volunteer force higher priority was given to
the [testing] program and efforts were made to improve its management." Statistics bear this out. During the 1968–69 school year, the high school testing program reached approximately 350,000 students in 7,200 high schools; by 1974–

75, nearly 1.3 million high school students took the ASVAB in more than 15,000 schools nationwide.[28]

Although the Pentagon expanded its high school outreach in several ways during this period, the expansion of JROTC attracted the most critical attention. Spurred by increased funding and legislative support, between 1971 and 1974 the number of students in army JROTC grew from 93,843 to 114,012. Between 1971–72 and 1978–79, enrollment in air force JROTC increased 40 percent. Meanwhile, the number of students participating in the navy's version of the program more than doubled, rising from 9,000 in 1971–72 to 23,000 at the end of the 1970s. In 1976 the program had received a boost when President Gerald Ford signed Public Law 94–361, which raised the ceiling on federally funded JROTC units from twelve hundred to sixteen hundred.[29]

Because schools were not required to accept new JROTC units, the tradition of local control of U.S. public education meant that these programs could be created only by a vote of local school boards. Many boards approved new JROTC units because of vocal support from educators and other school stakeholders. Principals and board members often viewed JROTC as complementing a school's existing job-training programs and saw it as an opportunity to provide students with more choices. Teachers who supported Junior ROTC often believed that it would reduce discipline problems at school. Indeed, the program's expansion in high schools was largely the result of its alleged ability to instill discipline— transforming sullen teens into obedient citizens. Parents and teachers believed that newly ingrained habits would carry over into increased economic opportunities for youth. "Both historically and in the present," the anthropologist Gina Perez argues, "supporters of JROTC have pinned their hopes on the rehabilitative power of military discipline . . . as a way to address social upheaval in the midst of intense social and political transformation as well as growing economic and social inequality."[30]

High schoolers themselves had a variety of reasons for participating in JROTC. For many it was the allure of a uniform. Naval JROTC cadets, to take one example, were decked out in blue blazers with gold buttons; if they had senior rank, their blazers bore special chevrons and other eye-catching insignia that boosted students' status among their peers. "You get satisfaction walking down the hall and everyone stares at you," one female naval JROTC cadet told a reporter. "You feel special. It makes you feel impressive." Junior ROTC also afforded cadets the opportunity to compete with other schools in drill and marksmanship. In 1976, when female cadets accounted for nearly a third of the total enrollment in army JROTC, an army representative reported that a major reason young women joined JROTC was the desire to perform in drill teams during football half-time shows.

Thus youth participated for many of the same reasons that they engaged in sports and other extracurricular activities—they saw JROTC as both a status booster and as an outlet for their social, creative, and competitive energies.[31]

But the rapid expansion of JROTC had an unforeseen effect: it spurred creation of a national network of anti-JROTC activists, with organizations like the American Friends Service Committee (AFSC) leading the charge.[32] Given the growing militarization of high schools, and the possibility of open debates about it, the emergence of an anti-JROTC backlash is easy to understand. Where some saw a much-needed addition to traditional schooling, critics perceived a covert military recruiting program. "The Pentagon sees JROTC as a recruitment tool, nothing else," one AFSC staff member wrote in a letter to the *Baltimore Sun*. Although many school stakeholders embraced JROTC, military officials promoting new school units worked hard to reassure the public that the program was simply a form of citizenship education. "We're not trying to play up militaristic objectives at all," the commander in charge of the navy's high school program told an interviewer in 1968. "Joining Navy Junior ROTC is like joining an extracurricular activity—like joining band." At a 1971 meeting of a Parent-Teacher-Student Association in Hagerstown, Maryland, a regional director of army JROTC painted a compelling picture of the program as at once able to instill discipline and self-confidence in students and help those of lesser means attend college on an ROTC scholarship. The military aspect was merely a footnote. "All we do," the officer claimed, "is make it a little bit military by putting on a uniform."[33]

While they stressed the nonmilitary aspects of JROTC in public, in trade journals and other venues out of public view, military officials cast JROTC in a much different light. A September 1969 article in *All Hands*, a navy publication, made this disclosure: "Like every education program sponsored by the Navy, NJROTC has a mission: to develop and motivate young men toward careers in the Navy." In a 1971 military briefing, the commander of air force ROTC concluded, "The favorable impact of the junior [*sic*] ROTC program on the military services seems undeniable." A 1977 article in *All Hands* further noted that the naval JROTC program "has exceeded all predictions" about its utility as a recruitment tool. Such insights illustrate how JROTC was indeed viewed as a funnel for teenagers' entering the military.[34]

This was not lost on critics of JROTC who portrayed the U.S. military as an invading force, breaching the sanctity of educational spaces. In this depiction public schools were replacing draft offices as the new beachheads in the Pentagon's manpower strategy. For example, the headline on a 1974 article in *America Report*, published by Clergy and Laity Concerned, proclaimed: "U.S. Military Plans Silent Invasion of Schools." To representatives of bellwether pacifist organizations like

Fellowship of Reconciliation (FOR), JROTC was an effort to inoculate America's youth against the germs of pacifism. "What is happening," the group's executive secretary said in 1974, "is that young people are being trained to respect the military outlook, to accept the military as a normal part of life and not to become resisters if we ever have to go back to the draft." The official of the Fellowship of Reconciliation also saw high school military training as subverting the traditional mission of public education—teaching children to think on their own—and replacing it with a system designed to churn out "a bunch of little robots who are taught to respond to their commanding officer, to the government or to the president." The following year criticism of JROTC also emerged in mainstream media. Nicholas von Hoffman, a syndicated writer whose column appeared in dozens of U.S. newspapers, mocked the Pentagon's various strategies to reach youth: "The new beachhead is in secondary education, and if that doesn't work, they'll land in grammar schools."[35]

The Emergence of Counter-recruitment

As part of this growing backlash, national peace organizations shifted focus from draft counseling to school militarism. This transition had begun as soon as the draft ended: Peace activists and the alternative press began framing school militarism as a vital post-Vietnam issue. "The draft has been declared officially dead," read a June 1973 dispatch from the radical Liberation News Service, but with JROTC expanding the "ghost [of the draft] lingers on." In the pages of its magazine, and later at its national convention in 1974, the War Resisters League (WRL) identified counter-recruitment—which it described as "a relatively new aspect of peace movement activity"—as a critical focus for peace activism.[36]

Unlike other national organizations, the league emerged from the Vietnam era stronger, bolstered by a quintupling of its membership.[37] Experience with anti-JROTC activism, along with its strengthened membership, placed the league in a good position to contribute to the nascent counter-recruitment movement. As early as 1973, organizers from the War Resisters League worked with the AFSC to begin a long-term campaign to eliminate JROTC from the San Francisco city high schools. By the middle of the decade, the league was distributing its four-page *Counter-recruiting Action Outline* pamphlet to members of its massive mailing list. Before presenting a series of suggestions for counter-recruitment goals and strategies, the pamphlet sketched some of the theoretical foundations of the work. "Since agitation has brought the end to the draft," it read, the military was therefore "trying to maintain its full-force strength through recruiting." For the peace movement to consolidate its gains, it would be necessary to counter the military's vast recruitment apparatus. The group suggested it was possible to conceive of counter-recruitment as both a way to weaken the military by targeting its soft underbelly (recruiting and ROTC), while at the same time helping people think more critically about U.S. militarism.[38]

While WRL was one of the long-standing peace organizations with relatively deep pockets and national reach, the most prominent group to address school militarism during the 1970s was the Philadelphia-based Central Committee for Conscientious Objectors (CCCO). When Congress passed the first peacetime military conscription law in 1948, representatives of churches and civil liberties groups formed the CCCO as a means of offering legal assistance and counseling to American conscientious objectors. During the Vietnam War the committee was busy training draft counselors, circulating thousands of copies of its guidebook on conscientious objection, and advocating amnesty for war resisters. Bob Seeley, a CCCO staff member, produced much of that literature. Seeley was a Quaker conscientious objector who performed his two years of alternative service by working with the AFSC in Sumter, South Carolina. He joined the CCCO in 1968 and would remain with the organization throughout the 1970s, working initially as a draft counselor and later as editor of *CCCO News Notes*.[39]

Shortly after the draft ended, Seeley urged peace activists to hold their applause. Cleverly appropriating the language of war, he noted: "The plain fact is this: We have won—we have forced the military to end inductions—but it is the most Pyrrhic of victories. Our city has burnt down around us, while our opponent glories in his surrender, [and] repairs those ramparts which we have barely touched," including high schools, where "the military has an easy entry" because JROTC programs were growing at a rapid clip. Seeley advised other activists that repealing the draft was not enough. "We must begin to counteract the noxious growth of Junior ROTC," he urged, "and, even though our resources are pitifully few, try to counteract the flood of misleading propaganda which the military is putting out in the name of recruiting."[40]

At the same time the head of the CCCO's regional office in the Midwest described the "continued expansion of high school ROTC and other teenage military programs" as "one of the greatest long-term threats we face." Although the committee would later confront severe funding shortages, for much of the 1970s the CCCO was in a position to meet this challenge. It dispatched field organizers across the United States in an attempt to persuade former Vietnam era draft counselors to move into counter-recruitment; kept activists informed of changes in military enlistment law and other developments through regular periodicals like

CCCO News Notes and *Counter Pentagon*; and committed its human and financial resources to building a viable national network of activists fighting JROTC and other forms of school militarism.[41]

Together with the American Friends Service Committee and the Women's International League for Peace and Freedom, the CCCO and the War Resisters League represented a major force in the emerging counter-recruitment movement. They provided financial and moral support to the parents, veterans, peace activists, and clergy who formed ad hoc groups to oppose what they perceived to be the military invasion of their public schools. These collectives had various names: Citizens Concerned with JROTC (Fairfax County, Virginia), Committee for Abolition of JROTC in Maricopa County (Arizona), Citizens Coalition Against Military Training in the Public Schools (Philadelphia). But opposing JROTC was only part of the way this national network of activists resisted the increased presence of the military in schools. Counter-recruiters also sought to check school militarism by distributing information about conscientious objection; traveling to professional educators' conferences to share alternatives to the military recruiting pitch; and attempting to eliminate military aptitude tests in America's high schools. In the coming years their work would generate impressive results.

Turning the Tide

To counter-recruiters and their allies, JROTC represented a brazen attempt by the Pentagon to indoctrinate the nation's children about war and militarism. When it came to strategy, groups like the CCCO tended to repeat the tried-and-true tactics used by the Committee on Militarism in Education in the 1930s, namely trying to support local activists or parents who wanted to prevent JROTC from coming to their communities. The tradition of local control of public schools, coupled with growing opposition in the 1970s to the militarization of education, created ideal conditions for battles about JROTC. Local campaigns against JROTC occurred in Norfolk, Virginia (1972), where vehement faculty and student protests torpedoed a proposed navy JROTC unit; Phoenix, Arizona (1973), where opposition came from an interfaith coalition of local clergy; and Philadelphia (1974–75), where parents and other activists were concerned about the way JROTC channeled Black youth into the military.[42]

Many of those opposing JROTC in the 1970s lived far from city centers. In part this was because JROTC came late to America's cities—the public schools of Baltimore, New York City, and Miami were largely free of military influence until the early 1980s.[43] By that time successful anti-JROTC campaigns had occurred in rural and suburban locales, including conservative strongholds. Many of these campaigns assumed a familiar pattern. At school board meetings parents and concerned citizens objected to the military character of the program, while school boards avoided ideological attacks and voted against JROTC by claiming that it was too costly.[44] Two case studies illustrate this point.

In 1974 a large number of parents and community members raised concerns about militarism in schools during a six-week, bitterly fought battle about whether to bring the Marine Corps JROTC to a high school in suburban Fairfax County, Virginia. Ultimately the school board's 6–5 vote against the program came down to money, though other issues were raised. To one parent the proposed JROTC unit at their children's high school was an "attempt to predispose 14-year-olds to a military career," while another objected to "the sight of kids in uniform, with guns, practicing a drill." Although it supported the school board's economic argument, the *Washington (D.C.) Star-News* sympathized with the more ideological activists, editorializing that military training made sense for college youth but was inappropriate for high schoolers. What made the school board's rejection of JROTC notable is that it came despite pressure from the *Navy Times*, whose editors urged Fairfax County to welcome high school military training.[45]

During the 1974–75 school year, the conservative Philadelphia exurb of Upper Perkiomen became another site of fierce opposition to a proposed marine JROTC program. As one community activist involved in that campaign later recalled, she was at first unsure of her ability to build an opposition movement in what she termed a Republican stronghold. However, she and the other activists would soon learn that there was plenty of "latent hostility toward bringing American militarism back home," which she attributed to the influence of the anti–Vietnam War movement.[46] Although most dissent from parents and community members focused on the economics of JROTC and the loss of community control, some voices were more militant. "Any more money spent on education," one resident wrote to their local newspaper, "should be to show that peace is possible, not that war is inevitable."[47] After hours of testimony from citizens, the school board "overwhelmingly rejected" the program on the basis of cost alone. Steve Gulick, editor of *Counter Pentagon*, later interpreted the lesson of Upper Perkiomen to be that American conservatism "ought not to be simply written off" and that under the right conditions, traditionally promilitary Republicans might be willing to join forces with counter-recruiters.[48]

Campaigns against the ASVAB

The same year activists in Virginia and Pennsylvania were opposing JROTC was also the peak period for military aptitude testing in the nation's high schools.

During the 1974–75 school year, nearly 1.3 million students took the exam, a nearly fourfold increase since 1968. During its first five years the school testing program had run into little opposition from parents and teachers.[49] This was at least partly because the marketing of the test was deceptive. For example, an informational pamphlet distributed by the military to parents and teachers in that period said the ASVAB had no link to military recruitment. By fall 1974 that picture began to change when a constituent of U.S. Representative Charles Mosher, an Ohio Republican, complained about how their child's taking of the high school test had led to disruption of their home life with insistent phone calls from recruiters. Intrigued, Mosher followed up by requesting a General Accounting Office study of the Pentagon's ASVAB program. The ensuing report focused attention on the issue of student privacy rights and the question of whether administering a military aptitude test in public schools was appropriate. Mosher's collaboration with Tom Conrad, a staff member at the Philadelphia-based Friends Peace Center who was active in counter-recruitment, led to investigations by Mosher's office. By the following year Mosher had succeeded in garnering more negative publicity for the Pentagon's prized testing program, noting that "the military's primary objective in offering [the tests] to high schools is to get their foot in the door for purposes of recruiting."[50]

At the same time the American Civil Liberties Union (ACLU) also began investigating use of the test in high schools, even devoting a special issue of its monthly magazine, *Privacy Report*, to the topic.[51] Between 1975 and 1976 the ACLU sought plaintiffs for a potential lawsuit that would have charged that the Pentagon's high school testing program was a wholesale violation of the 1974 Privacy Act. However, perhaps as a way to head off further controversy and avoid an embarrassing legal battle, the Pentagon decided to follow Mosher's recommendations and institute major reforms to the program. The Pentagon subsequently revised its ASVAB-related marketing materials to more explicitly state the recruiting purpose of the test. Schools implementing the test were also allowed to refuse to send students' test results to military recruiters. As a result of the public criticism, many school officials sought to avoid controversy associated with the aptitude test and stopped participating altogether. Between the peak year of 1974–75 and 1977–78, the number of students tested dropped by 16 percent.

Although Tom Conrad was pleased with this result, during a counter-recruitment retreat in 1976 he urged his colleagues to aim higher than mere regulation of the ASVAB, which he considered "an insidious tool for militarism." Counter-recruiters, he added, "must work to remove it completely and immediately! Be offensive!"[52] Not surprisingly, many activists did not cotton to the idea of military testing in public schools and began to organize to raise public awareness of this stealth recruiting program. In Wilmington, Delaware, a small group of local citizens contacted guidance counselors at seventeen high schools in their area to raise questions about the use of the ASVAB. In Erie, Pennsylvania, three teachers who wrote a letter to their headmaster stating that "Catholic schools should in no way support the military structures of the state," helped bring an end to ASVAB testing at their parochial school.[53]

Growth of a Network

Far from being isolated, activists in rural and suburban locations were well connected to a growing grassroots national network of counter-recruiters. Those new to the work could be initiated into the movement through contact with the CCCO's field organizers. Alternatively, they could learn from documented case studies of community resistance to JROTC. One of the first examples was a booklet published in the early 1970s (and later distributed in pamphlet form by the CCCO) that detailed a high school French teacher's successful campaign to oppose JROTC in Salem, Oregon. Another resource for activists was *Military Training for 14-Year-Olds: The Growth of High School JROTC*, a guidebook produced in 1974 by the National Interreligious Service Board for Conscientious Objectors. Hailed in the pages of *Counter Pentagon* as "the most complete usable study of JROTC in print," throughout the 1970s larger national organizations like AFSC distributed the manual to grassroots groups.[54]

While this information was helpful, the leading source of education and information for activists of the 1970s was *Counter Pentagon*, a bimonthly CCCO publication and the only periodical to focus solely on counter-recruitment. *Counter Pentagon* provided an ideological and intellectual framework for opposing school militarism, tracked school district policy and state laws that pertained to military recruiting in schools, and provided a forum for readers to share news about their work. Steve Gulick, a former draft resister from Philadelphia who later became a social worker, served as editor from 1974 to 1977, a period of vital activity for the counter-recruitment movement. A self-described radical with socialist sympathies, Gulick's first task was to redesign the publication's distinctive logo, by placing a raised fist in the middle of the simple Pentagon design that had been on the masthead during the first few months of the journal's existence. "I wanted it to be vigorous," he later recalled. Through its lively design and spirited coverage, *Counter Pentagon* was critical to the formation of movement identity among counter-recruiters. It enjoyed a nearly ten-year print run before ceasing publication amid the committee's funding difficulties in the early 1980s.[55]

The upsurge of local activism, as well as the circulation of periodicals like

Counter Pentagon, led to the first attempt at national coordination among counter-recruitment and anti-JROTC organizers. An early indication of the strategic sophistication within the budding activist community was the inaugural counter-recruiting conference, held in February 1974 at the Stony Run Friends Meeting House in Baltimore. It drew more than one hundred people from as far away as Maine, Georgia, and Iowa. In a report on the conference, a special issue of *Counter Pentagon* offers a snapshot of the issues and questions that motivated activists.[56]

Why engage in counter-recruiting at all, when other issues may have seemed more urgent? In a panel discussion of the philosophy behind counter-recruitment, the army veteran and activist David Cortright addressed this question. In his talk Cortright noted that recruiting enough personnel was the "weakest link" in the all-volunteer force, adding that counter-recruitment "attacks this link." He also suggested that the effectiveness of counter-recruiting cannot be measured by counting the number of people who do or do not enlist, since information about conscientious objection or GI rights could still be useful for someone committed to enlisting.[57]

Several conference workshops explored how school militarism intersected with issues of race and class. Many counter-recruiters had come out of the Vietnam era draft resistance movement and were therefore keenly aware of the racial bias baked into conscription. The military draft had long been subject to criticism. In his antiwar speeches Dr. Martin Luther King Jr. condemned the hypocrisy of a system that denied Black Americans full citizenship at home while asking them to fight in Vietnam—where twice as many Blacks died in proportion to their share of the U.S. population. In a session called "Counter-recruitment in the South: A Broad Offensive against Injustice," Walter B. Collins of the Southern Conference Educational Fund noted the dire economic straits that forced many young people in the South to join the military. Given the reality of racial and class oppression, Collins argued, counter-recruiters in this region would be most effective if they reframed the armed services not as an "employer of last resort" but as a form of "brain drain" and "a way for taking people away from the struggle for jobs and for social services" in their communities.[58]

Collins's remarks pointed to a key dilemma for counter-recruiters: how to dissuade youth in low-income communities and communities of color from joining the military without being able to offer them nonmilitary alternatives to higher education or job training. In a workshop devoted to this theme, George Velasquez of the AFSC Mexican American Project in San Antonio questioned whether the conference's predominantly white attendees were capable of understanding the needs of people of color. One of Velasquez's main points—which, as one observer reported, left several in the audience "feeling defensive and guilty"—was that "the military is an economic alternative that offers more to Third World people than [does the] civilian economy, and it is unrealistic to expect to dissuade Third World people from entering the military."[59]

Conference attendees were also involved with one of the first attempts at forming a network of counter-recruiting activists, the Inter-Faith Committee on Draft and Military Information. During the Vietnam War the interfaith committee—composed of representatives of the CCCO, Fellowship of Reconciliation, the Episcopal Peace Fellowship, and others—had been devoted to draft counseling. Starting in 1974 its primary activity was to support counter-recruitment efforts with a presence at the annual convention of the American Personnel and Guidance Association.[60]

Since the end of the draft, all branches of the military were heavily lobbying the guidance association. Because it was the main professional association representing high school guidance counselors, all military recruiting services tried to make their presence known at its conventions with recruiters and displays.[61] One member of the interfaith committee, Bill Offenloch of Catholic Peace Fellowship, cast the guidance association convention as part of the military's "behind-scenes-maneuvers" to use educators as a means of "rebuilding the military's fallen image among youth." Although N. W. Ayer, the army's advertising agency, had described the 1974 guidance association gathering in New Orleans as "a launching base for Army liaison activities with the educational community," the convention was ecumenical in its militarism. Admiral Elmo Zumwalt Jr., outgoing chief of naval operations, delivered the keynote address, and school counselors could interact with the navy's life-size robotic display of John Paul Jones, the marines' Revolutionary War scene with brass cannons and marines in period-appropriate uniforms, or the air force's six-foot scale model of the B-1 bomber. Anticipating the need for an organized response, interfaith committee representatives had paid a substantial sum for travel, lodging, and booth rental at the convention. According to accounts in the activist press, their display—featuring literature with facts about navy careers and the realities of military life—was well received by school counselors in attendance. In fact, following Zumwalt's address, guidance association delegates lined up in front of the counter-recruiting booth.[62]

By the fall of 1975 the interfaith committee had dissolved and a new counter-recruiting network was in the works—one that would prove to be far more durable and influential. An announcement in the November issue of *Counter Pentagon* described the Task Force on Recruitment and Militarism (TFORM) as channeling the organizing energies of interfaith committee activists and taking over what had been a primary organizing initiative: outreach to school counselors. Coordinated by the CCCO, and heavily represented by groups affiliated with historic peace churches, TFORM went far beyond an annual presence at guidance association conventions.[63] Its meetings allowed activists to discuss counter-recruitment strategy and stay abreast of developments in school militarism. Over time the task force also coordinated campaigns to get rid of the military aptitude test (at meetings, Tom Conrad regularly briefed members on his work with Representative Mosher) and JROTC. The task force also hosted special guest speakers like the Fellowship of Reconciliation's John Swomley, a seminary professor and long-time pacifist who at a 1976 meeting gave a speech on the history of the Committee on Militarism and Education. Swomley's topic was a timely one, as he was at that moment helping FOR to revive Dewey and Sayre's committee.[64]

Restarting the Committee on Militarism in Education (CME) was initially funded and overseen by the FOR, which began publicizing the project at task force meetings in 1975. The aim was to form a network of notable national educators willing to "take a stand and produce literature of validity for other educators" on the subject of school militarism. The CME project got off to a good start, publishing a newsletter—*Militarism Memo*—and nearly doubling the size of its mailing list between 1976 and 1978 to more than eighteen hundred educators; it also attracted support from renowned left-wing educators like Jonathan Kozol, author of *Death at an Early Age* (1967), a widely read memoir of his time teaching in the segregated Boston public schools. Although it did not last long enough to have much influence on policy, the revived CME could claim some organizing success, including a campaign to block the formation of a military-run public school in Cincinnati. The problem was that the scope of the CME was so limited—conceived as an organization for educators rather than peace activists—that it had difficulty raising money and gaining support from those who would be its natural allies: peace organizations. By the end of the decade, CME was gone for good.[65]

Responding to Repression

While counter-recruiters organized for the postconscription era, their opposition also mobilized. In February 1974 a resident of Oakland, California, wrote a letter to the Department of Defense "offering to report on the anti-JROTC programs of the AFSC," which was then holding its annual meeting in San Francisco.[66] While it is not clear whether the Pentagon responded to the offer, it is worth noting that it originated in the Bay Area, the center of anti-JROTC campaigns led by AFSC, the War Resisters League, and the Ecumenical Peace Institute, which was affiliated with Clergy and Laity Concerned.[67]

On occasion, military recruiters wrote threatening letters or made harassing phone calls to counter-recruiters, ostensibly to challenge the veracity of their literature. In July 1976 *Counter Pentagon* excerpted a letter sent to a high school principal by an air force recruiting commander who asked that the school's guidance department stop distributing counter-recruitment brochures. A guidance counselor at the school wrote to *Counter Pentagon* to "make other counselors aware of the harassment that is in store for them should they deny the military entrance to their schools."[68] This behavior by recruiters resulted from pressure by their commanding officers to meet monthly recruiting goals. That October a Marine Corps recruiting officer called the CCCO's headquarters in Philadelphia to complain about the content of the group's pamphlet, *What I Learned in Today's Military*. After a representative explained that the committee did not have the resources to solicit the military's point of view for all of its literature, the officer acknowledged his true motive: "When something like this gets into a high school, we can't recruit anyone. They don't believe us."[69]

The case of the Portland Military and Veterans Counseling Center in Oregon may best illustrate the lengths taken by the military and its allies to thwart counter-recruiting. Founded in 1967, the center mainly provided draft counseling services until conscription ended, at which point its mission pivoted to helping Vietnam veterans with "bad paper" win discharge upgrades. Operating out of the campus ministry offices at Portland State University, the group was successful at applying for grants, and by the late 1970s its annual budget of about $75,000 was bolstered by funding from the National Council of Churches.[70]

In 1977 the center began an ambitious program of counter-recruiting in Portland area high schools. The outreach effort required three new staff members, overseen by a project coordinator, Bob Gould; the funding came almost entirely from a $20,000 grant made available under the federal Comprehensive Employment and Training Act (CETA). The center soon became a source of concern to agents in the Portland Police Department's intelligence division, which had long monitored social change movements. In a June 1978 intelligence report, one officer speculated that the center must have "perpetrated a rip-off of tax money given" through CETA. The report ended with an unsubstantiated, if not unsurprising, tirade. "The people who staff and run this organization are full-fledged Communist revolutionaries and are working toward revolution in this country," it stated without evidence. "One of their tactics is by undermining the military programs and creating as much dissention [*sic*] as possible.[71]

By September 1978 counselors from the center had presented their counter-recruitment slide show at dozens of local high schools. The group's printed literature also sought to educate youth about the less rosy aspects of military life, such as the discomfiting reality that military service entails "risk of death or injury in training or combat." As one local journalist described the group: "Program workers consider themselves a type of consumer rights organization, protecting the rights of unwitting high school students against the false advertising schemes the recruiter feels compelled to use in order to meet her/his quota."[72]

The center also played a role in uncovering military recruitment fraud by local recruiters. After learning that Pentagon officials were investigating recruiter improprieties in the Portland area, the group asked Portland's congressional representative to look into the number of cases of suspected fraud and the outcome of any completed investigations. Just weeks after that request, suspicious and threatening phone calls started coming in to the center, and local military recruiters confronted staff members at the center's offices. Recruiters also pressured the county agency charged with distributing CETA funds to cut off support to the organization, while the national head of recruiting for the marines contacted the county agency and raised questions about the center.[73]

In fall 1978 local military recruiters started to investigate the center's funding sources after reading an *Oregon Times* article about the center's counter-recruitment program. An anonymous person also sent the article to an aide to U.S. Representative Robin Beard of Tennessee, a Republican member of the House Armed Services Committee. Beard then contacted the local CETA administrator for Portland and asked her for the center's original funding proposal. As an investigation by *Willamette Week* concluded, this was nothing less than a campaign of "willful harassment" by local military recruiters. As the newspaper noted, the CETA administrator was one of several local officials who felt intimidated by such requests.[74]

In 1979, with its CETA funds exhausted, the center closed its doors. Did the military recruiters' harassment have anything to do with its demise? "Maybe to some extent, yes," Bishop Cochran, a staff member, later acknowledged. But he also noted that by the end of 1970s it was getting harder to raise money.[75] For Bob Gould the center's closure was the logical outcome of the peace movement's waning energy. "After the war and the draft were over," he told the *Oregonian*, "we lost a lot of our support, both in people and money." Interviewed in 2011, he recalled that a changing climate for organizing had as much to do with the center's closure as any harassment by recruiters: "It was just getting harder and harder to find the support of sympathetic people in the community. There was no war going on and we had had minimal support even when the war was raging."[76]

If at times activists had to endure harassment or arrest, they took it in stride.

Many of those targeted were of the Vietnam generation and had experienced even greater repression. "That was the life of a draft counselor," Bishop Cochran later recalled. "For those of us doing counter-recruiting, it was the same thing. You just assumed that your phone was being tapped and assumed that that sort of thing was going on all the time. It wouldn't scare or surprise you, since during that time the government was seriously opposed to what we were doing."[77]

Since the heyday of the CME, military officials felt deeply threatened by critics of school militarism. The military, along with various patriotic organizations, slammed its critics through the press, placed them on blacklists, and sent moles to spy on their conferences. As the preceding examples suggest, new forms of repression surfaced during the transition to an all-voluntary armed forces in the 1970s. As the military placed schools at the center of its recruiting strategy, counter-recruiters were like uninvited guests at the ball. Military recruiters and their allies in law enforcement thus sought to neutralize critics of school militarism precisely because they threatened the supply of volunteer recruits.

Conclusion

Looking back at the 1970s, what is most striking is how deeply anti-JROTC sentiment appeared to penetrate American culture. This was no doubt helped by widespread opposition to U.S. military involvement in Vietnam. Historians have noted how the Vietnam War encouraged Americans to view the military more critically, a sentiment that played out during the 1970s in debates about the military's involvement in public schools.[78] The anti–Vietnam War movement, with its targeting of ROTC and on-campus recruiting, provided counter-recruiters with experience in nonviolent protest, lobbying, and media outreach—what the sociologist Christian Smith has called an "activist script."[79] In the early 1970s, as the Pentagon transitioned from reliance on the draft to a need for militarized public schools, activists were quick to mobilize grassroots groups and begin lobbying school board members, parents, and students.

Despite being numerically small, the counter-recruitment movement achieved a number of local victories to limit JROTC and helped regulate a pervasive military testing program. These activists found support for their goals in mainstream American culture. This is evident in the willingness of large religious bodies to publicly caution against introducing military training in high schools. Thus the New York State Council of Churches, in a 1971 statement, characterized JROTC as "preliminary instruction in the fine art of killing." The church group also questioned why it was considered proper to ban prayer in schools but allow military training. "Not being able to bow before God," they asked in their statement, "shall we now kneel to the Pentagon?" Perhaps the most notable of these interventions by religious groups was the 1978 resolution by the Pennsylvania Council of Churches that condemned JROTC as a threat to the "integrity of public education and the quality of life which such education should enhance."[80]

During this period mainstream media were also willing to question the JROTC program. In March 1971, during a debate in the New York State Legislature about lifting a decades-old ban on establishing JROTC units at public high schools, the Rochester *Democrat & Chronicle*'s editors objected to the "intrusion of the military into high schools." Two years later virtually the same piece of legislation reappeared—to even stronger denunciations in the press. "This is not the Third Reich," a suburban daily newspaper, the *Journal-News* of Nyack, editorialized, "and there is no valid reason for military indoctrination at the secondary level of public education." In New York City the *Daily News* covered a candidate running for city council who characterized the JROTC legislation as a plan that "would raise our youngsters to be illiterate, gun-carrying automatons." Although lawmakers later approved JROTC for New York State, media criticism continued in 1975, with the broadcast of an hour-long CBS documentary examining the JROTC controversy, cleverly titled, "Reading, Writing and Recruiting."[81]

The 1970s also saw members of Congress take courageous action to curb school militarism. In 1976, the same year Representative Mosher was crusading against the use of ASVAB testing in high schools, Representative Ron Dellums of California, a self-described democratic socialist, proposed an amendment to the annual defense authorization bill that would have effectively dismantled the JROTC by cutting its funding. The provision failed but not before Dellums attracted attention to the issue by declaring: "It is more important that Johnny learn to write than that he get his gun." Dellums was joined in his anti-JROTC advocacy by Representative Parren Mitchell, his colleague in the Congressional Black Caucus. Mitchell, a Maryland Democrat, supported peace activists who sought to prevent JROTC from gaining a foothold in Baltimore. In a 1979 letter to the city's school board, Mitchell recognized that many urban youth needed assistance finding jobs and avoiding gangs but rejected the idea that JROTC was the proper way to address their problems. "There are those," he wrote, "who believe that by having military training for students, it will dissipate underlying currents of unrest, anger or frustration. This is a poor solution to a serious problem. . . . You do not solve problems of our young people by teaching them to march and shout, 'Yes sir!'"[82]

As these examples suggest, the 1970s could be described as the decade activists and their allies almost defeated school militarism. But the moment would not last.

By the 1980s rising conservatism would usher in a renewed embrace of militarism, creating a difficult organizing environment for counter-recruiters. If anti-JROTC sentiment was somewhat mainstream in the 1970s, the next decade would witness increased public acceptance of military power and a challenging climate in which to resist school militarism.

CHAPTER 5

Resisting School Militarism
in the Reagan Era

For most of her childhood, Fran Donelan lived with her family in working-class
South Baltimore. Donelan's father, a machinist by trade, was a shop steward at a
local plant and active in the Democratic Party, at times working on the campaigns
of several local candidates. "Politically, he was a union man," Donelan recalled.
While all three of her brothers served in the navy, including one who dropped out
of high school to join at seventeen, Fran followed a different path. With help from
her father, who nurtured a class analysis, she would eventually enjoy a long career
as a peace activist and community organizer.[1]

During the 1960s, when Donelan attended Johns Hopkins University as an
undergraduate, she picked up a job in one of the university libraries. There she began serving as a de facto counselor, speaking regularly to male students who, as the
war in Vietnam raged, came to the library seeking information about the draft. In
1967 she started volunteering as a draft counselor at what was then the Middle At-
lantic Regional Office of the American Friends Service Committee (AFSC), located on East Twenty-Fifth Street in Baltimore. Three years later the AFSC hired
her full time, the start of a more than thirty-year career with the organization.
While she worked on various issues with the AFSC—GI rights and military counseling, apartheid, Central America—none was as meaningful as her work with
young people.[2]

Throughout the 1980s Donelan engaged in a campaign against the presence of
Junior Reserve Officers' Training Corps units in Baltimore city high schools and
became one of the most prominent figures in the national counter-recruitment

movement. With other organizers in the AFSC, Donelan recruited teachers, veterans, and others to speak against the program in an effort to stop further incursions of the military into public schools. Although it was not enough to undermine JROTC, grassroots opposition can be credited with forcing the Baltimore school board to place a temporary cap on the number of JROTC units operating in the city. Organized resistance to school militarism, in Baltimore and across the country, also contributed to the adoption in 1987 of an army JROTC mission statement that deemphasized the program's militaristic aspect.

This chapter examines anti-JROTC activism in Baltimore to assess public attitudes about the military in America during the Reagan years and the challenges facing counter-recruiters. Historical scholarship has examined the ways in which the war in Vietnam damaged military-public interactions and how those relations were subsequently restored.[3] As Gina Perez suggests, analyzing high school military programs provides an "important lens through which to observe shifting public sentiment about the military and its role in society."[4]

Baltimore merits special attention for two reasons. First, the city was a hub of peace activism. During the peak years of anti–Vietnam War protest, Baltimore saw national media coverage of high-profile actions, such as those by the Baltimore Four in 1967 and Catonsville Nine in 1968. In the former a group of activists, among them Rev. Philip Berrigan, were arrested for breaking into and damaging records in a Selective Service Board office in downtown Baltimore.[5] Donelan remembers that following the arrests, there was a "sense that the city was a real breeding ground for antimilitary activism." This agitation for peace even found its way into the local school system, where antiwar ferment helped birth new organizations like Baltimore Teachers Concerned about Vietnam and the High School Student Union.[6] Moreover, Baltimore activists were leaders in the nascent counter-recruitment and anti-JROTC movement. Both Donelan and Chip Cole, her colleague in the Baltimore AFSC office, were instrumental in organizing a pair of national conferences, in 1974 and 1981, for activists concerned about school militarism. In 1975 Cole and Donelan were also founding members of the Task Force on Recruitment and Militarism, the first regional network of such activists.

In addition, the military's emphasis on expanding JROTC in Maryland created ideal conditions for a confrontation once the first city schools installed JROTC units in 1979. In the early 1980s geographic distribution of JROTC was heavily skewed, with southern states home to about 60 percent of all JROTC units. According to one researcher, applications for JROTC units from the Northeast (including Maryland) were "favorably weighted." Military officials who were promoting new JROTC units in Carroll County, Maryland, in 1984 spoke of the need to strengthen the JROTC's presence in the state.[7]

Led by a superintendent who was also an officer in the U.S. Army Reserve, the Baltimore city school district began to advocate for more JROTC units in 1975, the same year the United States left Vietnam and two years after Congress refused to renew the draft. In response to the push for JROTC, Donelan and her colleagues condemned the military's invasion of high schools. In particular, activists questioned the diversion of resources to JROTC and from traditional academic programs, and they decried how the lack of economic opportunities forced young Black men into military training programs. Framing their message with a diverse range of approaches, anti-JROTC activists effectively built coalitions with teachers' unions and members of Congress, as well as traditional peace organizations—an impressive coalition at a time when criticizing the military was becoming increasingly difficult.

JROTC Comes to Charm City

Baltimore, also known as Charm City, was a relatively late adopter of JROTC. The city's embrace of the program appears to have begun with the installation of Dr. John Crew as schools superintendent in 1975. Crew was clearly sympathetic to the military. He had attended the historically Black Morgan State College (now a university) on an ROTC scholarship and served in the U.S. Army Reserve while schools chief.[8] In June 1979 the city school board, without seeking public comment, approved an air force JROTC program for Northwestern High School. Board members later said that they avoided public participation because they were not aware that JROTC was controversial. But it is difficult to imagine how the school board would not have been familiar with the JROTC debate in nearby Howard County, which the *Baltimore Sun* and *Howard County Times* had covered regularly for two years. A more likely explanation would be that school officials wished to minimize public scrutiny of a program they knew was divisive.[9]

In what would become a recurring theme, those in favor of the program were the first to get their message publicized. In an August 11 article announcing the JROTC program at Northwestern High, the *Sun* allowed Major Robert A. Dash, the program's senior officer at the high school, to reject claims that JROTC was an "attempt to militarize the schools." "Of course," he noted, "we'd like to see the best students choosing a career in the Air Force. But whatever they choose, it's good for them that these choices are laid out to them."[10] Framing the program as providing a unique opportunity to students helped secure critical support for the expansion of JROTC in Baltimore and throughout the country.

To counter Dash's claims, Donelan noted the breadth of opposition to JROTC during a September 6, 1979, school board meeting by reading statements from

John Bethea, president of the Baltimore Teachers' Union, and U.S. Representative Parren Mitchell, Democrat of Baltimore. Mitchell was a noted civil rights activist, the first Black member of Congress from Maryland, and a friend of Donelan's.[11] Don Patterson, a Black city resident opposed to the program, argued to the school board that JROTC would "force a single point of view—militarism"—on teenage cadets. As a former teacher in the Baltimore city schools, Patterson lent significant credibility to opponents of the program.[12]

However, these largely philosophical and ideological arguments were made within a negative frame of reference, offered no alternatives to the military-run program, and ultimately failed to persuade the school board. According to the *Sun*, the board "took no action" on citizens' complaints. In this early phase of the JROTC controversy, supporters effectively rebutted charges of militarism with stern speeches about discipline, softened by the rhetoric of free choice and by pointing out social mobility opportunities for local youth. Moreover, JROTC proved so popular with students that enrollment had doubled since the beginning of the 1979 school year. Baltimore's other daily newspaper, the *News-American*, described cadets who would "eagerly await" the beginning of JROTC every day. The perceived appeal of the program created momentum for an expansion of JROTC to other schools and challenged local activists.[13]

In October the school board debated a motion to establish a navy JROTC unit at Walbrook High in West Baltimore. During a two-hour public discussion, critics articulated philosophical objections to military training in schools, while supporters spoke enthusiastically of enhancing the "options" available to students. Donelan argued that JROTC was "youth indoctrination masquerading as vocational education and training." Marguerite Vlasits, president of the Baltimore chapter of Women's International League for Peace and Freedom (WILPF), urged that "this low-keyed infiltration . . . into our schools must be stopped here and now." In contrast the principal of Walbrook High echoed Major Dash when she cast JROTC as simply "another option for her students." The principal also identified the economic realities encouraging youth to enroll in the program, suggesting that since "inner city youth can't afford college," JROTC was critical to their future success because ROTC scholarships might be the only way for them to pursue higher education. While the school board ultimately approved a navy JROTC unit for Walbrook High, the diversity of opposing views led the board president to ask that staff monitor the program to ensure that "schools are not being used unwittingly" to recruit for the military.[14]

Given these sharply divergent opinions, that a June 17, 1981, forum on a proposed third JROTC unit for Baltimore schools led to the lobbing of "verbal hand grenades" is not surprising. By that time the list of individuals and groups opposing JROTC had grown impressively long and included the regional chapter of the National Association of Concerned Veterans, Mitchell, the city's teachers' union, local chapters of AFSC and WILPF, and prominent clergy, including the chaplain at Johns Hopkins. During three hours of testimony more than forty speakers—professors, parents, and activists—addressed school board members. They included Bruce Parry—University of Baltimore economist, West Point graduate, and regional leader of the veterans' group—who described JROTC as "an extension of... the militarization of our economy and our society."[15]

Despite the well-reasoned critiques by a decorated military veteran like Parry, those in favor of JROTC again marshalled an equally impressive roster of speakers who appealed to the board members' interest in offering additional "choices" to students. Persuaded by parents of cadets and cadets themselves, the board later voted 4–3 to approve the new military unit. Although local activists had assembled a strong coalition and refined their antimilitarist message, they had again failed to prevent JROTC from moving into another city school.[16]

Race, Poverty, and JROTC

In Baltimore and other cities, counter-recruiters sought to link school militarism to the related issues of poverty, race, segregation, and lack of postsecondary opportunities for low-income and minority youth.[17] Nationwide, Blacks participated in JROTC in far greater numbers than their share of the population; by 1975 members of minority groups accounted for 43 percent of all participants nationally. In Dallas, which had the highest level of JROTC enrollment in Texas, 66 percent of JROTC cadets were Black, although they accounted for only 50 percent of the total student population. The *Dallas Morning News* described the largest JROTC unit in the Dallas schools as "all black." These trends were mirrored in Baltimore city schools, where by 1975 Northwestern, Walbrook, and Edmondson high schools all had student bodies that ranged from 95 to 99 percent Black, according to the school district.[18]

JROTC's expansion in Baltimore schools with high concentrations of Black students provided a strategic opening for activists. As Marguerite Vlasits, the president of the Baltimore WILPF chapter, argued, Superintendent Crew used JROTC as a cynical way to "motivate minority students" into "highly glamorized" armed forces careers.[19] Parren Mitchell, a champion of the Black community, openly worried about how the program was effectively "steering low-income and black kids" into the military.[20] By emphasizing the connection between different forms of oppression, activists anticipated what became a common strategy of the contemporary peace movement and other social justice struggles.[21]

By the early 1980s the country was in a deep recession—the jobless rate reached nearly 11 percent in 1982, the highest level since the Great Depression. A bad economy, however, was a boon for the military, with one analyst noting that rising unemployment "contributed to a more favorable recruiting environment." In the Pacific Northwest, where joblessness was higher than the national average, headlines like "High Unemployment Spurs Military Recruiting" and "Recession Assists Military Recruiters" spelled out the inverse relation between economic woes and recruitment success.[22] As in other parts of the country, recruiters in Maryland attributed their achievements to economic hardship, including the downturn in manufacturing. Between 1970 and 1984 Baltimore lost more than seventy-three thousand entry-level jobs, many of which had been unionized factory positions offering good wages and benefits. By 1981 Charm City had the highest poverty rate for cities of its size in the Northeast and was home to more than twenty-five thousand unemployed youth. School officials estimated that 15 percent of high school graduates went on to careers in the military.[23] Thus, it is likely that many Black youth enrolled in JROTC to compete for an ROTC college scholarship and to receive training for a future military career. Donelan would later recall that while JROTC was promoted in diverse ways in different communities, in Baltimore "the appeal was the military presenting a vision of choice about the economic future for students." In response she and others challenged the belief that JROTC would lead to better economic opportunities: "For minority children, they [recruiters] make them feel like they have a leg up for college," she told a reporter for the *Philadelphia Inquirer*. "It [ROTC] doesn't. ROTC scholarships are competitive. These children ought to be taking math and science and English rather than ROTC."[24]

Racial and economic themes emerged again in 1983, when Baltimore's school board held hearings on bringing yet another JROTC unit—this one run by the marines—to another low-income, mostly Black Baltimore school. According to one newspaper report, Southern High School drew its student body from an "uneasy mix" of four neighborhoods: two "poor black neighborhoods" and two "white neighborhoods, blue collar and poor." When the *Baltimore Sun* interviewed Southern's acting principal, Lloyd Blumenfeld, he recalled that his school was considered an appropriate venue for JROTC because of the student body's proclivity for military careers and disinterest in academics. As he told the paper, a key reason for community acceptance of high school military training was the way neighborhood residents had traditionally viewed the armed forces: as a reliable employer, especially during times of economic distress. In Blumenfeld's view, the large numbers of South Baltimore residents who had always gone into the military raised the question: "Why not have them as best prepared as possible for that?" The principal also hoped that the JROTC would ameliorate some of the perceived deficiencies of his students. "Maybe they'll raise their kids better," he said. What Blumenfeld did not make clear, however, was how the typical JROTC curriculum—with a substantial part of the instructional time devoted to military training and drill—would translate into parenting skills.[25]

The minimal opposition to this proposal came only from peace activists—Donelan among them—who were not well known in South Baltimore. At an open forum on the JROTC plan at Southern High School, these opponents of JROTC were "shouted down" by local residents. That Donelan had been raised in these same South Baltimore neighborhoods and had assembled a multiracial coalition did not seem to matter. As she later recalled: "Even when we had a Black veteran, teacher, student, parent or politician testifying, there would be some parents who would challenge us as 'outsiders.'" Nor was it surprising when subsequent media coverage portrayed those attempting to block the JROTC unit as a group of agitators meddling in the affairs of a majority Black neighborhood. "The media," Donelan continued, "would emphasize the Black against White, Insider/Outsider aspect whether it was true or not."[26]

While Donelan's outsider status was certainly a factor, another reason her message was unwelcome may have been that Baltimore's sizable Black community actually liked what JROTC had to offer. More than a decade before the first JROTC unit was established in the city, the editorial board of the weekly *Afro-American* newspaper noted that a high school cadet corps program—with its promise to teach skills like "coordination, drill, how to give orders as well as how to obey them"—would benefit the city's youth, who tended to forgo college and "spend a great deal of time in the streets."[27] If JROTC was associated with such positive outcomes as improved discipline, enhanced socioeconomic mobility, and equal opportunity, activists would face long odds in their efforts to keep the program out of America's schools.

The "Stunning Rebirth" of JROTC

The forces opposing JROTC in Baltimore had dwindled by the time of the Southern High School proposal in 1983, and they proved unequal to the task of convincing parents that a military training program did not belong in their child's school. When Southern's program began the next year, activists had to contend not only with difficulties in organizing across racial and class divides but also with powerful social and cultural forces that were contributing to a surge in popular support for JROTC. In the view of Southern High's principal, there was "a trend towards conservatism," including a withdrawal from "some of the anti-Vietnam sentiment that used to exist in society."[28] This shift—evident in the increasing enrollments of high school military training programs, in survey data of youth and adult attitudes toward the military, and in local and national media coverage—placed yet another formidable obstacle in the path of anti-JROTC organizing.

In his cultural history of the post-Vietnam years, Christian Appy notes that by the 1980s "Americans were learning to stop worrying and once again love the machinery of war and the handsome, heroic Americans who knew how to use it." This assessment is supported by public opinion polls, which found that between 1969 and 1980 the percentage of Americans who believed military spending should be cut dropped sharply, from 52 to 14 percent. During the same period the share of those who felt the Pentagon was underfunded increased from 8 to 49 percent.[29] These changing beliefs were also evident among the young. A respected longitudinal study of youth attitudes found the proportion of male high school seniors who expected to serve in the military rose for three straight years in the early 1980s (1980–82) after experiencing a decline from 1976 through 1979. The historian Lawrence Wittner finds that this "hawkish tide" played a role in the 1980 election of Ronald Reagan, who campaigned on the need for increased military spending and "peace through strength."[30]

The cultural tilt toward militarism was increasing public acceptance of high school military training. The expansion of JROTC units nationwide demonstrates this. By the mid-1980s army JROTC—by far the largest program of the military branches—was approaching its highest recorded enrollment levels. In the early 1980s the army's high school program grew by 35 percent; by 1985, 863 units were enrolling about 135,000 high school cadets throughout the United States. The program increased so rapidly, noted its official historians, that it "overwhelmed the management capabilities" of regional commanders.[31]

In this period of intense growth, school administrators were also learning "to love the machinery of war." School districts across the United States that previously had little contact with the Pentagon began applying for JROTC units. Some of the largest districts added JROTC programs beginning in the early 1980s, including Miami-Dade, Florida. In the 1982–83 school year Miami-Dade's schools had no JROTC units. Two years later the district had four programs. This was typical of all of South Florida, where by 1984 one in ten youths was enrolled in JROTC. Another previously untapped area experiencing such growth was New York City. Between 1980 and 1982 three new JROTC units were added—all in schools with overwhelming majorities of minority students. A press report from 1983 noted that JROTC's expansion in the Big Apple illustrated the "stunning rebirth in recent years" of high school military training.[32]

The Fight for Equal Access in Public Schools

As JROTC experienced increased popularity during the 1980s, another development attracted little notice: the growth of active military recruiting in high schools. Two factors drove this trend: the growing need to recruit qualified applicants—especially high school graduates—to fill positions in an increasingly tech-savvy military, and the presidency of Ronald Reagan, whose policies led to an emphasis on armed forces recruiting and advertising.[33]

The U.S. military was now recruiting in a variety of ways, but as the *Baltimore Sun* reported, most of its resources were directed at high schools.[34] Although comprehensive data are lacking, news reports from the period suggest that military recruiters were visiting high schools in some cities dozens of times per year. One army recruiter's "constant presence" at a Pennsylvania school caused a student to remark, "Man, you're at school even more than I am!" Military recruiters found particularly fertile recruiting grounds in rural parts of the country, where they sometimes succeeded in enlisting 20 to 25 percent of a single year's graduating seniors.[35] Many educators seem to have embraced this trend, with one principal going so far as to call military recruiters "an appendage of our guidance department," while counselors in large urban districts routinely worked in close partnership with the armed forces. By 1982, according to the U.S. Army's public relations department, approximately 95 percent of American schools were placing few (if any) restrictions on military recruiter visits to campus.[36]

The school outreach plan worked, and between 1979 and 1983 all branches of the military exceeded their recruiting goals. In June 1984 the American School Counselor Association joined four other national organizations of educators and school administrators in signing a voluntary agreement with the heads of recruiting for the army, navy, coast guard, air force, and Marine Corps. The text of the nonbinding compact, which encouraged schools to formulate guidelines to facilitate military recruiters' access to students, was mailed to every high school in the nation and met with alarm in the counter-recruiting community.[37]

As the military presence increased, activists began to see access to high schools as essential to their own work. The *Objector*, a publication of the Central Committee for Conscientious Objectors (CCCO), devoted a special issue in 1981 to counter-recruitment in high schools.[38] Rick Jahnkow, an antidraft and counter-recruitment organizer who became active in the 1980s, later suggested that as the level of high school organizing increased, school officials—sometimes in collaboration with law enforcement—sought to block students' access to counter-recruiters. San Diego police, for example, arrested activists while they were trying to speak with students on public sidewalks.[39] During the 1980–81 school year alone, staff of the Chicago chapter of Clergy and Laity Concerned (CALC) contacted dozens of schools with requests to provide students with information about conscientious objection; in return for their efforts, they received sixty-six rejection letters from school officials. Faced with consistent pushback from school administrators, those challenging school militarism revised their strategy.[40] To overcome these barriers, the counter-recruitment movement needed a legal determination that they merited as much access to schools as military recruiters.

The staff member responsible for counter-recruitment work at Chicago CALC, Rev. Andrew Skotnicki, was a devoted Catholic priest who often worked sixteen-hour days, splitting his time between CALC and his parish on Chicago's low-income South Side. Skotnicki's work in these neighborhoods helped him recognize a need to provide students with a "balanced picture" of military life. In a letter to school officials, he noted that many of the district's poor and minority students were "slowly resigning themselves to military service . . . because military recruiters have had virtually unmonitored access to their hearts and minds via the high school."[41] Army recruiters assigned to Chicago saw teenagers as their target market and therefore focused their outreach on high school students.[42] Moreover, approximately half of all Chicago high schools had JROTC units, enrolling more than fifty-five hundred students, many of whom performed uniformed "courtesy patrols" in their school hallways.[43]

In November 1981, after a year of failing to make headway in the public schools, Skotnicki sent a letter to the district superintendent requesting permission to distribute leaflets and make presentations to students about conscientious objection and the realities of military service. This resulted in an invitation for Skotnicki to speak to a large group of Chicago's high school guidance counselors. As he prepared his talk, Skotnicki proposed to education officials that literature on conscientious objection and the realities of military service be made available in local schools; he also asked that CALC and other peace groups be allowed to deliver this information in person through student assemblies.[44] His subsequent presentation was well received, and in the weeks that followed, letters supporting the proposed counter-recruitment plan arrived at the office of the schools' superintendent. In one, a member of the Chicago CALC advisory board pointed out that such a service was an important step for racial justice, given the disproportionate number of "inner-city youngsters" being recruited by the military.[45] But despite such support and the positive response to Skotnicki's speech, the superintendent declined to advance CALC's proposal. "It didn't take long to realize that we weren't going to get anywhere without legal action," Skotnicki later recalled.[46]

On April 15, 1983, Clergy and Laity Concerned, Skotnicki, and two students from the Chicago schools and their parents filed suit in U.S. District Court against the Chicago school board. At issue, they argued, was the fundamental unfairness of schools' providing military recruiters access to students while excluding those with alternative opinions. This not only infringed on activists' rights under the First and Fourteenth Amendments, the plaintiffs averred, but was also educationally unsound. On December 19 Skotnicki and another CALC staff member elaborated on this theme—and riffed on the army's popular advertising slogan— in an opinion piece for the *Chicago Tribune*: "We, too, would like our students to be all that they can be. However, we question the notion that this is fulfilled primarily by military service." They argued that if the Chicago schools prevented peace groups like CALC from presenting students with an opposing view, "there is no longer dialogue—only monologue, and a frightening one at that."[47]

On January 20, 1984, U.S. District Judge George N. Leighton agreed and ruled in favor of Chicago CALC. The case rested on the idea that by granting access to the military, school officials had created a public forum on the controversial topic of military service. When the school board then denied access to groups with alternate views, it was on the constitutionally shaky ground of "picking and choosing which views may or may not be expressed to its students."[48] The Chicago CALC case had an immediate and powerful effect on the counter-recruitment movement. As one activist noted, the ruling was a key to "be duplicated and tried in the locks of school systems nationwide."[49]

In mailings sent to local chapters across the country, CALC's Midwest office encouraged local affiliates to take the news to their school boards and request access equal to that accorded military recruiters. The precedent-setting case, *In These Times* reported, "has opened the country's school systems to an extent never before possible." "We've been doing high school classroom presentations for years," one Oregon activist later noted, "but now, thanks to Chicago CALC's legal challenge to the Chicago board of education, we also have access for counseling which is equivalent to the access available to military recruiters." Activists across New York State also successfully used the Chicago ruling in their fight for equal access. Significantly, for the rest of the 1980s, subsequent court decisions strengthened the legal basis for counter-recruiting in schools.[50]

Youth Leadership and Arts-Based Outreach

Although some organizers continued to have trouble accessing local schools, overall the Chicago case had a liberating effect on counter-recruitment activity. After the ruling new activist groups sprang up while existing organizations were able to increase their work. Yet counter-recruiters were experiencing limited return on their investment of time and money; given the power of the military, their message was often faintly heard. As one reporter who observed Fran Donelan in action noted, "their mimeographed pamphlets can easily get lost in the shuffle of the armed services' glossily printed, dramatically illustrated literature." Organizers slowly recognized that lecturing youth about the dangers of military service was not enough. The activists needed new strategies to generate support. In an interview with *Education Week*, Donelan said that the majority of anti-JROTC campaigns failed because adult activists failed (or never even tried) to give an organizing role to students themselves. At a CCCO-sponsored conference later in the decade, Rev. Emory Searcy—lead plaintiff in an equal access lawsuit brought against the Atlanta public schools—emphasized the strategic importance of building youth leadership in the counter-recruitment movement: "Our children are our future. We need to guide them, teach them well, then get out of their way and let them lead the way." In this context some counter-recruiters began to view arts-based, participatory activities as an effective way to get youth involved in efforts to address school militarism.[51]

One local organization that was on the cutting edge—both in terms of having youth directly involved in organizing and in using the arts—was Youth Against Militarism. Formed in 1985 in Cincinnati, the CALC-affiliated group was led by two local clergy, Dr. Daniel Buford and Dr. Michael Washington. Through strategic partnerships with the local teachers union, parents, the Fellowship of Reconciliation, and Cincinnati CALC, Buford and Washington had helped to defeat two earlier efforts to turn failing Cincinnati high schools into publicly funded military academies.[52] Building on this momentum, they sought to train local youth to become counter-recruiters. To educate their peers about militarism, young activists produced videos and a weekly program on community radio. They also used rap music. As one of the group's fifteen-year-old members, Maisha Pesante, told a Youth and Militarism Conference in Chicago, "You gotta work with the kids ... and one of the ways to get to our audience is to try to make them feel what we are saying ... through rap." She then proceeded to demonstrate her skills in a performance that "compelled [the audience] to take youth leadership seriously."[53]

Other groups used music to sensitize youth to issues of war and militarism. In 1986 a youth theatre group affiliated with a Seattle community center developed a rap video to address military recruitment.[54] Skits were the creative outlet of choice for youth in Oakland's Peace and Justice Youth Outreach Project. Two recent high school graduates who attended an AFSC "summer workshop on militarism and yearned to spread their knowledge" had organized the youth-run group in 1982.[55] The AFSC later provided seed money for the project, hired an adult coordinator, and paid youth activists to make presentations—which included "improvisational theatre"—to an average of fifty high school classes each year.[56]

In the 1980s several national peace organizations had the resources to cultivate innovative forms of arts-based outreach to youth. The CCCO's role in creating the *Real War Stories* comic book in 1987 is instructive. The organization worked with Joyce Brabner, a veteran activist, to raise money and recruit artists for the project. Brabner was in a unique position to assist because of her activism and significant media skills. Her husband was the underground comic artist Harvey Pekar, and she used her experience promoting his *American Splendor* comic books for a new project: *Real War Stories*. Brabner recruited more than twenty-five artists to work on the comic book, "many of them among the best in the field," including Mark Farmer, a British artist who worked on the *Incredible Hulk*.[57] Farmer said he considered his contribution to *Real War Stories* "one-in-the-eye for the Careers Officers at school who 'suggested' I consider the Police or Armed Forces whenever I mentioned commercial art as a means of making a living."[58]

Based on the testimony of people fleeing conflict in Central America, as well as the autobiographies of American draft resisters, *Real War Stories* was a powerful tool to help youth think critically about the decision to enlist in the military. According to the San Diego activist Rick Jahnkow, the comic book's design and backing by well-known artists helped give it an auspicious start at the annual Comic Con in San Diego. However, the original plan to distribute the comic to students backfired when school administrators balked at a panel that graphically depicted a sailor being sexually assaulted by another sailor. Still, Jahnkow viewed *Real War Stories* as one of the significant counter-recruitment undertakings of the 1980s and among the most influential in terms of arts-based outreach.[59]

An Expanding Network

Many of the same organizations involved in post-Vietnam counter-recruiting remained active during the 1980s. Although church bodies did not make bold statements about JROTC in this period, people of faith played an influential role in the movement to confront school militarism. Nearly one-fifth of the more than sixty counter-recruiting groups responding to a CCCO survey in 1986 reported some affiliation with faith-based organizations. Many were, like Skotnicki and his Chicago colleagues, part of Clergy and Laity Concerned. In addition to CALC, large and well-established organizations like the CCCO and War Resisters League (WRL) had the resources to devote full-time staff to counter-recruitment. During the 1980s Ed Hedeman, a WRL staff member, researched and wrote about JROTC for progressive publications, and he helped the organization serve as an information clearinghouse. Moreover, the WRL-produced "ROTC Dismantling Kit" offered grassroots groups a step-by-step guide to eliminating high school or college ROTC

programs. In 1986, when Glen Anderson, a Vietnam veteran and conscientious objector, wrote an account of his successful campaign to block an army JROTC unit
from starting at the high school in Lacey, Washington, he made sure to mention
the "helpful information and encouragement" he found in the WRL kit.[60]

During the 1980s military veterans like Anderson also played a key role in
seeking to reduce the military footprint in schools. Veterans have long been essential to maintaining ideological support for U.S. militarism. Since the first half
of the twentieth century, the American Legion has organized groups of veterans to silence dissent and endorse American wars. Veterans have an even longer
history of promoting militarism in schools: following the U.S. Civil War, veterans of that conflict met regularly with schoolchildren to relate "thrilling stories
of heroic deeds, brave encounters, desperate battles, . . . and wondrous suffering."
Throughout the 1920s and 1930s the American Legion bitterly opposed any effort to reduce the ROTC presence on college campuses. With their involvement
in counter-recruitment efforts, military veterans were boldly rejecting the legion's blind patriotism, choosing instead to confront an essential feature of U.S.
militarism.[61]

Some veterans involved in counter-recruitment were motivated by a sense of
duty to repair the harm they had caused in combat. When Rob Pfeiffer, a former marine officer, had gone to fight in Southeast Asia, he embraced the American mission of winning hearts and minds. By the 1980s, at the height of the U.S.
government's involvement in proxy wars in Central America, Pfeiffer and a dozen
other veteran friends in Maine formed the state's first chapter of Veterans for Peace
(VFP). Years later Pfeiffer said his experience in Vietnam had led him to work
with VFP: "We were embarrassed and shocked by what we had been involved in."
During the 1980s, as the military distributed free book covers festooned with recruiting messages, Pfeiffer partnered with art teachers to organize a peace-themed
book cover contest.[62] More than a dozen schools in the state participated. Thanks
to VFP's largesse, twenty thousand copies of the winning submission were printed
and distributed to every high school in Maine. By creating and using the book
covers, Pfeiffer recalled, students themselves "became counter-recruiters."[63]

Other veterans were simply outraged by what they viewed as military recruiters' cynical methods of exploiting youth. The idea for the Veterans Education
Project, based in rural western Massachusetts, grew out of veterans' learning that
the army was regularly bringing war materiel—including small arms, a howitzer,
and a helicopter—to its high school recruiting exhibitions. In response Vietnam
veterans and teachers partnered with a local peace center to establish the Western Massachusetts Committee on Peace Education. The new organization eventually became the Veterans Education Project, which published a pamphlet criticiz-

ing the "one-sided, violent demonstrations" at local schools and sought to balance the military's perspective with classroom presentations and other forms of public education.[64]

Similarly, the Madison, Wisconsin, chapter of Vietnam Veterans Against the War (VVAW) sought to curb recruiting activities in its city's schools. After filing public records requests, the group learned that military recruiters visited some local high schools as often as every other day during the school year. Armed with this data, VVAW helped elect two candidates to the Madison school board who supported the group's aims; in August 1985, in a unanimous vote, the board approved a new policy that limited military recruiters to twice-yearly school visits. As local activists later related, the key to their campaign's success was avoiding antimilitarist rhetoric and instead using arguments—like parents' rights to influence their child's career path—that would have broad appeal. For the Madison veterans group, theirs was a "great victory" that would protect high schoolers "from abuse and misinformation from the military."[65]

The Task Force on Recruitment and Militarism continued to meet during the 1980s, although its influence was largely limited to the East Coast. Meanwhile, the decade also saw newer groups rise to prominence along the West Coast, including San Diego's Project on Youth and Non-Military Opportunities. Rick Jahnkow, the group's chief organizer, became a national leader in the movement against school militarism, regularly contributing thought-provoking articles to the *Objector*, *On Watch* (a publication of the National Lawyers Guild's Military Law Task Force), and other periodicals important to the counter-recruitment community.

Despite its national influence, however, counter-recruitment and anti-JROTC work competed for the attention of peace activists during the 1980s, a period marked by struggles against U.S. involvement in Central America, the nuclear freeze movement, and other social justice issues.[66] Counter-recruiters had to vie for funding and other forms of support with groups doing antinuclear work. Peace activists also had to contend with significant cultural and political changes that limited what they could achieve in an increasingly conservative, promilitary America.

A Resurgence of Patriotism

After the 1960s youth rebellion, older Americans were quick to see JROTC as capable of molding teens into patriotic, flag-waving adults. Although readers could find criticism of JROTC in mainstream media during the early part of the 1970s, it had all but disappeared by the 1980s. Indeed, most news reports about the program were favorable and often expressed astonishment at the "increasing number of teenagers" who were setting aside their blue jeans and "donning military fatigues."[67] Newspapers all but competed to offer the most fulsome praise of JROTC. In 1979, at the height of the debate about Walbrook High in Baltimore, a *News-American* editorial approved of the way JROTC programs "point boys and girls toward civilian careers—and even toward military careers—a prospect "perfectly horrible to the pacifists," of course. Two years later, amid an unprecedented expansion in local JROTC enrollment, the *Dallas Morning News* editorial board hailed what it called the "comeback for high school soldiering."[68]

Mainstream media coverage of JROTC during the early 1980s attributed its surging popularity to the "new generation" of high school youth. The *Christian Science Monitor* noted that military training programs were commanding "new attention" from a cohort of students "more interested in training for careers than protesting war." Those in the military also tended to share the view that youth of the 1980s were "showing more pride for the red, white and blue."[69] When a *New York Times* reporter visited Long Island high schools in 1981, she found a "resurgence of patriotism" making the borough's JROTC programs "bigger and better than ever." "Students today are different than students of the 1960s," observed the commander of one JROTC unit. "There's a lot more flag-waving going on." Distance from Vietnam certainly helped sustain this "resurgence of patriotism." According to another JROTC commander, youth coming of age in the early 1980s "have very little recollection of Vietnam." Consequently, with America's role in the carnage increasingly forgotten, JROTC enrollment was rising because youth were no longer "afraid of being laughed at for wearing a uniform."[70] When the commanding officer of the JROTC department in Omaha, Nebraska, was asked in 1985 about the program's growing enrollment, he had a pithy reply: "The Vietnam syndrome is gone."[71]

Economic factors provided additional incentive for youth to join JROTC during this time. As college costs soared along with rates of youth unemployment, the Pentagon increased the amount of scholarship money it awarded to ROTC cadets. An economic recession combined with cultural trends to create a situation in which high school military training was unremarkable. Lacking concrete alternatives to a program that promised opportunities—educational and vocational—that appealed to parents, educators, and students, counter-recruiters realized they could accomplish only so much.

Conclusion

The anti-JROTC campaigns yielded mixed results. Was the opposition, as one columnist predicted in 1975, really "too weak, too poor, and too obscure" to stop the spread of school militarism?[72] Despite the various obstacles blocking their efforts to evict the military from schools, counter-recruitment activists were nonetheless able to make modest, yet measurable, gains. Donelan and her colleagues at the Baltimore AFSC were members of one of the only organizations researching JROTC in the late 1960s. That made them a pivotal—and national—resource for local citizens, grassroots groups, and media covering the JROTC issue. The Baltimore AFSC office used the local and national media to foster public debate. At the same time these activists also increased pressure on the army to restructure the JROTC program and make it less militaristic. According to the official history of the U.S. Army Cadet Command, the first JROTC mission statement ("To Motivate Young People to Be Good Americans") was adopted in 1987 in response to growing anti-JROTC activism, which by then was a nationwide phenomenon. This wording was intended "as much to deflect political criticism as it was to express the actual purpose of the program."[73]

While Baltimore activists can rightly take some credit for stimulating a national debate about high school military training, the local results of their organizing are less clear. Years of campaigning and coalition building ultimately failed to prevent JROTC from coming to Northwestern, Walbrook, Edmondson, and Southern high schools. Yet Donelan considered it an important concession when the school board eventually limited JROTC units in city schools to five. However, the board later abandoned this restriction, and by 1996—at the peak of a new period of JROTC expansion—Maryland had among the most inner-city JROTC programs in the country.

Baltimore's anti-JROTC activists used a variety of messages to build awareness of their campaigns. One of their more effective strategies was highlighting the program's exploitation of problems of race and poverty. Donelan consistently noted that ROTC scholarship money was limited and that schools were unfairly channeling young Black youth into JROTC while their white peers took college prep classes. However, activists' inability to articulate a viable alternative to JROTC meant that they were often perceived as simply being against something and unable to offer better options to economically desperate youth.

Although Donelan had Black leaders like Parren Mitchell on her side, activists were not able to overcome racial and class divisions. The anti-JROTC coalition became painfully aware of its alienation from Baltimore's Black community during the 1983–84 Southern High School campaign, when activists were unable to shed their outsider status and local residents even shouted them down at a public forum. Donelan's experience was not unique. In the mid-1970s the campaign to prevent a JROTC unit at Philadelphia's majority-Black Overbrook High School encountered difficulty organizing across racial differences. Stephen Gulick, a former CCCO organizer and editor of *Counter Pentagon*, was involved in the campaign and would later recall that Overbrook's Black teachers were angered by anti-JROTC activism, which they perceived as "whites wanting to take away opportunities from Blacks."[74]

By equating military training programs with indoctrination, peace activists were able to argue that JROTC conflicted with traditional educational values like critical thinking. However, by failing to offer viable alternatives, they usually were unable to persuade parents and other school stakeholders. In Baltimore, JROTC supporters, with their rhetoric of enhancing student choice and opportunity, found their message well received in a city beset by economic distress. Further, activists' ideological opposition to JROTC surely alienated conservative, promilitary forces in the community like the *News-American*'s editorial board. School board members, who were generally more pragmatic than ideological, and more easily swayed by financial arguments, saw JROTC as a low-cost vocational education program that offered greater postgraduation prospects for many of their students.

The counter-recruitment movement thus found itself at a crossroads by the end of the 1980s. It could continue to repeat its moral arguments against JROTC, but those seemed to hold diminishing appeal. Conversely, activists could adopt a broader message that eschewed antimilitarism, emphasizing instead issues like curriculum control and the economic cost to schools of maintaining JROTC programs. During the next wave of anti-JROTC mobilizing in the 1990s, activists would organize a truly national network and score victories in more than a dozen communities. Significantly, the most effective of these campaigns avoided the usual ideological emphasis.

CHAPTER 6

A Resurgent National Movement

The fall of the Berlin Wall in 1989 triggered a series of events that would lead to the end of the Cold War. Lawrence Wittner finds that the subsequent fall of eastern Europe's Communist regimes and the signing of nuclear disarmament treaties encouraged many U.S. peace activists to "put the nuclear issues behind them."[1] If these historic events had a paradigm-shifting effect on the peace movement writ large, they did for counter-recruiters as well. Writing in *Draft Notices* later that year, Rick Jahnkow argued that, given the decreasing danger of a nuclear war and recent progress in arms control, prospects were "better for achieving a number of the peace movement's short-term goals." It was thus "essential . . . to give more attention to the root causes" of war. Jahnkow argued that the peace movement needed to resist the spread of militaristic values in society, specifically by focusing its efforts on public schools. Despite the end of the Cold War, he suggested, peace activists could not afford to rest. Shifting their emphasis to working with youth would go a long way toward preventing wars of the future.[2]

By the end of the 1980s, counter-recruiters had the support of the courts, as witnessed by favorable equal access rulings in Chicago and Atlanta, but they were not well organized on a national or regional level. Some initiatives were promising—well-established regional groupings like the Task Force on Recruitment and Militarism (TFORM) and newer groups like Project YANO (the Project on Youth and Nonmilitary Opportunities)—but nothing was likely to connect activists across the country and unite them in common struggle. At the National Conference on Youth, Militarism and Alternatives, in Chicago in 1988, which was organized by the WRL and CCCO and attended by more than two hundred people, Jahnkow asked attendees to consider the need for a cohesive strategy: "How can all of us become more aware of the many different groups and efforts which exist all over the country? Is there a communications tool which could be created to do this, possibly by a national group?" The question became more urgent in future years, as TFORM ceased to be an active network for counter-recruiters.[3]

An answer came in the form of the National Campaign to Demilitarize Our Schools (NCDOS), an organizing network that during the 1990s was critical to the development of policy campaigns with national coordination. Planning for NCDOS had begun shortly after the U.S. invasion of Panama in December 1989, when Gary Wolf of the Western Region office of the Central Committee for Conscientious Objectors (CCCO) wrote a memo to Jahnkow and other key organizers in the counter-recruitment movement. The list of recipients included Michael Marsh, chief organizer for counter-recruitment for the War Resisters League; Leonard McNeil of the Peace and Justice Youth Outreach Project, an AFSC-affiliated Oakland group known for its innovative youth-led organizing model; Harold Jordan, an AFSC staff member in Philadelphia responsible for the organization's handling of school militarism issues; and Kathy Gilberd, an attorney with the National Lawyers Guild's Military Law Task Force who was interested in recruiting fraud.

Wolf's memo outlined an agenda for the national campaign planning meeting in San Francisco the following February that was timed to coincide with a national conference for activists in the peace and antinuclear movements. While he expected the strategy session to last no more than a few hours, Wolf recommended that the group produce a mission statement for a cooperative venture, an agreement among the different organizations to work jointly on at least one specific project and develop a plan to raise money for it. Wolf enclosed Jahnkow's recent commentary, "The Peace Movement Needs to Shift Its Emphasis," and suggested that the article could "serve as a starting point for discussion of a unified mission statement."[4]

At the February 1990 meeting, participants began by taking stock of their movement. They agreed that counter-recruiters would be operating from a position of strength, given that the military was trying to stave off post–Cold War budget cuts. Participants also agreed that a joint campaign to address militarism would correct a perceived lack of coordination among national organizations and allow them to develop a "division of labor and a method of ongoing communication." Another strength they identified was the legal victories in the push for counter-recruiters to have equal access to local schools. However, participants recognized that they did not "sufficiently address alternative careers for youth," lacked "a clear message," and fell short of having "a strategy for building a multi-cultural movement." In addition, they recognized that a joint campaign to address militarism could allow them to develop a "division of labor and a method of ongoing communication." Such a campaign would also have the clear advantage of improving their ability to collaborate on fund-raising campaigns.[5]

The "Draft Proposal for a Joint Youth Peace Campaign" emerged from the February meeting. The document noted three goals for what activists later christened the National Campaign to Demilitarize Our Schools: raising awareness of the negative influence of militarism (defined as "pro-military values") in schools; freeing schools from "direct military influence" by restricting military recruitment; and attracting more activists—particularly youth—to participate in counter-recruitment efforts. In addition to such typical forms of activism as handing out leaflets and letter writing, attendees identified a need for student-led actions like "guerrilla theater" as important to the campaign. This approach would be a means of "confront[ing] recruiters and JROTC campaigns" directly in schools and involve more youth by channeling their creative talents into antimilitarist activism.[6]

Throughout 1990 participants in NCDOS planning sessions continued to discuss how to initiate their campaign. Several ideas enjoyed broad agreement: the importance of youth as the primary constituency, for example, and the idea that arts-based activism was an excellent way to attract them to the campaign. However, participants voiced concerns as to whether organizing efforts should seek to demilitarize schools by barring military recruiters or allow local groups the flexibility to determine their own tactics (e.g., those trying to focus on "equal access" for counter-recruiters).

Although the name of the organization suggested that the goal was not equal access but rather complete demilitarization of schools, the draft proposal that emerged from the February meeting struck a balance between the two positions. A revised version circulated to NCDOS planners in the summer of 1990 echoed this view: "Alongside the movement for equal access, it is felt that there should be a movement which asserts that militarism and education are antithetical, and which calls for schools to be *completely demilitarized*." The minutes from a subsequent meeting in July note that "concern was raised about the focus being on 'demilitarizing' our schools," with some in attendance suggesting that an emphasis on demilitarization "might conflict with our equal access arguments and victories." Leonard McNeil of Oakland's youth outreach project stated his case for such a two-pronged approach: planners would make the campaign primarily about demilitarizing schools while keeping equal access as an alternative approach. The final NCDOS proposal formally adopted in December 1990 used this approach—parallel struggles for change in the schools.[7]

Although coordinated campaigns had shown promise in the past, NCDOS would be the first formal attempt at a national strategy for school demilitarization, focusing not only on JROTC but all the methods the military used to gain access to youth. Throughout the 1990s NCDOS convened biannual meetings and built a supportive environment for local organizations engaged in anti-JROTC work and other forms of counter-recruitment. Affiliated groups produced literature, including a booklet, *Making Soldiers in the Public Schools* (1995), that attracted national media attention and forced changes in the JROTC curriculum; monitored the growth of JROTC nationally; and assisted local communities in resisting the entry of JROTC into their schools. Fortuitously, the group's first year of existence was a time of U.S. military buildup in the Persian Gulf. When the United States invaded Iraq in January 1991, NCDOS was able to channel public opposition to that war toward interest in the ongoing campaign against the expansion of militarism in schools.

The Gulf War

On January 17, 1991, U.S. and coalition forces began bombing Iraq in response to that country's annexation of neighboring Kuwait. What became known as the Gulf War lasted little more than a month and was judged a resounding victory for the U.S.-led coalition. But this so-called war was grossly one-sided—fewer than 150 American service members died in combat, whereas more than eighty thousand Iraqi civilians were thought to have died as a result of the U.S. invasion and its immediate aftermath.[8] The Gulf War was significant for being the first large-scale U.S. military deployment in the post-Vietnam era and led to unprecedented cultural veneration of the U.S. military.

For weeks before the invasion of Iraq, U.S. public schools largely fell in line to support the emerging war effort. In Baltimore army recruiters started a campaign that enlisted elementary school students to collect donated items and care packages to send to troops in the Persian Gulf.[9] Students across the country, including fifty thousand in Boston alone, wrote letters to American soldiers stationed in Saudi Arabia.[10] One schoolteacher's testimony from 1991 illustrates the way this played out:

> Immediately following the initiation of hostilities in mid-January the schools were adorned with ribbons, banners, and displays which glorified a military solution to the [Gulf] crisis and war. Assemblies soon followed exalting the role of soldiering, cookies were hurriedly baked to send to the troops, and letters were written to members of the armed forces exalting the use of force. In not

one case do I recall a single educational endeavor to assess why soldiers were being asked to give up their lives.[11]

In this atmosphere educators raised scattered protests and made attempts to foster public debate about the question of American military intervention. Shortly before the U.S. military began air strikes against Iraq, *Education Week* surveyed teachers to find out how schools were addressing the crisis. In Ann Arbor and Chicago some high schools organized teach-ins, while in Oakland, California, pressure from parents and students led the school board to pass a resolution condemning U.S. military actions against Iraq. Although major cities and college towns like Ann Arbor held educational forums for high school students, in other parts of the country the situation was quite different. Most teachers said that student protest was nonexistent at their schools.[12]

While little concern about the war was evident within schools, public opposition to the looming U.S. invasion led to massive street demonstrations in Washington, D.C.; New York; San Francisco; and other major cities. Americans' opposition also encouraged peace activists to pay attention to school militarism. "One positive result of the Gulf War," wrote Rick Jahnkow in the inaugural issue of the *NCDOS Newsletter*, "is the growing number of groups forming to challenge the military's presence in high schools and colleges." In San Diego, Project YANO, the effort to counter school militarism, recorded an unprecedented spike in activity following the Gulf War and greater involvement from veterans. In Portland, Oregon, counter-recruiters cited the Gulf War as the reason they were booking twice the usual number of classroom presentations. A coalition of Philadelphia college and high school students, formed in reaction to the U.S. invasion, spent the remainder of the 1991 school year distributing literature and petitioning school officials to offer students more nonmilitary paths to job training and college scholarships.[13]

In Houston a former conscientious objector and draft resister named Bob Henschen was teaching high school during the Gulf War. Angered at how "warfare had been glamorized and made to look antiseptic and high-tech" on television, he wanted to do something about the military recruiters who regularly cornered his students, as well as the presence of JROTC units in the Houston school system. Months after the war faded from the headlines, he and some friends formed the Committee for Youth & Non-Military Opportunities that for years provided Houston guidance offices with information about alternatives to military service.[14]

New Allies in Antimilitarism

Opposition to the Gulf War and growing parental concerns about their children's privacy led local school boards to begin to reconsider their relationship with the military. In January 1991 school boards in Los Angeles, Oakland, and San Francisco voted to stop supplying student information to military recruiters.[15] In Rochester, New York, activists went even further. Members of the Rochester Peace and Justice Center had been trying to organize a ban on military recruiters in schools since the late 1980s. In the summer of 1991, after they decided to collaborate with the Gay Alliance of the Genesee Valley, activists stopped using antimilitarist language and instead framed their campaign around the military's practice of barring openly gay service members. The strategy worked. That December the school board passed a policy banning in-school recruitment by any organization that used discriminatory hiring practices. Five of seven school board members voted for the ban, with the board president giving an implicit endorsement of how activists described the issue: "It's not an anti-military policy, but an anti-discrimination policy."[16]

Although the school board had carefully managed its message, the policy faced immediate backlash. Angry letters to the editor sought to equate the recruiter prohibition with a ban on books; one columnist condemned the school board's decision as "absurd" and "boneheaded." Meanwhile, the parents of a Rochester student sued the school district, claiming that the policy violated a 1984 state law that required that military recruiters have access to public schools. After a pair of setbacks in lower courts, the school district persisted until the state's highest court sided with activists and upheld the recruiter ban in May 1994. While counter-recruiters recognized the national significance of the victory—Rochester was the first U.S. city to effectively bar military recruiting in schools—they also fretted about the "mixed message" the school board had sent: that militarism was acceptable so long as it was not homophobic. "It is up to us," one CCCO staff member wrote in the *NCDOS Newsletter*, "to build on this message by illustrating that both homophobia and militarism are deadly, oppressive, and mutually reinforcing."[17]

In 1992 the school board in Oregon's largest city enacted its own ban on military recruiters. The Portland victory followed a trajectory similar to that in Rochester: after years of using ideological arguments, activists formed an alliance with the city's LGBTQ+ groups and successfully argued for a prohibition on antidiscrimination grounds. The recruiter bans of Portland and Rochester were unique because of their explicit linking of school militarism to the issue of discrimination against LGBTQ+ individuals. As a gay rights advocate in Rochester said at the time, the policy forced the Pentagon "to realize that the gay and lesbian community will not tolerate the oppression they are subjected to."[18] The dual recruiter prohibitions also had remarkable longevity. Schools in both cities remained free of military recruiters until 2002, when Congress passed the No Child Left Behind Act and the threatened loss of federal funding forced the school districts to rescind these policies.

Throughout the 1990s activists continued to see the military's antigay stance as a potential organizing handle. As noted in a CCCO press release, LGBTQ+ rights groups were "central to the struggle" to stop the spread of JROTC in Minneapolis. The San Francisco office of the Gay & Lesbian Alliance Against Defamation called for the removal of JROTC units from city schools. The group noted that "by allowing the JROTC to continue, the school district willingly invites homophobic bigotry directly into our classrooms." Meanwhile, at a 1993 meeting of NCDOS, activists discussed how another San Francisco–based group, Lesbians and Gays Against Intervention, had produced counter-recruitment materials tailored to LGBTQ+ youth.[19]

Organizers also realized that the same strategy worked well in the college arena, where it gave a significant boost to activists who had long struggled in their fight against ROTC. In a 1994 article a professor of social work who had been involved with anti-ROTC organizing at her Iowa university wrote: "The best chance of removing the ROTC presence will be through the gay/lesbian rights arena." During the 1990s college activists followed that advice and used antidiscrimination arguments to pass campus referenda against ROTC at large public universities like San Jose State; California State University, Sacramento; and the State University of New York's Cortland campus, as well as at Pitzer College, one of the prestigious Claremont Colleges in California. LGBTQ+ groups were key allies in many of these struggles.[20]

The campaigns to ban military recruiters help illustrate how counter-recruiters incorporated inclusive messages and brought new allies into the struggle against school militarism. In this respect they reflected broader changes occurring in the peace movement (and other national organizing efforts). Scholars have noted that after the Gulf War, the U.S. peace movement became more likely to emphasize the participation of Blacks, Latinos, and other groups focused on social justice.[21] Indeed, one of the initial goals of NCDOS was to publicize how school militarism had a disproportionate influence on Black and Latino youth. In the CCCO's second edition, published in 1991, of its *Youth and Militarism Directory* of organizations and their contact information, an announcement concerning NCDOS describes the group as giving "special attention to the impact of the military on low-income communities and people of color." Rick Jahnkow also mentioned this goal in 1992 in the *NCDOS Newsletter*, when he noted that school militarism is "not just a peace issue, since militaristic values reinforce racism, sexism, homophobia, and a variety of other attitudes that are the cause of injustice in the world."[22]

Although NCDOS envisioned the construction of a more diverse movement, the group lacked a strategy for getting there. The reality was that most of its key members represented groups and organizations without significant racial and ethnic diversity. One of the most vocal critics on this issue was Harold Jordan, who at the time led the AFSC's Youth and Militarism program. As a Black man working with veterans during the 1980s, Jordan had firsthand experience with the lack of diversity in the U.S. peace movement. He was pleasantly surprised when he joined AFSC in 1987 and found that the traditionally Quaker-affiliated organization had a much more diverse staff than any other major peace organization. For this reason he believed AFSC was well positioned to conduct counter-recruitment work in communities of color.[23]

At the July 1990 meeting of NCDOS, Jordan noted that if the organization adopted a rigid demilitarization approach, it would have trouble becoming a truly "multicultural effort" because that emphasis might not make sense to all constituencies. In his view NCDOS should encourage demilitarization but also allow flexibility so that culturally diverse communities could better respond to local needs. Although Jordan did not articulate it then, this was the lesson of earlier counter-recruitment campaigns in the majority-Black schools of Baltimore and Philadelphia, where anti-JROTC activists had faced community support for a program seen as offering economic opportunities to youth. Jordan's generation of organizers would have to learn from those experiences and exercise restraint and respect if their efforts to reach a broader audience were to succeed. In 1992, when the U.S. Congress approved the largest expansion in the history of JROTC, it effectively gave NCDOS activists an issue around which to effectively mobilize in diverse communities.[24]

Operation Young Citizen

After a swift victory in Iraq, the American military enjoyed a surge of public confidence, to its highest level in decades.[25] In this climate of adulation, the Pentagon had no difficulty asking Congress to double the number of JROTC units nationwide. In his published memoirs, General Colin Powell, then chair of the Joint Chiefs of Staff, wrote that he first proposed the idea for expansion in the spring of 1992. An ROTC college graduate himself, Powell viewed JROTC as a program that could prevent the urban unrest that had unfolded in Los Angeles in late May and early June, after a jury acquitted police officers caught on video as they beat

Rodney King, a Black motorist. Powell acknowledged the program's militarism, but he emphasized the social benefits of high school soldiering: "Yes, I'll admit, the armed forces might get a youngster more inclined to enlist as a result of Junior ROTC," he wrote. "But society got a far greater payoff." When in a speech later that year President George H. W. Bush announced the plan to expand JROTC, he also stressed that the program was capable of instilling discipline in youth and providing an antidote to social instability. For the president JROTC was "a great program that boosts high school completion rates, reduces drug use, raises self-esteem and gets these kids firmly on the right track."[26]

One of the most fervent champions of an expanded JROTC was U.S. Senator Sam Nunn, the Georgia Democrat who chaired the Senate Armed Forces Committee. With the Cold War over, Nunn encouraged Americans to recognize the role soldiers could play in mentoring young Americans and addressing a range of social ills. Like Powell, Nunn viewed the Los Angeles riots as the type of domestic emergency that the military could help to address. In a widely cited Senate speech, he elaborated on his proposed Civil-Military Cooperative Action Program. "While the Soviet threat is gone," he declared, "we are still battling at home drugs, poverty, urban decay, lack of self-esteem, unemployment, and racism. The military certainly cannot solve all of these problems and I don't stand here today proposing any magic solution to the numerous problems we have at home. But I am totally convinced that there is a proper and important role the Armed Forces can play in addressing many of these pressing issues." He envisioned, for example, mobilization of national guard units to address the nation's hunger crisis by assisting local relief agencies in distributing surplus food.[27]

By using the language of educational and social opportunity, Powell, Bush, and Nunn were drawing on a long tradition of casting JROTC as the solution to social problems. Catherine Lutz and Lesley Bartlett, in their study of the cultural politics of JROTC, found that military programs in high schools have often been promoted as a way to assimilate unruly urban youth and address a perceived plague of "moral/psychological decay."[28] During the 1990s the military touted JROTC as a way to reduce the high school dropout rate, although Lutz and Bartlett found no evidence that branches of the armed forces were collecting data to back up such claims. Similarly, despite a lack of published research comparing the job prospects of JROTC students and those of students not in the program, JROTC promotional literature consistently linked participation in the program with enhanced employment opportunities for minority cadets.[29]

Given the strong favorability ratings for the military, and that the JROTC expansion was couched in the historically resonant language of moral uplift, the expansion plan faced little opposition in Congress.[30] During the next two years hundreds of new units were added to U.S. high schools. Between 1992 and 1996 the number of JROTC programs nationwide increased by 60 percent, from 1,481 to nearly 2,400.[31] During this period underresourced schools received up to five years of special financial aid for agreeing to host a JROTC unit; more than a third of the new JROTC units created between 1992 and 1995 benefited from such assistance. Because many of those schools had high proportions of students of color, Black enrollment in JROTC rose from 25 percent in 1994–95 to 33.21 percent in 1995–96. (Blacks represented just 15 percent of the total high school student population at the time.)[32] Although the service branches did not fully meet their expansion goals, the increase in JROTC units changed the face of education in many parts of the country that had previously been free of high school military training. The Pentagon particularly wanted to see the expansion extend to regions long underrepresented in JROTC, such as the Northeast and some of the plains states. The biggest increase by far occurred in New England, where the number of high schools with JROTC more than doubled between 1992 and 1996.[33]

Resistance Mounts

Proponents of JROTC were effective at portraying its expansion as a boon for American education and an antidote to youth alienation. Echoing the arguments used by Colin Powell and others, the pro-JROTC forces pitched the program as a solution to broken families and social fracture. "Their parents are working or they're separated," one marine JROTC instructor said of his cadets. "They need somebody to say: 'Left face! Right face!'" Educators proved particularly receptive to this message, much to the chagrin of counter-recruiters and their allies. In focus group research Chicago principals and counselors praised JROTC for its ability to discipline and motivate youth. When asked about his newly installed marine JROTC unit, one Massachusetts school principal gushed: "I'll tell you, I've never been called 'sir' so much in my life as I have in the last four weeks." In the pages of the nation's leading journal for educators, the executive director of the National School Boards Association doubted whether the anti-JROTC message of NCDOS would ever "comport with the general beliefs of school boards around the country."[34]

The arguments of those supporting school military training had paid off. "School districts, by and large, bought the argument that JROTC was not a recruiting tool," the AFSC's Harold Jordan later recalled. But some were not having it. For instance, teachers played a key role in a significant anti-JROTC campaign in working-class Bethlehem, Pennsylvania. Beginning in April 1993, peace activists began to educate their local teachers' union about the implications of a proposed navy JROTC program at Liberty High School. Allowing JROTC into the school, they argued, would result in a loss of curriculum control and the hiring of instructors who were not unionized yet received higher pay than other faculty. While the peace group's contacts with students also helped, educators' opposition led the Bethlehem school board to revisit the issue and ultimately vote 5–4 to cancel JROTC. "With the union throwing their significant weight against the program," a CCCO staff member later wrote in the *Objector*, "the tide turned."[35]

Vocal opposition to JROTC once again emerged in the mainstream media. Counter-recruitment campaigns received favorable press coverage in national publications, most notably *Education Week* and *Time* magazine. In an opinion piece for the *New York Times*, Eugene Carroll, who had retired from the U.S. Navy as a rear admiral, called JROTC units "living relics of the cold war" and rejected the idea—promoted by Senator Nunn and others—that JROTC could address the urban crisis. "It is appalling," Carroll added, "that the Pentagon is selling a military training program as a remedy for intractable social and economic problems in inner cities. Surely, its real motive is to inculcate a positive attitude toward military service at a very early age, thus creating a storehouse of potential recruits." The public seemed to take notice. "One of the founding principles of our republic," read a subsequent letter to the *Times*, "is civilian control of the military. With the growing presence of the military in our country's education system, this principle is eroding."[36]

Grassroots groups, many of them aligned with NCDOS, also mounted significant opposition to school militarism. Both AFSC and CCCO remained active in the 1990s and became key organizations working under the NCDOS umbrella. Using the Freedom of Information Act as well as public affairs contacts at military branches, CCCO regularly obtained the "target lists" of schools that had expressed interest in JROTC. This information was published in early Internet forums to help activists in these targeted communities agitate against the proposed high school military units. CCCO also provided support to local anti-JROTC campaigns across the country and monitored their progress. AFSC produced counter-recruitment literature distributed by community groups and dispatched organizers to "hot spots" of anti-JROTC organizing.

In one of the decade's more memorable struggles, in the fall of 1994 AFSC's Harold Jordan went to Seattle, where the majority-Black Rainier Beach High School was the site for a proposed "JROTC academy." The Department of Defense, working with the U.S. Department of Education, had selected several locations in high-poverty urban areas to pilot a new type of school that offered an expanded JROTC curriculum. Drawing on his experience in organizing across racial lines, Jordan assembled a diverse coalition that included antiwar veterans, the National Organization for Women, and teachers. The campaign made an issue of the Pentagon's apparent targeting of majority-Black schools for its JROTC units.[37]

Although many efforts to block JROTC failed, Rainier Beach was one of more than a dozen campaigns that succeeded. By avoiding strident antimilitarist appeals, activists were able to keep JROTC out of Seattle as well as more conservative parts of the country. In Waterboro, Maine; Sioux Falls, South Dakota; and Roane County, West Virginia, community members—often working closely with the AFSC and CCCO—found that economic arguments and cost-benefit analyses resonated with school boards and parents and could effectively delay or thwart proposed JROTC programs. By the mid-1990s places like Sioux Falls were well represented under the NCDOS banner. Between 1991 and 1994 the number of local organizations affiliated with NCDOS doubled, with many of the new coalition members located in rural and suburban areas. Of the sixteen activists who gathered in Philadelphia for an October 1992 NCDOS meeting, six were organizing in their communities exclusively against JROTC. "Without NCDOS," Harold Jordan said at the gathering, the various groups that collaborated on anti-JROTC campaigns "might never have contacted each other around this issue."[38] Anti-JROTC sentiment was no longer a bicoastal phenomenon, and NCDOS provided the perfect platform for coordinating a national campaign against high school military training.

A Successful Scholar-Activist Collaboration

As activists with the Committee on Militarism in Education had emphasized during the 1920s and 1930s, grounding a campaign in credible research was crucial, which NCDOS members recognized. "One of the things we noticed was that no one had actually looked at what was being taught in JROTC," Harold Jordan recalled years later. "It was clear to us that there was not the usual accountability mechanism when it comes to bringing curriculum into the schools. While it was true that other antimilitarists were doing critical work on JROTC, we thought that AFSC's contribution as one of the leaders in the network would be to take on a big piece of work that a small group couldn't do." What the organization lacked, however, was someone with the training and credentials to research the JROTC curriculum. Catherine Lutz, an anthropologist then at the University of North Carolina who was interested in researching U.S. militarism, fit the bill.[39] During her inquiry she went to Philadelphia to meet with Jordan, whose name kept coming up whenever she talked about the subject with colleagues. "We had a long discussion in my office," Jordan recalls. "It turned into, 'Can we do each other a favor here?'" When she agreed to work with AFSC, the organization had found its expert. The outcome of the eighteen-month collaboration of Lutz and Jordan was their 1995 report, *Making Soldiers in the Public Schools*.

Although he was not credited as Lutz's coauthor, Jordan assisted Lutz in writing and researching key sections of the report. "We simply had to address the arguments that were being made by the military to school authorities," Jordan said. To this end he filed numerous Freedom of Information Act requests and did "a lot of digging around in strange places." They mined sociology journals, doctoral dissertations, and think-tank reports for their potential to undermine the standard pro-JROTC arguments. As Jordan recalled, the use of this diverse material was motivated by their sense that "we had to get it right. We didn't want anything published that would be open to question or attack based on factual errors." He added, "In the end there was never any attack on the basic interpretations." Ultimately this approach paid off as stories about the report appeared in the *Washington Post* and *Time* magazine.

Meanwhile, Lutz and one of her graduate students, Lesley Bartlett, teamed up to analyze the army's JROTC curriculum. Their research took aim at the way JROTC textbooks presented the notion of leadership; they found that the books usually equated the term with "respect for constituted authority." They also found that the army JROTC curriculum treated U.S. history as a series of triumphant military maneuvers, rarely questioning whether war was a desirable or legally justified option, nor did the curriculum discuss who was victimized by these actions. Overall, Lutz and Bartlett's analysis pointed to the propagandizing function of JROTC and seriously weakened the argument that JROTC primarily trained youth in citizenship and leadership skills.[40]

Studded with footnotes, their study threw a wrench into a Pentagon marketing machine that was trying to sell JROTC as an effective way of dealing with "at-risk youth" in American schools. Indeed, *Making Soldiers in the Public Schools* garnered favorable press in national publications, demolished key arguments used by supporters of the program, and cast the JROTC curriculum in such a negative light that it forced the army to withdraw and later revise the textbooks it used in its JROTC classrooms. For Lutz the experience highlighted the key ingredients of successful collaboration in addressing school militarism: "Activists bring their knowledge of the political landscape as well as their deep knowledge about the issue. What the academic brings are both analytic skills and academic credentials or cultural capital—which helps bring credibility to the knowledge that they both generate."

Making Soldiers in the Public Schools was a boon to anti-JROTC campaigns. Activists in local communities often provided copies of the report to school officials who were contemplating a new JROTC program. Jordan also noted that ac-

tivists used the report "to raise questions with educators about JROTC. Whenever we heard of school boards considering JROTC, we got reports, information,
and analysis into their hands." While the short-term effects of their research were
impressive and largely beneficial to the counter-recruitment movement, over the
long term the military actually benefited the most. In response to the report, the
army revised the JROTC curriculum and expunged some of the more offensive
parts of the texts—such as one section that appeared to justify the so-called In-
dian Wars, a series of U.S. military campaigns that many historians now view as
part of a genocidal campaign against indigenous people. Ironically, an army historian observed, by forcing the army to remove such sections, "the critique of Lutz
and Bartlett probably strengthened JROTC offerings."[41]

Despite the Pentagon's enjoying a substantial increase in recruiting resources
during the 1990s, its recruitment efforts faced other challenges. Throughout the
decade, especially during the later years, a booming economy spelled trouble for
recruiters. In 1999 the army experienced its worst recruiting year in two decades.[42]
Troubled by the challenges of meeting recruitment goals, U.S. Senator Tim
Hutchinson, an Arkansas Republican who chaired the Armed Services Committee's Subcommittee on Personnel, blamed school officials' reluctance to open their
doors to the military. However, the claim had virtually no basis. A 2001 RAND
Corporation assessment of several years' worth of recruiter surveys showed "no
evidence of a negative trend in access" to schools. In fact, the proportion of military recruiters who said they were able to speak directly with high school seniors
and display brochures and other materials remained constant during the period of
study. Moreover, the percentage of recruiters who said high schools in their area
administered the Armed Services Vocational Aptitude Battery without any privacy safeguards for students also held steady at about 85 percent. Rather, as the
Pentagon's own research found, recruiters' biggest problem was teenagers' declining interest in military service. Between 1989 and 1999 the percentage of males
aged sixteen to twenty-one who expressed an interest in military service dipped
from 17 to 11.3 percent, while the rate for Blacks also fell dramatically, from 53 to 37
percent.[43]

Undeterred by the lack of data to support his claims, in February 2000
Hutchinson held Senate hearings on the issue of school access that directly
blamed schools and education officials for the military's recruiting woes. After
hearing testimony from recruiters and military officials, Hutchinson announced
on the Senate floor that in 1999 alone military recruiters had encountered nearly
twenty thousand instances of "denial of access." While the term conjures images
of physical confrontations at the schoolhouse door, the military recruiting services
seem to have applied the label to anything that was less than carte blanche access.

If a school allowed recruiters on campus but limited the number of visits to twice a year, the recruiting services would cry foul and report it up the chain of command as a denial of access. However, the twenty thousand figure was a misleading statistic that made for compelling headlines. As important, it ultimately led to an amendment to the No Child Left Behind Act of 2002 that tied federal funding for public high schools to a requirement that they provide military recruiters with access to campus and student information.[44]

As numerous scholars have shown, No Child Left Behind had a dramatic influence on U.S. education. That schools would be graded based on students' performance on standardized tests in math and reading encouraged the practice of "teaching to the test" and left little room for teachers to be creative in designing their curriculum.[45] No less radical was the requirement that schools allow military recruiters access to campus and individual student contact information. Schools that failed to comply risked losing valuable federal funding. However, as Brian Lagotte has shown, most school administrators have at best an imperfect grasp of the law; many believed that they had to grant the military as much access to their campus as possible. Consequently, at many schools in the United States military recruiters make weekly visits to set up information tables, volunteer to coach sports, and deliver guest lectures to history classes—all in a bid to achieve what the U.S. Army refers to as "school ownership." For example, a U.S. Army Recruiting Command handbook that we obtained shows that recruiters visited certain schools as often as one hundred times in a 180-day school year.[46]

The Iraq War

In February 2003 millions marched worldwide to protest the planned U.S.-led invasion of Iraq. When the Bush administration started the war anyway, the decision demonstrated the limits of street protests and forced many to question their involvement in politics. Yet some—like an army veteran, Yvette Richardson—were moved to pursue forms of activism that promised a direct influence on American militarism.

Shortly after the Iraq War started, Richardson began thinking of the young people serving and dying in the U.S. armed forces. When she served as a Military Police officer from 1992 to 1997, she had been stationed at the massive Fort Hood army base near Austin. Her path to resistance started there as well, at Under the Hood Café, a nearby coffee shop that provided support for veterans, including those opposed to U.S. wars. Talking with active-duty war resisters she met at the café, Richardson eventually became part of the growing antiwar movement. The transition from soldier to activist was not easy. "I was this whole different person in the military," she said in an interview, "doing what I was supposed to do, doing what I was told to do, and following what's going on around me instead of pushing up against things."[47]

At one rally she made contact with Peaceful Vocations, a group that went into local schools and shared information with students about the realities of military service and nonmilitary career options. After joining the group for several visits to high schools in Fort Worth, Richardson felt she had found her calling. Central to her transformation was the realization that "standing on the corner with a protest sign" had limited effect. Instead, she and other counter-recruiters emphasized "grassroots, one-on-one conversations" with students targeted by military recruiters. Although this required more time and energy than she—a single mother attending school part time—was sometimes able to muster, her participation was important to counter what she viewed as the military's skewed perspective.[48]

According to one survey, 86 percent of Texas high school students who reported having contact with a military recruiter said they were never told about the risks of military service.[49] One egregious example Richardson cited was when— in 2006, with the Iraq War raging—she spoke with a high school student who was told by a recruiter, "We're not even in a war anymore." "You think," Richardson said, "'How can these kids not know we're in a war?' But when you're sixteen or seventeen years old, and if you're not watching the news and somebody in that position of authority tells you we're not in a war anymore—especially if it's a military person—you're going to believe it." Such examples illustrate why Richardson felt a duty to challenge the information the military presented. "I'm a veteran," she noted, "so I have this knowledge that these kids don't have, and they're not going to get it from the recruiter."[50]

In their embrace of counter-recruitment as a way to fight war where it begins— in local schools where military recruiters enjoyed wide-open access—veterans like Richardson joined other activists disillusioned by what they perceived as the failure of traditional antiwar efforts. Many believed that if they could convince enough students not to enlist, and erect obstacles to recruiting in schools, activists could sap the military's strength and affect its ability to prosecute the war in Iraq.

As one researcher found, during the Iraq War years antiwar activists viewed counter-recruitment as a way "to move beyond the 'symbolic protest' of antiwar marching and demonstrating" and "interfere directly and 'materially' with the inner workings of U.S. military aggression."[51] If enough people undertook such interference, these activists believed, they could have an immediate and negative effect on the military's ability to enlist the number of young people necessary for U.S. imperial adventures. Fueled by anger at the Iraq War, counter-recruitment was most active and visible between 2005 and 2009. During this period counter-recruitment trainings in the Midwest, hardly a breeding ground of antimilitarist sentiment, could attract dozens of attendees, and, in the words of an AFSC staff member, "it was sexy to do counter-recruitment." As one prominent observer wrote in 2007, counter-recruitment campaigns were one of the "few good efforts" remaining in an otherwise moribund peace movement.[52]

But by the end of new century's first decade, activists had learned that it was unrealistic to measure success by how effective they were at reducing the military enlistment rate. As the Iraq War experience showed, when military recruiters fail to "fill boots," they simply make it easier to enlist. For example, when the U.S. Army Recruiting Command faced unprecedented recruiting difficulties in 2006, it addressed the problem by issuing so-called moral waivers to thousands whose criminal records normally would have prevented them from enlisting.[53] As two authors of this book noted in 2014: "A fight with the Pentagon is not a fair fight, nor is it one that counter-recruiters are likely to win."[54]

Rather than focusing on curtailing recruitment, many counter-recruiters during the Iraq War period focused instead on trying to mentor youth activists. As early as the 1980s, organizers understood that their message was more likely to be accepted when youth delivered it. Thus, as the Iraq War persisted, Peaceful Vocations held poetry slams in Fort Worth that students, teachers, and parents attended. The group saw such events as an effective way to reach students who typically bypass a literature table set up by counter-recruiters in local schools. The slams also helped activists maintain visibility in the Fort Worth educational community and facilitated new contacts with teachers. "The poetry slams," one group member observed, "are how we've found our biggest supporters in the schools."[55]

A similar cross-generational organizing effort occurred in San Diego, where students and adult allies formed the Education Not Arms Coalition to counter the military presence at Mission Bay High School. With support from a popular teacher and seasoned activists at Project YANO like Rick Jahnkow, students at Mission Bay implemented a multidimensional campaign to do what many considered impossible: uproot an established JROTC unit. Racial and class appeals proved to be most effective in this effort. As the student leaders publicized how the school's lauded college preparatory curriculum had to surrender classroom space to the JROTC, they demonstrated how militarism effectively starved the largely Hispanic student body of academic resources. Through intensive leafletting and peer education, youth activists were able to, as they termed it, "un-cool" JROTC. When in 2012 student enrollment in the program dipped below the minimum number required to receive federal funding, the school abolished its JROTC unit.[56] Although San Diego offered the most dramatic example of youth-led counter-recruiting, other notable campaigns during the period occurred in

New York City and Oakland, where grant funding allowed paid youth interns to organize for the passage of citywide policies to curb military recruitment in schools.[57]

Conclusion

Since 2000, local campaigns to limit on-campus military recruiting have been the most visible form of counter-recruitment organizing. However, the formation in 2003 of the National Network Opposing the Militarization of Youth (NNOMY) has also contributed to maintaining movement consciousness among activists. A 2009 national counter-recruitment conference, which the network organized, brought together more than 250 activists from across the country for a series of workshops on ways to address school militarism. Several surprisingly effective initiatives, including the National Coalition to Protect Student Privacy, developed from that crucial meeting.

Although few groups have had the vision or resources to conduct effective state-level campaigns, throughout much of the 2010s the coalition used grant money and private donations to assist counter-recruiters in several states on issues related to the military's aptitude testing. The results of these campaigns have been impressive. After activists organized for years, in 2010 the Maryland legislature passed a law that bars schools from automatically funneling test results to the military. In New Hampshire local activists subsequently forced that state's commissioner of education and state board of education to rein in the use of military aptitude testing in high schools and encourage schools to prevent the automatic transfer of student test results to the military.[58]

Given the level of support for high school military training among educators and parents, it is not surprising that the 2012 victory at San Diego's Mission Bay High School was one of the only successful anti-JROTC campaigns. But one other California effort is also worth mentioning. Largely in response to public anger about the Iraq War, in 2006 the San Francisco school board voted to gradually eliminate JROTC by 2009. Despite San Francisco's reputation as a liberal city, military training had been a component of the city's public school experience since early in the twentieth century. Given the city's prominence, and its long history of support for JROTC, the school board's action created a stir. The JROTC vote earned generous coverage in periodicals read by the national military and defense community, including a cover story in the March 2007 issue of *U.S. Naval Institute Proceedings*. As a high-level JROTC official later claimed, this was the "first time anywhere in the country that JROTC has been kicked out of a school district solely on ideological grounds."[59]

The issue soon generated an outpouring of support for high school military training that led to the election of all new members to the city school board. Opposing JROTC, as the then mayor of San Francisco (and current governor of California), Gavin Newsom, put it, was tantamount to "disrespecting the sacrifice of men and women in uniform."[60] In May 2009 JROTC's advocates persuaded the new school board to reverse course and return military training to the city's high schools. The lesson here was clear: opposition to school militarism can be political poison in even the most liberal surroundings.

Beginning in the 1990s, activists learned to overcome what had been their biggest organizing hurdle—isolation. Between 1990 and 1996, as JROTC programs rapidly multiplied, groups affiliated with NCDOS recorded major breakthroughs: military recruiter bans in two of the country's major school districts and national visibility (for the first time since the 1970s) in mainstream media. Most significant was the nationally coordinated campaign against JROTC that recorded at least a dozen victories by local groups of teachers, veterans, clergy, and LGBTQ+ rights groups. During AFSC's successful effort in Seattle, activists demonstrated that they had learned from earlier struggles in the 1980s and could now better harness the potential of organizing multiracial coalitions.[61]

Although activists fought valiantly against a rising tide of militarism, with help along the way from groups like AFSC, they ultimately failed to prevent JROTC from nearly doubling in size during the decade.[62] As other issues stole activists' attention, NCDOS held meetings with less regularity, and by the end of the 1990s the coalition would be no more.

Instead of condemning the JROTC as a "military invasion of high schools," a common rhetorical strategy during the 1970s and 1980s, counter-recruiters would find greater success discussing practical issues that were more likely to resonate with school stakeholders. Through 2010 and beyond, when pitched battles erupted over JROTC, activists debated in online forums whether sticking to a principled antimilitarism or reframing their work was more likely to succeed at thwarting militarism in schools.[63]

Most of the counter-recruitment movement ultimately chose to embrace the latter approach, and in this the activists reflected broader changes occurring within other social movements for peace and justice. The declining relevance of moral language in the peace movement can also be seen in U.S.-based campaigns against military toys, in opposition to domestic and foreign U.S. military bases, and in global organizing to recognize the rights of conscientious objectors to war.[64] This rhetorical shift may have made strategic sense. But in return for a greater likelihood of success, counter-recruitment activists jettisoned the moral discourse that had long animated traditional peace movement activities.[65]

CONCLUSION

Much has changed since John Nevin Sayre and his colleagues formed a committee to oppose ROTC and JROTC. Policies and practices initiated during the early 1920s were entrenched by the end of the century, as the military's recruiting services increasingly sought to capture the teenage mind. When the Committee on Militarism in Education (CME) formed, the country had about one hundred Junior ROTC units. Today high schools have about thirty-four hundred. Military training is now such a permanent feature of the U.S. educational landscape that one in six public high schools has a JROTC unit. In some parts of the United States—including most of the Southeast—the density is far greater, with JROTC present in 30 to 60 percent of public high schools.[1]

This book has emphasized how military recruiting in schools and JROTC allow the military to reach the all-important high school market. But that is just the most visible part of the story. Today the Pentagon markets itself to youth in other ways as well. Many are local under-the-radar efforts, whereas others are more national in scope and represent a long-term investment. For example, the U.S. Army has been able to use the new emphasis on standardized testing in schools to promote March 2 Success, an army-sponsored website designed to help students hone their test-taking ability. While the army depicts March 2 Success as a community service, evidence suggests that recruiters are using it to gain access to schools and thus be able to better befriend and recruit young people. In Jackson, Mississippi, community members tasked with promoting army recruiting in the city pushed for the deployment of a van outfitted with March 2 Success workstations that would visit local schools. The army's recruiting commander for Jackson boasted that the so-called Mobile Learning Unit "will increase our recruiters' footprint in the Jackson public school district."[2]

The military has also been quick to capitalize on the widespread interest in the fields of science, technology, engineering, and mathematics. The Pentagon spends roughly $20 million every year to support STARBASE, a program that brings at-risk fifth-grade students to military bases for a week of hands-on science instruction. Civilians teach the courses, but at least one full day consists of uniformed military personnel extolling the benefits of a career in the armed forces. One indication of how seriously the Pentagon takes the ideological function of this program is that it tests all the fifth-graders before and after their participation to assess—among other things—whether STARBASE is effective at making children think more positively about the military.[3]

The exponential growth in the number and variety of military partnerships with public schools during the past one hundred years has been accompanied by a qualitative change in the way the issue is debated. In the twenty-first century, STARBASE, March 2 Success, and similar efforts have attracted little attention from parents or peace activists, least of all educators. In fact, whereas left-wing teachers like Jessie Wallace Hughan organized against military drill during the 1920s, and teachers' unions were vocally opposed to JROTC at key moments following the Vietnam War, today classroom teachers rarely are involved with counter-recruitment. In the early part of the twentieth century, socialists were among the first to condemn the increase of high school and college military programs. Today U.S. Senator Bernie Sanders, a self-described democratic socialist, touts the benefits of the STARBASE program.[4] Indeed, the military's ever-growing presence in American schools may appear to be a natural component of public education. But, as we have demonstrated, military training and recruiting in schools has historically been an unstable and highly contested proposition. In each period of that history, vibrant collectives were seeking to undermine school militarism.

During the 1920s increasingly bold military maneuvers in schools and colleges led some of the nation's leading intellectuals, clergy, and peace activists to form an organization devoted to uncovering and critiquing school militarism. Before the Committee on Militarism in Education ceased operations in 1940, these activists and their allies won state and local victories against high school ROTC and forced more than a dozen colleges and universities to abolish compulsory military instruction. Although the CME failed to roll back the tide of militarism that would eventually lead the country to war, committee members successfully shifted the terms of debate with the aid of a highly sophisticated research and publicity apparatus. Some of the leading periodicals of the day discussed the CME's ideas, which provoked a backlash from public officials who sometimes resorted to surveillance and skullduggery to stop activists' activities. The CME even forced a sitting president—Calvin Coolidge—to take a public stand against compulsory ROTC.

During the 1960s, when an unpopular war in Southeast Asia encouraged Americans to shed their traditionally warm embrace of the military, campus protests rocked the country. Although high school militarism was less pronounced during this era, antiwar activists relentlessly targeted ROTC units at colleges and universities. By the early 1970s, with college ROTC enrollment cratering and the military about to shift to relying on an all-volunteer military, the Pentagon identified high schools as their new recruiting stations. Standing in the way of military officials was a diverse coalition of parents, church groups, and peace organizations that would have made John Sayre and other CME founders proud. Drawing on its experience in Vietnam-era draft counseling, and using antimilitarist rhetoric, the nascent counter-recruitment movement achieved significant victories in the fight against JROTC and effectively limited the Pentagon's high school testing program. Along the way, activists enlisted allies in Congress, academia, and the press—achieving the most mainstream support for military-free schools in America's history.

But the Reagan era began a new period of cultural veneration of all things military. Aided by creative efforts at regional coordination such as the Task Force on Recruitment and Militarism, counter-recruiters of the 1980s made valiant attempts to resist JROTC in places like Baltimore. With studies showing that JROTC churned out youth more inclined to serve in the military, the Pentagon viewed the high school program as essential to maintaining its all-volunteer force. The 1991 Gulf War created a brief opening for activists to challenge this system and led to a surge of resistance to school militarism. This infusion of talented activists, the establishment of local groups in places like Houston, Texas, with little history of peace activism, and the formation of a national network of counter-recruiters (the National Campaign to Demilitarize Our Schools—NCDOS), put the movement in a position of strength. In their quest to thwart the Pentagon's ambitious plans to double the size of JROTC, most activists made the strategic decision to limit their antimilitarist language and imagery, instead emphasizing issues—like school financing and curriculum control—that could appeal to school board members and parents in Middle America.

Between 1990 and 1996 NCDOS-affiliated groups opposing the incursion of Junior ROTC notched at least a dozen victories. Collaboration on research by activists and scholars furthered the cause of counter-recruitment by generating national news coverage critical of JROTC. And for the first time activists used an alliance with gay rights groups to prohibit high school recruiting in two major U.S. cities and to ban ROTC at several large universities. In contrast, activists in the post–9/11 era have found success more elusive in their battles against school militarism.

Following the terrorist attacks of September 11, 2001, public approval of the military reached record levels as the country's chief institutions—industry, schools, media—settled comfortably into a permanent war footing.[5] Outrage at the invasion of Iraq initially led to renewed interest in school militarism and counter-recruitment, notably from youth of color and military veterans. Bellwether peace organizations like AFSC also responded to the Iraq War by devoting more resources to support counter-recruiters. During the late 2000s coastal urban centers like New York and San Diego became hubs of innovation for counter-recruiting, offering mentoring and (in some cases) paid internships for youth activists. But this infrastructure relied on consistent funding. Once school militarism and the Iraq War were less frequently in the headlines, many progressive funders lost interest in supporting counter-recruitment. The Great Recession of 2008 also forced AFSC to close several of its local chapters and stop publishing literature that counter-recruiters used, dealing a blow to the movement.

Thus, counter-recruiters today are almost all volunteers, and demographically speaking they skew older and whiter than they did during the 2000s. These activists have struggled to maintain support from teachers and organized labor, and it has been more than forty years since a large religious body in the United States made a statement against ROTC or some other aspect of school militarism. This challenge is not new: the ability to create broad-based, sustainable partnerships has long been the Achilles heel of the counter-recruitment movement. During the 1970s organizers had support in Congress, the media, and the pulpit, but they also faced pushback from communities of color, which saw military service as a path to a stable job. With notable exceptions like Project YANO in San Diego, today's counter-recruiters struggle to build multiracial coalitions when they are unable to offer viable economic alternatives to programs like JROTC.[6]

When it comes to ROTC on college campuses, dissent is especially hard to find. In a 2010 *Washington Post* column, one university professor predicted that faculty and students at elite schools would embrace the revival of ROTC and only a "tiny minority of the professionally discontented" would oppose it.[7] He was right. The return of ROTC to Ivy League schools like Columbia University caused barely a murmur among student activists. The ease with which universities remilitarized is partly because of the cheerleading of then-president Barack Obama. Although he had never served in the military, Obama advocated a greater military presence at the nation's most prestigious universities. As he declared in his 2011 State of the

Union address: "I call on all of our college campuses to open their doors to our military recruiters and ROTC."[8]

While anti-ROTC campaigns never materialized at Ivy League schools in this period, they were successful at a few institutions like California State University, San Marcos, in 2009. Activists also had mixed success trying to prevent ROTC from establishing a beachhead in the City University of New York (CUNY), whose sprawling system includes twelve colleges. The Pentagon considered the Big Apple, which has the largest population of college students in the country, to be underserved by ROTC. The military therefore tried in the 2010s to start ROTC chapters on four of the CUNY campuses—City College, York College, Medgar Evers, and the College of Staten Island. Although units were eventually established at City College and York, opposition from faculty blocked ROTC at Medgar Evers and Staten Island. The CUNY struggle was noteworthy for the strong opposition mounted by the Professional Staff Congress, the union that represents thirty thousand CUNY faculty and staff. This partial victory was one of the few bright spots in an era marked by growing acceptance of ROTC.[9]

As our account suggests, the history of opposition to the militarization of U.S. educational space is complicated. School militarism germinated for decades as the Pentagon sought to expand its influence in schools and in society at large. Examining anti-ROTC and counter-recruiting efforts reveals that the conflict about a military presence in schools at times has been a Sisyphean struggle. Nonetheless, to tell this story is to revisit the ways a surprisingly diverse range of Americans have intervened to limit the military's influence in U.S. schools and colleges. Their voices remind us that war commences not in the White House or even in the boardrooms of scheming multinational corporations. Rather, war begins in the shaping of what George Coe and his CME colleagues called the psychological mindset that creates young people submissive to authority and in thrall to military symbolism.

Today's counter-recruitment movement is animated by the same spirit as its predecessors': activists believe that to challenge school militarism is to "stop war where it begins"—in the JROTC classroom and high school cafeterias, hallways, and athletic fields where military recruiters hold sway. The prospects for the counter-recruitment movement are bound up with its past. By examining the history of these struggles for military-free schools, we believe the future can be made more peaceful. This book represents one contribution to that effort.

NOTES

Introduction

1. *Army and Navy Register*, October 9, 1926, 340.

2. David Vine, *Base Nation: How U.S. Military Bases abroad Harm America and the World* (New York: Metropolitan, 2015).

3. Cynthia Enloe, "The Recruiter and the Sceptic: A Critical Feminist Approach to Military Studies," *Critical Military Studies* 1, no. 1 (2015): 6.

4. This figure comes from calculations made by the noted peace scholar David Cortright, based on the Department of Defense budget for FY2014. For a discussion of this portion of the defense budget, see Cortright's foreword to Scott Harding and Seth Kershner, *Counter-recruitment and the Campaign to Demilitarize Public Schools* (New York: Palgrave Macmillan, 2015), vii–x.

5. U.S. Army Recruiting Command, *Recruiter Handbook*, USAREC Manual no. 3-01 (Fort Knox, Ky.: USAREC, 2011), 3.

6. After filing FOIA requests with the recruiting services of several branches of the military, we obtained more than two thousand pages of reports documenting what recruiters do on high school recruiting visits. For discussion of this data, see Scott Harding and Seth Kershner, "A Borderline Issue": Are There Child Soldiers in the United States?" *Journal of Human Rights* 17, no. 3 (2018): 322–339.

7. Emma Moore and Andrew Swick, *Leveraging ROTC to Span the Civil-Military Gap* (Washington, D.C.: Center for a New American Security, 2018).

8. Michael Winerip, "The ROTC Dilemma," *New York Times*, October 26, 2009; Moore and Swick, *Leveraging ROTC*, 15; Cheryl Miller, *Underserved: A Case Study of ROTC in New York City* (Washington, D.C.: American Enterprise Institute, 2011), 8.

9. Statistics on JROTC program are drawn from Charles A. Goldman et al., *Geographic and Demographic Representativeness of the Junior Reserve Officers' Training Corps* (Santa Monica, Calif.: RAND, 2017), ix; Andrew Morgado, "Junior ROTC Offers Opportunities, and Results, for Students," *Minneapolis Star-Tribune*, December 1, 2016; Elda Pema and Stephen Mehay, "Career Effects of Occupation-related Vocational Education: Evidence from the Military's Internal Labor Market," *Economics of Education Review* 31, no. 5 (2012): 682.

10. The "one in four figure" comes from Goldman et al., *Geographic and Demographic Repre-*

sentativeness, xii. The best recent example of the "school-to-military" argument is Suzie M. Abajian, "Drill and Ceremony: A Case Study of Militarism, Military Recruitment and the Pedagogy of Enforcement in an Urban School in Southern California" (PhD diss., University of California, Los Angeles, 2013).

11. Lesley Bartlett and Catherine Lutz, "Disciplining Social Difference: Some Cultural Politics of Military Training in Public High Schools," *Urban Review* 30 (June 1998): 119–136; Erica Meiners and Therese Quinn, *Flaunt It! Queers Organizing for Public Education and Justice* (New York: Peter Lang, 2009), 19.

12. Donald Downs, "ROTC and the Future of Liberal Education," *Chronicle of Higher Education*, May 15, 2009, https://www.chronicle.com/article/rotc-and-the-future-of-liberal -education/.

13. Horace Mann, *Lectures on Education* (Boston: Ide and Dutton, 1855), 53; Aline M. Stomfay-Stitz, *Peace Education in America, 1828–1989: Sourcebook for Education and Research* (Metuchen, N.J.: Scarecrow Press, 1993), 23.

14. Lawrence Cremin, *American Education: The National Experience, 1783–1876* (New York: Harper & Row, 1980), 513, 515.

15. Thomas Curran, "Love, Alfred Henry (1830–1913)," in Mitchell K. Hall, ed., *Opposition to War: an Encyclopedia of U. S. Peace and Antiwar Movements* (Santa Barbara: ABC-CLIO, 2018), 2:399–400.

16. Peter Brock, *Pacifism in the United States: From the Colonial Era to the First World War* (Princeton, N.J.: Princeton University Press, 1968), 927, 929.

17. Thomas F. Curran, *Soldiers of Peace: Civil War Pacifism and the Postwar Radical Peace Movement* (New York: Fordham University Press, 2003), 145–146.

18. Robert H. Wiebe, *The Search for Order, 1877–1920* (New York: Hill & Wang, 1967), 57.

19. David B. Tyack, *The One Best System: A History of American Urban Education* (Cambridge, Mass.: Harvard University Press, 1974), 230, 232.

20. Tara M. McCarthy, "'The Humaner Instinct of Women': Hannah Bailey and the Woman's Christian Temperance Union's Critique of Militarism and Manliness in the Late Nineteenth Century," *Peace & Change* 33 (April 2008): 200–201.

21. "Address of Mrs. Hannah J. Bailey," *Report of the First Annual Meeting of the Lake Mohonk Conference on International Arbitration*, 1895, 68, 88, copy in authors' possession.

22. "Notes and Comments," *Advocate of Peace* 57 (November 1895): 256.

23. Space does not allow a full catalog of incidents of labor violence. Suffice it to say, as do two prominent historians, that America boasts the "bloodiest and most violent labor history of any industrial nation in the world." Philip Taft and Philip Ross, "American Labor Violence: Its Causes, Character, and Outcome," in Hugh Graham and Ted Gurr, eds., *Violence in America* (New York: Bantam, 1969), 281. See also Robert Goldstein, "Political Repression of the American Labor Movement during Its Formative Years—a Comparative Perspective," *Labor History* 51, no. 2 (2010): 271–293.

24. "Notes and Comments," 255.

25. Craig Karpel, "Teenie Militarists," *Ramparts*, September 28, 1968, 43–50.

Chapter 1. Making Citizen Soldiers

1. Stephan Brumberg, "New York City Schools March off to War: The Nature and Extent of Participation of the City Schools in the Great War, April 1917–June 1918," *Urban Education* 24, no. 4 (1990): 449.

2. *American Jewish Chronicle*, July 6, 1917, 268; *Brooklyn Eagle*, January 11, 1917.

3. Brumberg, "New York City Schools March," 451–452. See also Diane Ravitch, *The Great School Wars: New York City, 1805–1973* (New York: Basic Books, 1974), 225.

4. Arthur A. Ekirch Jr., *The Civilian and the Military* (New York: Oxford University Press, 1956), esp. chap. 1.

5. James Madison, *The Writings of James Madison: 1787–1790* (New York: G. P. Putnam, 1904), 5:193.

6. Donald Alexander Downs and Ilia Murtazashvili, *Arms and the University: Military Presence and the Civic Education of Non-military Students* (New York: Cambridge University Press, 2012), 78. On students' response to military instruction, see Willard Nash, *A Study of Military Science in the Land-Grant Colleges* (New York: Columbia University Press, 1934), 18–25.

7. For an overview of this period, see chap. 3 in Nash, *A Study of Military Science.*

8. "Military Drill in Public Schools," *Journal of Education* 61, no. 14 (1905): 369; Louis H. Chaney, "Military Training in the Secondary Schools," (master's thesis, Butler University, 1940), 19.

9. Lesley Bartlett and Catherine Lutz, "Disciplining Social Difference: Some Cultural Politics of Military Training in Public High Schools," *Urban Review* 30, no. 2 (1998): 122–123; Leigh Robinson Gignilliat, *Arms and the Boy: Military Training in Schools and Colleges, Its Value in Peace and Its Importance in War, with Many Practical Suggestions for the Course of Training, and with Brief Descriptions of the Most Successful Systems Now in Operation* (Indianapolis: Bobbs-Merrill, 1916), 253.

10. Ralph Barton Perry, *The Plattsburg Movement: A Chapter of America's Participation in the World War* (E. P. Dutton, 1921), 14. See also John Garry Clifford, *The Citizen Soldiers: The Plattsburg Training Camp Movement, 1913–1920* (Lexington: University Press of Kentucky, 1972).

11. Daniel Barthell, "The Committee on Militarism in Education, 1925–1940" (PhD diss., University of Illinois, 1972), 10–12.

12. Bartlett and Lutz, "Disciplining Social Difference," 124.

13. Eric Fisher Wood, "A Proposed Military System," in Agnes Van Valkenburgh, ed., *Military Training in Schools and Colleges, Including Military Camps* (New York: H. W. Wilson, 1917), 101.

14. Alan Penn, *Targeting Schools: Drill, Militarism, and Imperialism* (London: Woburn Press, 1999), xi, 169.

15. A. C. F. Beales, *The History of Peace* (New York: Dial Press, 1931), 186–193, 245–250; Claire Hirschfield, "Randall Cremer," 181–183, in Harold Josephson, ed., *Biographical Dictionary of Modern Peace Leaders* (Westport, Conn.: Greenwood, 1985); Penn, *Targeting Schools*, 137.

16. Beales, *History of Peace*, 167–169, 284; Thomas C. Kennedy, "The Ubiquitous Friend: Edward Grubb and the Modern British Peace Movement," *Peace Research* 17 (1985): 1–4, 6–9.

17. Richard A. Cloward and Frances Fox Piven, *Poor People's Movements: Why They Succeed,*

How They Fail (New York: Vintage, 1979), 102; Ryan Shafto, "The Socialist Party of America and the Campaign for Military Preparedness, 1914–1917," unpublished manuscript in authors' possession, 15; *Appeal to Reason*, November 23, 1895, 2.

18. Shafto, "Socialist Party of America," 13; *Shawnee County Socialist*, March 14, 1914, 4.

19. Aline M. Stomfay-Stitz, *Peace Education in America, 1828–1990: Sourcebook for Education and Research* (Metuchen, N.J.: Scarecrow Press, 1993), 42. See also Susan Zeiger, "Teaching Peace: Lessons from a Peace Studies Curriculum of the Progressive Era," *Peace & Change* 25 (January 2000): 52–69.

20. Zeiger, "Teaching Peace," 55.

21. Beales, *History of Peace*, 259.

22. Jennifer Curran, "To Make War Unthinkable: The Woman's Peace Party of New York, 1914–1919" (master's thesis, Memorial University of Newfoundland, 1997), 75.

23. David Starr Jordan, "Military Training in High School," *Humanitarian*, February 1917, reprinted in *Labor Journal* (Everett, Wash.), February 16, 1917, 1.

24. Charles Howlett and Audrey Cohan, *John Dewey: America's Peace-Minded Educator* (Carbondale: Southern Illinois University Press, 2016), 34–35.

25. Ibid., 99–109.

26. Edward B. DeGroot, "Physical Education versus Military Training in Secondary Schools," *American Physical Education Review* 22 (1917): 304.

27. Ekirch, *Civilian and the Military*, 218.

28. *Labor World* (Duluth, Minn.), December 18, 1915, 4; *Appeal to Reason*, February 24, 1917, 4.

29. Students' Anti-Drill Society, "Compulsory Military Drill—A Great College Menace," in Van Valkenburgh, *Military Training in Schools and Colleges*, 179.

30. "Princeton Students Opposed to Military Training," *Advocate of Peace*, April 1916, 113.

31. H. C. Peterson and Gilbert Fite, *Opponents of War, 1917–1918* (Seattle: University of Washington Press, 1957); David M. Kennedy, *Over Here: The First World War and American Society* (New York: Oxford University Press, 1980); "Compulsory Military Training in Schools and the National Need for Physical Preparedness," *Current Opinion*, August 1916, 115.

32. Brumberg, "New York City Schools March," 466; Ravitch, *Great School Wars*, 229.

33. *School and Society*, April 28, 1917, 495; *Brooklyn Eagle*, editorial, March 3, 1917. For more on Hughan, who was a noted activist and perennial congressional candidate for the Socialist Party, see Scott Bennett, "Radical Pacifism and the General Strike against War: Jessie Wallace Hughan, the Founding of the War Resisters League, and the Socialist Origins of Secular Radical Pacifism in America," *Peace & Change* 26, no. 3 (2001): 352–373.

34. "Why the War Should Be Studied in Schools," *National School Service Magazine* 1, no. 1 (September 1, 1918): 5. According to George Creel, who headed Wilson's propaganda agency: "We published *The Study of the Great War*, by Professor Harding, which became a textbook in schools, colleges and cantonments." George Creel, *How We Advertised America* (New York: Harper, 1920), 108.

35. Peterson and Fite, *Opponents of War*, 102–109; Kennedy, *Over Here*, 56–59.

36. An extensive scheme of military training for boys that had been instituted at a Wyoming high school before the war and publicized widely as the "Wyoming idea" served as a model

for the War Department after the formal establishment of Junior ROTC programs. See E. Z. Steever, "The Wyoming Plan of Military Training for Schools," *School Review*, March 1917, 145–150; George Creel, "Wyoming's Answer to Militarism," *Everybody's Magazine*, February 1916, 150–159.

37. Barthell, "Committee on Militarism in Education," 16.

38. *New York Times*, January 7, 1917; *Appeal to Reason*, January 8, 1916.

Chapter 2. Postwar Peace Activism and the Committee on Militarism in Education

1. See Charles DeBenedetti, *The Origins of the Modern American Peace Movement, 1915–1929* (Millwood, N.Y.: KTO Press, 1978); and Charles F. Howlett and Glen Zeitzer, *The American Peace Movement: History and Historiography* (Washington, D.C.: American Historical Association, 1985).

2. Linda Kay Schott, *Reconstructing Women's Thoughts: The Women's International League for Peace and Freedom before World War II* (Stanford, Calif.: Stanford University Press, 1997), 13. According to another historian of the era, "suffrage and peace were linked in the minds of many" female activists. See Herbert Janick, "An Instructive Failure: The Connecticut Peace Movement, 1919–1939," *Peace & Change* 5, no. 1 (1978): 12.

3. Charles Chatfield, *For Peace and Justice: Pacifism in America, 1914–1941* (Knoxville: University of Tennessee Press, 1971), 152.

4. John Charles Paige, "The American University and the Student Peace Movement" (master's thesis, Oklahoma State University, 1973), 7; Roswell P. Barnes, *Militarizing Our Youth: The Significance of the Reserve Officers' Training Corps in Our Schools and Colleges* (New York: Committee on Militarism in Education, 1927), microfilm reel 20, box 35, Records of the Committee on Militarism in Education (hereafter Records of the CME), Swarthmore College Peace Collection (hereafter SCPC), McCabe Library, Swarthmore, Pa.

5. Reinhold Niebuhr, "The Threat of the ROTC," *World Tomorrow*, October 1926, 155; Ronald Schaffer, "The War Department's Defense of ROTC," *Wisconsin Magazine of History* 53, no. 2 (winter 1969–70): 108–120; Paige, "American University and the Student Peace Movement," 7–8.

6. As late as 1963, the air force maintained segregated ROTC units at such large universities as Auburn, Baylor, and Mississippi State. Michael S. Neiberg, *Making Citizen-Soldiers: ROTC and the Ideology of American Military Service* (Cambridge, Mass.: Harvard University Press, 2009), 63.

7. James C. Evans and Albert J. Parker, "ROTC Programs and Negro Youth," *Journal of Negro Education* 25, no. 2 (1956): 136. See also Marcus S. Cox, *Segregated Soldiers: Military Training at Historically Black Colleges in the Jim Crow South* (Baton Rouge: LSU Press, 2013).

8. John Nevin Sayre, "The Altars of Freedom," *World Tomorrow*, October 1926, 156–157; Daniel Barthell, "The Committee on Militarism in Education, 1925–1940" (PhD diss., University of Illinois, 1972), 36–37; Committee on Militarism in Education, executive board meeting minutes, November 24, 1925, microfilm reel 2, box 2, Records of the CME; "Anti-militarists," *Pax Special*, June 1925, microfilm reel 130.93, Records of the Women's International League for

Peace and Freedom U.S. Section, SCPC. See also "Howard Students Strike: 400 at Negro University Oppose Compulsory Military Drill," *New York Times*, May 8, 1925.

9. Winthrop D. Lane, *Military Training in Schools and Colleges of the United States*, 2d ed. (New York: Committee on Militarism in Education, 1926), 20, microfilm reel 21, box 36, Records of the CME; Walter C. Longstreth, *Regarding Military Training at Universities* (Philadelphia: Peace and Service Committee of Philadelphia, 1925). We have relied on a later edition of this pamphlet, reissued by the CME, that we found in its records (microfilm reel 21, box 36) in the SCPC.

10. Barthell, "Committee on Militarism in Education," 44, 46.

11. Edward Hachtel, John Nevin Sayre, and Tucker P. Smith, *Reserve Officers' Training Corps and Citizens Military Training Camps*, July 1, 1925, 1–2, microfilm reel 21, box 36, Records of the CME; Nathan Andrew Long, "The Origins, Early Developments, and Present-Day Impact of the Junior Reserve Officers' Training Corps on the American Public Schools" (Ed.D. diss., University of Cincinnati, 2003), 156–158; Barthell, "Committee on Militarism in Education," 40–41; Hachtel, Sayre, and Smith, *Reserve Officers Training Corps*, 2–4, 5–6. See also Arthur A. Ekirch Jr., *The Civilian and the Military* (New York: Oxford University Press, 1956), 222–226.

12. During the 1920s Congress had thwarted repeated attempts by the War Department to promote universal military training. In a 1922 report to President Warren Harding, General John J. Pershing showed that the War Department viewed ROTC as a substitute for the peacetime draft: "That we have not adopted the principle of universal military service renders it highly essential that training which leads up to, and as far as possible includes preparation for military service should be popularized by all available methods." Barnes, *Militarizing Our Youth*, 26.

13. Winthrop Lane, *Military Training in Schools and Colleges in the United States* (New York: Committee on Military Training, 1926), 18–19.

14. Ibid., 24.

15. Evidence that local organizing campaigns used the Lane pamphlet is supported by a letter from a Houston, Texas, schoolteacher who sought the CME's help in preventing the implementation of military training in her city's school system. "Last week I presented the dangers of the [ROTC] system to the staff and board of the local Y.M.C.A.," she wrote. "My opponent, a Captain in the Reserves (one of the high school instructors of drill) deplored my use of the Lane pamphlet." The CME then contacted the American Civil Liberties Union on her behalf for the names of residents in the Houston area who might be able to assist her. Edith E. Osborn to CME, December 3, 1928, and Tucker P. Smith to Forrest Bailey, December 22, 1928, both in box 336, American Civil Liberties Union Files, Seeley G. Mudd Manuscript Library, Princeton University, Princeton, N.J.

16. Barthell, "Committee on Militarism in Education," 66.

17. Ibid., 48, 74–75, 77, 78. In addition to having close links to FOR, the CME and the Fellowship of Youth for Peace had a shared ideology that made their alliance a natural fit. The latter was firmly opposed to school militarism and in October 1925 had passed a strongly worded resolution against compulsory military training.

18. Barthell, "Committee on Militarism in Education," 57.

19. Ibid., 79, 81.

20. According to the history of the CME, "Sayre was the exception" to this rule. As chair for

the first year of CME's existence, and as vice chair from then on, he remained closely involved in the organization's work. Barthell, "Committee on Militarism in Education," 83.

21. "E. Raymond Wilson," in *Guide to the SCPC* (Swarthmore, Pa.: n.p., 1981), 74–75.

22. "Military Training in Cleveland," *School Review*, March 1926, 164–165; George A. Coe, *The War Department as Educator*, microfilm reel 21, box 37, Records of the CME; Chatfield, *For Peace and Justice*, 153–154; Eileen Eagan, *Class, Culture and the Classroom: The Student Peace Movement of the 1930s* (Philadelphia: Temple University Press, 1981), 33, 110–111; Massachusetts Committee on Militarism in Education, *Military Training in the Schools and Colleges of Massachusetts: A Survey* (Boston: Century Press, n.d.), microfilm reel 20, box 35, Records of the CME; Morris R. Cohen, *A Dreamer's Journey* (Boston: Beacon, 1949), 151–152.

23. Ekirch, *Civilian and the Military*, 221.

24. Sayre quoted the editorial during his testimony before the House Committee on Military Affairs, on June 15, 1926. A copy of his testimony is available in series E, box 11, John Nevin Sayre Papers (hereafter Sayre Papers), SCPC.

25. Paige, "American University and the Student Peace Movement," 9–10. See also Sayre's testimony before the House Committee on Military Affairs.

26. Niebuhr, "Threat of the ROTC," 155; John Nevin Sayre to W. H. Hoover, March 25, 1930, series E, box 11, Sayre Papers; Lane, *Military Training in Schools and Colleges*, 30.

27. Eric Foner, *Give Me Liberty: An American History*, 6th ed. (New York: W. W. Norton, 2020), 2:714.

28. George A. Coe, "Shifting the National Mindset," *Religious Education* 18 (October 1923): 318–321.

29. Coe's views reflected those held by other progressive educators at the time. For example, in his book *Dare the Schools Build a New Social Order?* (New York: John Day, 1932), George S. Counts forcefully argued that teachers should serve as leaders of radical social change in America.

30. Coe, "Shifting the National Mindset," 321.

31. George A. Coe, "Training Citizens—for What?" *World Tomorrow*, October 1926, 151–154.

32. Paul Klapper, *The Teaching of History* (New York: D. Appleton, 1926), 114–116; Barthell, "Committee on Militarism in Education," 75–76.

33. *News Letter*, February 7, 1927, microfilm reel 21, box 36, Records of the CME. The first issue of the newsletter appeared on March 6, 1926, and the last in April 1927.

34. Barnes, *Militarizing Our Youth* 5–6. One particularly disturbing excerpt from the ROTC text read as follows: "During the course of a great war every government, whatever its previous form, should become a despotism."

35. Barnes, *Militarizing Our Youth*, 15–18. Barnes notes that the YMCA secretary, Paul Guthrie, had also run afoul of what southerners considered proper academic decorum through his role in organizing an interracial committee on campus.

36. Barnes, *Militarizing Our Youth*, 13.

37. Tucker P. Smith, *So This Is War: A Study of Popularized Military Training* (New York: Committee on Militarism in Education, 1929), 43, 41, microfilm reel 21, box 37, Records of the CME. According to Barthell, Smith's publication was probably "the most important single piece of CME propaganda since the Barnes pamphlet." Barthell, "Committee on Militarism in

Education," 130–131. For more on Smith, particularly his pre-CME involvement in organized labor, see Charles F. Howlett, *Brookwood Labor College and the Struggle for Peace and Social Justice in America* (Lewiston, N.Y.: Edwin Mellen Press, 1993).

38. Harriet H. Alonso, *Peace as a Women's Issue: A History of the U.S. Movement for World Peace and Women's Rights* (Syracuse, N.Y.: Syracuse University Press, 1993), 85–124. Alonso remains the standard historical treatment for the role of women in peace advocacy between the wars. Although it focuses on a much later period of history, one of the best discussions of maternal peace activism can be found in Amy Swerdlow, *Women Strike for Peace: Traditional Motherhood and Radical Politics in the 1960s* (Chicago: University of Chicago Press, 1993). On the absence of women in CME's leadership ranks, see Barthell, "Committee on Militarism in Education," 77.

39. Eric L. Hamilton, "Florence Brewer Boeckel," 80–81, in Mitchell K. Hall, ed., *Opposition to War: An Encyclopedia of U.S. Peace and Antiwar Movements* (Santa Barbara, Calif.: ABC-CLIO, 2018); Justus Doenecke, "Frederick Joseph Libby," 562–564, in Harold Josephson, ed., *Biographical Dictionary of Modern Peace Leaders* (Westport, Conn.: Greenwood, 1985); Bessie L. Pierce, *Public Opinion and the Teaching of History in the United States* (New York: Alfred A. Knopf, 1926), 254–257; Florence Brewer Boeckel, *Between War and Peace: A Handbook for Peace Workers* (New York: Macmillan, 1928), 326–328.

40. Maud C. Stockwell, *Some Facts Concerning Military Training at State Universities* (Minneapolis, Minn.: Women's International League for Peace and Freedom, 1926), 11, microfilm reel 21, box 36, Records of the CME.

41. Zona Gale, "Don't Be Silly," *Nation*, April 10, 1929, 422–423.

42. The public influence of clergy during this period is discussed in William H. Thomas, *Unsafe for Democracy: World War I and the U.S. Justice Department's Covert Campaign to Suppress Dissent* (University of Wisconsin Press, 2009), 4.

43. Niebuhr, "Threat of the ROTC," 156.

44. Joseph Kip Kosek, *Acts of Conscience: Christian Nonviolence and Modern American Democracy* (New York: Columbia University Press, 2009); Ray Abrams, *Preachers Present Arms: A Study of the War-time Attitudes and Activities of the Churches and the Clergy in the United States, 1914–1918* (Philadelphia: University of Pennsylvania Press, 1933), 245–246; Paige, "American University and the Student Peace Movement," 12. For more on the role of churches during the war, see John F. Piper, *The American Churches in World War I* (Athens: Ohio University Press, 1987).

45. "Shall Our Schools Be Militarized?" editorial, *Herald of Gospel Liberty*, December 10, 1925, 1195.

46. "The Churches and Student Military Training," editorial, *Herald of Gospel Liberty*, February 25, 1926, 173.

47. Harry Emerson Fosdick, *The Present Crisis* (New York: Association Press, 1918); Robert Moats Miller, *Harry Emerson Fosdick: Preacher, Pastor, Prophet* (New York: Oxford University Press, 1985), 520. Abrams observes how, more than any other denomination, Episcopalians "have been traditionally tied up with various military organizations and patriotic orders, either through chaplains or social affiliations." Abrams, *Preachers Present Arms*, 31.

48. Niebuhr, "Threat of the ROTC," 156. Formerly a Christian pacifist who chaired the FOR from 1932 to 1933, Niebuhr had become disillusioned with the peace movement by the end of

the 1930s. For more on Niebuhr's break with pacifism, see Lawrence Wittner, *Rebels against War: The American Peace Movement, 1933–1983* (Philadelphia: Temple University Press, 1984), 15–16. Discussion of how Niebuhr later resumed his support of the peace movement, during the U.S. wars in Indochina, appears in Richard Wightman Fox, *Reinhold Niebuhr: A Biography* (New York: Harper & Row, 1987), 284–285, 288. For critical surveys of Niebuhr's work that examine his views on war and militarism, see Bill Kellermann, "Apologist of Power," *Sojourners*, March 1987, 15–20; Noam Chomsky, "Reinhold Niebuhr," *Grand Street*, winter 1987, 197–212; and Jackson Lears, "American Oracle," *Commonweal*, October 21, 2011.

49. Dewey, introduction to Barnes, *Militarizing Our Youth*, 4; Barthell, "Committee on Militarism in Education," 94.

50. The American Legion, founded in 1919 by a young colonel in the American Expeditionary Force named Theodore Roosevelt Jr., has long been one of the leading veterans' organizations in the United States. For much of the twentieth century, one of its key roles has been to stamp out dissent and promote war and militarism. Obsessed with maintaining ideological purity of the populace—what it called "one hundred percent Americanism"—the legion assisted in the Red Scare hunt for radicals and so-called subversives following World War I and waged a decades-long campaign of slanderous attacks against the peace advocate and Socialist Party presidential candidate Eugene Debs. Eugene V. Debs and J. Robert Constantine, *Letters of Eugene V. Debs* (Champaign: University of Illinois Press, 1990), 3:185.

51. Barthell, "Committee on Militarism in Education," 94–96, 67.

52. Before World War II, the U.S. political surveillance apparatus was "fragmented and localized, with limited coordination among local and federal authorities and private agencies competing for business." Jennifer Luff, "Covert and Overt Operations: Interwar Political Policing in the United States and the United Kingdom," *American Historical Review* 122, no. 3 (2017): 740.

53. The spy's full report of Coe's activities at the National Student Conference, dated November 28, 1927, can be found in box 7 of the George Albert Coe Papers, Special Collections, Yale Divinity School, New Haven, Conn. Excerpts from Wooley's dossier appear in the *Springfield (Mass.) Union*, March 23, 1928. Information about the monitoring of Niebuhr appears in Roy Talbert, *Negative Intelligence: The Army and the American Left, 1917–1941* (University Press of Mississippi, 1991), 243.

Chapter 3. Successful Organizing
Confronts the Rising Tide of War

1. This biographical sketch draws largely from James C. Juhnke, "Rachel Weaver Kreider and the ROTC Controversy at Ohio State University 1934–35," *Mennonite Life* 57, no. 4, https://mla.bethelks.edu/ml-archive/2002dec/juhnke_kreider.php. Mennonites have their roots in the Anabaptist movement of sixteenth-century Europe, whose adherents felt that the Reformation did not go far enough toward renewing the Christian faith. Taking their name from the sixteenth-century Dutch religious leader Menno Simons, the Mennonites eschewed all forms of war and violence, even in self-defense, and have long been at the forefront of peace activism in the United States. The historiography concerning peace advocacy by Christians espousing the Anabaptist tradition is extensive. Some representative examples would include Guy Hershberger, *War, Peace, and Nonresistance* (Harrisonburg, Va.: Herald Press, 1944); Rachel Walt-

ner Goossen, *Women against the Good War: Conscientious Objection and Gender on the American Home Front, 1941–1947* (Chapel Hill: University of North Carolina Press, 1997); Duane Stoltzfus, *Pacifists in Chains: The Persecution of Hutterites during the Great War* (Baltimore, Md.: Johns Hopkins University Press, 2013).

2. Daniel Barthell, "The Committee on Militarism in Education, 1925–1940" (PhD diss., University of Illinois, 1972), 208.

3. Ronald Schaffer, "The War Department's Defense of ROTC," *Wisconsin Magazine of History* 53, no. 2 (winter 1969–70): 112–113; Arthur A. Ekirch Jr., *The Civilian and the Military* (New York: Oxford University Press, 1956), 226–227.

4. Barthell, "Committee on Militarism in Education," 87, 207–208.

5. This biographical sketch draws largely from James C. Juhnke, "Rachel Weaver Kreider and the ROTC Controversy at Ohio State University 1934–35," *Mennonite Life* 57, no. 4, https://mla.bethelks.edu/ml-archive/2002dec/juhnke_kreider.php.

6. Wittner notes that the 1930s peace movement "could boast an unprecedented organization and popularity in the United States," while in Barthell's view it was "the strongest it ever had been during the interwar period." Lawrence Wittner, *Rebels against War: The American Peace Movement, 1933–1983* (Philadelphia: Temple University Press, 1984), 1; Barthell, "Committee on Militarism in Education," 218.

7. Robert Cohen, "Student Movements—1930s," in Mari Jo Buhle, Paul Buhle, and Dan Georgakas, eds., *Encyclopedia of the American Left* (Chicago: University of Illinois Press, 1992), 753.

8. James Frederick Green, "Peace Movement and Allied Activities Win Followers on Many Campuses," *New York Times*, June 12, 1932. For the poll results see Brown University's *Brown Daily Herald*, March 23, 1933.

9. James A. Wechsler, *Revolt on the Campus* (New York: Macmillan, 1935), 132–175; "The Great Student Strike," *Student Outlook* (New York), May 1935, 3–8, 16; Dennis Mihelish, "Student Anti-war Activism during the Nineteen Thirties," *Peace & Change* 2, no. 3 (fall 1974): 29–40; Eileen M. Eagan, "War Is Not Holy—the American Student Peace Movement in the 1930s," *Peace & Change* 2, no. 3 (fall 1974): 41–47. Eagan expanded her analysis in *Class, Culture, and the Classroom: The Student Peace Movement of the 1930s* (Philadelphia: Temple University Press, 1981). The Los Angeles Junior College president made repeated attempts to drown out the chants of antiwar demonstrators by screaming into the microphone of the campus public address system. When that failed to have the desired effect, he enlisted the aid of the Los Angeles Police Department's Red Squad. Following a vicious assault in which police nightsticks left two female protesters unconscious, the college president used the college's sprinkler system to scatter the remaining protesters. See Robert Cohen, *When the Old Left Was Young: Student Radicals and America's First Mass Student Movement, 1929–1941* (New York: Oxford University Press, 1993), 105–106.

10. "Student Strike against War," *Student Outlook*, May 1934, 13; "Husky Guards for Pacifists," *Boston Globe*, April 12, 1935; Associated Press, "War Target of Students," *Los Angeles Times*, November 9, 1935; Joseph P. Lash, "500,000 Strike for Peace: An Appraisal," *Student Advocate*, May 1936, 3–5.

11. Richard Welling, "Defend the Public Schools against Militarism," *Junior-Senior High*

School Clearing House, December 1930, 243; "Horse Sense and ROTC," editorial, *Oregonian* (Portland, Ore.), September 27, 1936.

12. Ray Abrams, *Preachers Present Arms: A Study of the War-time Attitudes and Activities of the Churches and the Clergy in the United States, 1914–1918* (Philadelphia: University of Pennsylvania Press, 1933), 237–238.

13. H. L. Fraser, "Methodists Oppose Militarist Courses," *Boston Globe*, April 12, 1931; "First Blood in the Fight against Forced War Drill," *Literary Digest*, February 18, 1933, 19.

14. Associated Press, "Drill Curb Asked by Church Council," *New York Times*, December 6, 1934; "Another Denomination Renounces War," editorial, *Christian Century*, June 13, 1934.

15. "Says Church Group Menaces Reserves," *Boston Globe*, February 4, 1932; "The Legion and DePauw," editorial, *Springfield (Mass.) Republican*, September 5, 1935.

16. Major Ralph C. Bishop and U.S. Office of Education, *A Study of the Educational Value of Military Instruction in Universities and Colleges*, pamphlet no. 28 (Washington, D.C.: Government Printing Office, 1932), 17–19; "Hardly Decisive," editorial, *Knoxville News-Sentinel*, March 5, 1932.

17. Barthell, "Committee on Militarism in Education," 135–136; Charles Chatfield, *For Peace and Justice: Pacifism in America, 1914–1941* (Knoxville: University of Tennessee Press, 1971), 156.

18. Schaffer, "War Department's Defense of ROTC," 116; Associated Press, "ROTC Shows Gain of 5,000 Students," *New York Times*, September 30, 1935; Edwin Johnson, "$10,000 Yearly for Antisocial Education," *Forum & Century*, September 1935, 149; Barthell, "Committee on Militarism in Education," 282.

19. In 1940 Congress allocated $17 billion to the military, prompting the historian Lawrence Wittner to remark that "despite their desire to avoid war Americans readied themselves for it." Wittner, *Rebels against War*, 29.

20. Barthell, "Committee on Militarism in Education," 174–176; James H. Hawkes, "Antimilitarism at State Universities: The Campaign against Compulsory ROTC, 1920–1940," *Wisconsin Magazine of History* 49, no. 1 (fall 1965): 51. A joint poll conducted by the Intercollegiate Disarmament Council, the National Student Federation, and Brown University's student newspaper found that 39 percent of the 22,627 students polled would "refuse participation in any future war involving the United States," while one-third indicated they would participate in war only if the nation was invaded. As a result of the poll's results, CME believed that "if this sentiment is crystallized through enrollment in aggressive local and national organizations, the militarists will have a much more difficult time in continuing to deceive youth into supporting the outworn slogans of nationalism and militarism." Given the overwhelming antiwar sentiment of students, the committee observed, "it is logical to assume that the war-makers will be extremely chary about expressing their authority . . . when resort to war will directly involve the generation which has spoken so clearly through this student poll." Barthell, "Committee on Militarism in Education," 175.

21. Barthell, "Committee on Militarism in Education," 178–179.

22. "First Blood in the Fight against Forced War Drill," *Literary Digest*, February 18, 1933, 18. Also see George A. Coe, "Students as Conscientious Objectors," *Breaking the War Habit* 2, no. 5 (January 1, 1934), box 682, ACLU Records, Seeley G. Mudd Manuscript Library, Princeton University, Princeton, N.J.

23. "First Blood in the Fight," 19.

24. J. F. Essary, "Ulman Ruling Held Blow to Army Training," *Baltimore Sun*, January 25, 1933; "Maryland Court Upholds Compulsory Drill," editorial, *Christian Century*, July 12, 1933, 901; "Maryland Can Compel Military Training," editorial, *Christian Century*, December 6, 1933.

25. "Maryland Court Upholds Compulsory Drill." For more on the *Coale* case, see *University of Maryland v. Coale*, 167 A. 54 (Md. 1932); and Charles F. Howlett, "Case Law Historiography," *Peace & Change* 22, no. 1 (January 1997): 49–75. For more on the *Hamilton* case, see *Hamilton v. Regents of the University of California, et al.*, 293 U.S. 245 (1934); and Charles F. Howlett, "The Courts and Peace Activism: Selected Legal Cases Related to Matters of Conscience and Civil Liberties," *Peace & Change* 38, no. 1 (January 2013): 6–32.

26. "Drill Curb Asked by Church Council," *New York Times*, December 6, 1934; Ekirch, *Civilian and the Military*, 228–230; *New York World-Telegram*, editorial, December 6, 1934. See also Chatfield, *For Peace and Justice*, 154–155. For more on the California court case, see John Beardsley, "Conscientious Objectors and the Law," *Breaking the War Habit* 3, no. 2 (May 15, 1934), and correspondence between Edwin Johnson and the ACLU's A. L. Wirin, June–July 1934, box 679, all in ACLU Records.

27. Barthell, "Committee on Militarism in Education," 140–141.

28. Ekirch, *Civilian and the Military*, 231–232; *Report of the Secretary of War to the President, 1935* (Washington, D.C.: U.S. Government Printing Office, 1935), 13; Associated Press, "Educators Protest Dern's Criticism of Opposition," *Springfield (Mass.) Republican*, December 30, 1935.

29. "With the Organizations," *Living Age*, May 1936, 350; Ekirch, *Civilian and the Military*, 232; Charles F. Howlett and Audrey Cohan, *John Dewey: America's Peace-Minded Educator* (Carbondale: Southern Illinois University Press, 2016), 44–45.

30. Richard L. Neuberger, "Oregon's People Confront the Military Drill Issue," *Christian Century*, August 19, 1936, 1110.

31. Eunice Fuller Barnard, "Classroom and Campus," *New York Times*, July 5, 1936; Neuberger, "Oregon's People Confront the Military Drill," 1110; editorial, *Oregonian* (Portland, Ore.), October 29, 1936. "Military Training," editorial, *Baltimore Sun*, October 20, 1936.

32. Barthell, "Committee on Militarism in Education," 267; "Compulsory Drill in Oregon," editorial, *Christian Century*, December 23, 1936; Edwin Johnson to editor, *Christian Century*, January 13, 1937. At their respective annual conventions Oregon's Methodists and Presbyterians had unanimously passed resolutions backing the initiative. See Neuberger, "Oregon's People Confront the Military Drill," 1110–1111.

33. See Charles DeBenedetti, *The Peace Reform in American History* (Bloomington: Indiana University Press, 1980), 108–137; Chatfield, *For Peace and Justice*, 223–287; Wittner, *Rebels against War*, 1–33.

34. Barthell, "Committee on Militarism in Education," 250–251, 256; "1936 Financial Statement," box 7, George Albert Coe Papers, Special Collections, Yale Divinity School Library, New Haven, Conn.

35. Commenting on the divided peace movement in April 1939, James T. Shotwell, a leading internationalist who was instrumental in helping to formulate the Kellogg-Briand Pact of 1928, stated: "I have come to the conclusion that the effort of many years to try to bring into a single body those who hold divergent views concerning not only the way to get peace but the nature

of peace itself, is fruitless and simply leads to confusion and ineffectiveness." DeBenedetti, *Peace Reform in American History*, 135.

36. Schaffer, "War Department's Defense of ROTC," 119; Barthell, "Committee on Militarism in Education," 247. During the 1936–37 academic year, the War Department had formed fewer than ten new ROTC units, and most of those were at Catholic colleges and universities. Edwin Johnson, "The Junior ROTC Knocks at the High-School Door," *Clearing House*, April 1937, 460n.

37. As we noted in chapter 1, informal military drill instruction had had a presence in New York City schools since World War I. However, since New York State law prohibited such instruction during the school day, boys participating in military drill usually did so after school under a civilian teacher. Introducing JROTC units would have ended civilian-led instruction of the high schools' military drill program, bringing it firmly under the control of the War Department.

38. Johnson, "Junior ROTC Knocks," 461.

39. For more on this story, consult Charles F. Howlett, "Bickering over Brass Buttons," *New York Archives* 16, no. 1 (summer 2016): 31–35.

40. Johnson, "Junior ROTC Knocks," 461. Activists argued that by permitting War Department personnel to teach credit-bearing courses, the city school board would have been in violation of New York State law requiring teachers in public schools to hold a state teaching certificate. Activists also maintained that offering military instruction during school hours was a violation of section 713 of New York State Education Law. For more on the New York City campaign, see Johnson, "Junior ROTC Knocks," 461–462; and *The Committee on Militarism in Education: Its 1936 Activities, Its 1937 Prospects*, box 7, Coe Papers. One of the more dramatic battles waged over JROTC in New York City occurred in late 1929 when a unit was created at the city's largest high school, Jamaica High. Parents, community groups, and the CME, led by John Dewey, opposed its establishment. It was a partial victory for Dewey and other opponents of JROTC. After taking the heat from parents and others, the school board decided that in keeping with section 713 of the state's education law, military training would be conducted after school hours but only as an elective.

41. Johnson, "Junior ROTC Knocks," 463; *Committee on Militarism in Education.*.

42. "No R.O.T.C. for Carbondale," *Fellowship*, September 1936, 12–13, series E, box 11, John Nevin Sayre Papers, Swarthmore College Peace Collection (hereafter SCPC), McCabe Library, Swarthmore, Pa..

43. Johnson, "Junior ROTC Knocks," 461.

44. George Albert Coe to Edwin Johnson, February 26, 1937, and William Knowland to George Albert Coe, March 9, 1937, both in box 1, Coe Papers; "Wilkins Hits Military in School System," *Mercury Register* (Oroville, Calif.), April 10, 1937; *Report of Committee on Militarism in Education*, esp. pt. 1, "Review of 1937," box 7, Coe Papers.

45. Johnson, "Junior ROTC Knocks," 464. As early as spring 1935, Johnson had used the term "fascism" within the context of the ROTC debate. That April the Board of Trustees of Connecticut State College (now the University of Connecticut) reaffirmed its policy of compulsory military training by adopting a resolution stating that "any formal public agitations or formal public discussion on the campus promoted by individuals on the college staff or indi-

vidual statements, which reflect upon the college military instruction or training, will subject such individuals to cause for removal." In his correspondence with Walter Landauer, a faculty member at the college, Johnson characterized the board's gag order as "incipient Fascism and as such must be vigorously fought." A new college president eventually rescinded the resolution, but compulsory ROTC remained intact until the 1960s. "A Statement with Reference to the Situation at Connecticut State College (Storrs, Conn.)," April 25, 1935, Archives & Special Collections at the Thomas J. Dodd Research Center, University of Connecticut Library, Storrs, Conn., http://hdl.handle.net/11134/20002:860463786 (see p. 33).

46. Johnson, "Junior ROTC Knocks," 464; *The Smallest Cadet* (New York: Committee on Militarism in Education, n.d. [prob. 1938]), box 2, Coe Papers.

47. *17 Significant Victories against Militarism in American Education* (New York: Committee on Militarism in Education, n.d. [prob. 1938]), box 2, Coe Papers; Michael S. Neiberg, *Making Citizen-Soldiers: ROTC and the Ideology of American Military Service* (Cambridge, Mass.: Harvard University Press, 2009), 29.

48. Merle Curti, *Peace or War: The American Struggle, 1636–1936* (New York: W. W. Norton, 1936), 272. In a work he originally published in 1935, Curti advocated for a socially engaged pedagogy, criticized the view that educators cannot be antimilitarist in their orientation, and disputed the notion that teachers have "no right to teach anything contrary to the collective opinions or valuations of society, or its controlling majority." Merle Curti, *The Social Ideas of American Educators*, rev. ed. (Totowa, N.J.: Littlefield, Adams, 1959), 565–566. For more on Curti's significance to the field of peace history, see Charles F. Howlett, "Merle Curti and the Significance of Peace Research in American History," *Peace & Change* 25, no. 4 (October 2000): 431–466.

49. *Committee on Militarism in Education* and *Report of Committee on Militarism in Education*, esp. pt. 1.

50. Ekirch, *Civilian and the Military*, 224–225; John Nevin Sayre to Mrs. Gardiner Hammond, December 16, 1938, box 2, Coe Papers. "To keep our ship afloat has been a most difficult job at times," Johnson wrote to Coe, "particularly because of that large indebtedness for printing which my predecessor and good friend, Tucker Smith, ran up back in 1930 and '31." Edwin Johnson to George Albert Coe, February 17, 1939, box 2, Coe Papers.

51. Johnson to Coe, April 26, 1939, box 2, Coe Papers.

52. John Nevin Sayre, "Support of the Committee on Militarism in Education," May 4, 1939, box 11, Sayre Papers.

53. Wittner, *Rebels against War*, 15–16, 22; John Howard Yoder, *Christian Attitudes to War, Peace, and Revolution* (Grand Rapids, Mich.: Brazos Press, 2009), 284; Gerry Weaver, "Military Training Hit by Educators," *Oregonian* (Portland, Ore.), July 3, 1936. Johnson had first observed teachers' growing tendency to support JROTC during a failed campaign to prevent the school board of Peoria, Illinois, from accepting a JROTC unit for its local high school. During the 1938–39 academic year, educators from other communities had sent messages to Peoria teachers testifying to the benefits JROTC had brought to their own schools. When Peoria officials and educators heard positive statements about JROTC from colleagues in other schools, the Peorians seemed much more likely to welcome a military training program in their own school district. "Our problem . . . is to meet that kind of testimony," Johnson wrote Coe in November. The committee's difficulty in reaching teachers became more urgent, Johnson continued,

at a time when "public opinion, under the impact of the international crisis assumes a more and more emotional tone." Johnson to Coe, November 14, 1939, box 2, Coe Papers. For more on the Peoria campaign, including the role played by red-baiting, see Barthell, "Committee on Militarism in Education," 299–301.

54. Sayre to Friends of the CME, October 16, 1940, box 2, Coe Papers.

55. Barthell, "Committee on Militarism in Education," 222, 318.

Chapter 4. The Decade They Almost Stopped School Militarism

1. Charles F. Howlett and Robbie Lieberman, *A History of the American Peace Movement from Colonial Times to the Present* (Lewiston, N.Y.: Edwin Mellen Press, 2008), 317.

2. Arthur A. Ekrich Jr., *Man and Nature in America*, rev. ed. (Lincoln: University of Nebraska Press, 1973), 179. For more on Niebuhr's Cold War–era debates with pacifists, see Leilah Danielson, "Christianity, Dissent, and the Cold War: A. J. Muste's Challenge to Realism and U.S. Empire," *Diplomatic History* 30, no. 4 (2006): 645–669.

3. An exception to the silence surrounding high school militarism was the American Friends Service Committee's groundbreaking 1955 pamphlet, *Speak Truth to Power*, which says that JROTC was used to "prepare young people for conscription, and establish military points of view in the minds of thirteen-year-olds." American Friends Service Committee, *Speak Truth to Power* (1955): 19, http://afsc.org.

4. Henry Richard Maar III, "The Lost Years: The American Peace Movement, From Vietnam to Nuclear Freeze," *Peace & Change* 44, no. 3 (2019): 387.

5. For two notable exceptions, see Robert Surbrug, *Beyond Vietnam: The Politics of Protest in Massachusetts, 1974–1990* (Amherst: University of Massachusetts Press, 2009), and Michael Foley, *Front Porch Politics: The Forgotten Heyday of American Activism in the 1970s and 1980s* (New York: Macmillan, 2013).

6. The historian Robert Kirk has shown the variety of ways the government encouraged elementary school children to participate in the war effort. Through coordination with the War Production Board and the Treasury Department, schools became hubs for the collection of scrap metal and paper—highly prized materials at the time. Children were well suited for the job, since they frequently played in the vacant lots in their neighborhoods where discarded newspapers and tin cans tended to accumulate. The syndicated cartoon strip *Little Orphan Annie* provides a good example of how visual culture helped mobilize children for war. After the comic depicted Annie organizing a platoon of scrap-collecting youth, playfully dubbed the Junior Commandos, the idea took hold in the popular imagination. By the fall of 1942 Boston alone reportedly had twenty thousand Junior Commandos. Through participating in scrap hauls, and by wearing the arm bands and other military insignia that lent visual legitimacy to their cause, Junior Commandos were "foot soldier[s] in the children's war," according to Kirk. Robert Kirk, *Earning Their Stripes: The Mobilization of American Children in the Second World War* (New York: Peter Lang, 1994), 55–56, 66, 72.

7. Michael S. Neiberg, *Making Citizen-Soldiers: ROTC and the Ideology of American Military Service* (Cambridge, Mass.: Harvard University Press, 2009), 32–33; *The Junior ROTC Manual* (Washington, D.C.: Department of the Army, 1955), 8.

8. Information about the postwar decline of the peace movement comes from Maurice Isserman, *If I Had a Hammer: The Death of the Old Left and the Birth of the New Left* (New York: Basic Books, 1987), 131; Lawrence Wittner, *Rebels against War: The American Peace Movement, 1933–1983* (Philadelphia: Temple University Press, 1984), 182–239; Massimo Teodori, ed., *The New Left: A Documentary History* (Indianapolis: Bobbs-Merrill, 1969), 120; and John R. Salter provides a first-person account of the University of Arizona protests in "The Next Great Step of the Way," *Sojourners*, March 1981.

9. "Gray Board Report Dims Hopes for High School ROTC's," *Baltimore Afro-American*, August 21, 1948; Craig Karpel, "The Teenie Militarists," *Ramparts*, September 28, 1968, 43–50; Arthur T. Coumbe and Lee S. Harford, *U.S. Army Cadet Command: The 10 Year History* (Fort Monroe, Va.: Army Cadet Command, Office of the Command Historian, 1996), 259. A summary of McNamara's views on the JROTC appears in Nathan Andrew Long, "The Origins, Early Developments, and Present-day Impact of the Junior Reserve Officers' Training Corps on the American Public Schools" (PhD diss., University of Cincinnati, 2003), 164–166.

10. Karpel, "Teenie Militarists," 44. A good summary of the arguments for and against the 1964 legislation can be found in William H. Boyer, *Education for Annihilation* (Honolulu: Hogarth Press, 1972), 94–97 .

11. "Waste of Defense Money," editorial, *Hartford (Conn.) Courant*, March 12, 1963.

12. John Swomley, *The Military Establishment* (Boston: Beacon , 1964), 224–225. Educators came out of the World War II experience strongly in favor of nuclear disarmament. Yet by 1948 the National Education Association had thrown its support behind the Cold War arms race and couched its requests for greater federal investment in public schools as a way to strengthen the "nation's front lines of defense." Charles DeBenedetti, "Educators and Armaments in Cold War America," *Peace & Change* 34, no. 4 (2009): 433.

13. Maurice Isserman and Michael Kazin, *America Divided: The Civil War of the 1960s*, 2d ed. (New York: Oxford University Press, 2004), 148, 137; Christian Appy, *Working-Class War: American Combat Soldiers and Vietnam* (Chapel Hill: University of North Carolina Press, 2000); Isserman and Kazin, *America Divided*, 137. One example of anti-JROTC activism during the Vietnam War occurred in New Orleans in May 1966, when peaceful picketers faced off against angry counterdemonstrators to protest the establishment of a new marine JROTC unit at Jesuit High School. For a first-person account of this demonstration, see Jack Frazier's letter to the editor in the *Nation*, July 4, 1966.

14. Kirkpatrick Sale, *SDS: The Rise and Development of the Students for a Democratic Society* (New York: Vintage, 1973), 201, 358, 380. See also Wittner, *Rebels against War*, 285.

15. John C. Leggett and Janet Roach, "UConn Story: Rhetoric and Repression," *New Politics* 7 (1969): 68–83.

16. Appy, *Working-Class War*, 6; Penny Lewis, *Hardhats, Hippies, and Hawks: The Vietnam Antiwar Movement as Myth and Memory* (Ithaca, N.Y.: Cornell University Press, 2013). Appy estimates that 80 percent of all enlisted men serving in Vietnam were from working-class or poor backgrounds.

17. The activities of students at Dutchess Community College and New Paltz are detailed in surveillance reports and other materials attached to Case 238–652–1, December 26, 1967, box 48, and Case 238–329–1, March 13, 1968, box 89, Non-Criminal Investigations Files, New York

State Troopers Files, New York State Police Bureau of Criminal Investigation Reports, New York State Archives, Albany.

18. Richard E. Meyer, AP, "The Violent Spring of College ROTC," *Atlanta Constitution*, June 28, 1970; Peter Karsten, "Anti-ROTC: Response to Vietnam or 'Consciousness III?'" in J. P. Lovell and P. S. Kronenberg, eds., *New Civil and Military Relations* (New Brunswick, N.J.: Transaction, 1974), 119; James Kirkpatrick Davis, *Assault on the Left: The FBI and the Sixties Antiwar Movement* (Westport, Conn.: Praeger, 1997), 180.

19. Richard Peterson and John A. Bilorusky, *May 1970: The Campus Aftermath of Cambodia and Kent State* (Berkeley, Calif.: Carnegie Commission, 1971), 32; Christian Appy, *American Reckoning: The Vietnam War and Our National Identity* (New York: Penguin, 2015), 190; Meyer, "Violent Spring of College ROTC." For anti-ROTC protests on campuses in the South, see Christopher Broadhurst, "There Can Be No Business as Usual: The University of North Carolina and the Student Strike of May 1970," *Southern Cultures* 21, no. 2 (2015): 84–101.

20. Karsten, "Anti-ROTC," 113. While Karsten writes that the decline was "largely a function of the continued demise of compulsory ROTC," another military historian argues that the elimination of conscription and anti-ROTC campus protests also contributed to the drop in enrollment. See Arthur T. Coumbe, "Why ROTC? The Debate over Collegiate Military Training, 1969–1973," *Air & Space Power Journal* (1999).

21. Duncan Spencer, "Recruiting—Still the Big Problem," *Washington (D.C.) Evening Star*, May 2, 1974.

22. Ibid.; Betsy Mitchell, "Midlanders Explain Service Shortage," *Omaha (Neb.) World-Herald*, July 11, 1978; David S. Barrett, "Military Recruitment Problems Linked to Communications Gap," *Hartford (Conn.) Courant*, August 21, 1974. By the end of the decade, the Defense Department was spending $80 million annually (the equivalent of $280 million today) on recruitment advertising. But it was not enough to shore up the flagging volunteer military. In a widely read op-ed piece in October 1979, Senator Sam Nunn—then chair of the manpower subcommittee of the Senate Armed Services Committee—warned that the military recruiting services were still facing "increasing difficulty" in meeting their monthly and annual objectives. Joann Stevens, "Raising Questions to Ask the Recruiters," *Washington Post*, June 28, 1979; Sam Nunn, "Military Weak, U.S. in Danger without Draft," *Atlanta Constitution*, October 21, 1979.

23. As Beth Bailey has shown, the recruiting services of the 1970s frequently used "the language of the market" and described their trade as selling a product—military service—to the public. Beth Bailey, *America's Army: Making the All-Volunteer Force* (Cambridge, Mass.: Harvard University Press, 2009), 101. The analogy to sales work made perfect sense to the commander of one Marine Corps Recruit Depot, who supervised more than one thousand recruiters. "That's really what I am," Major General Kenneth Houghton told a reporter in 1977, "a regional sales director." The recruiters under his command completed a seven-week course during which they learned some of the same sales techniques used in private industry. UPI, "Selling Marines Takes Strategy," *Atlanta Constitution*, May 29, 1977.

24. Army-funded focus group research found that Washington, D.C., guidance counselors were "mildly antimilitary" and "very reluctant to actively suggest that a student enlist." Their reluctance was mainly the result of the perception (later documented to be true) that a disproportionate number of Blacks were being assigned to combat duty and dying in Vietnam. John

M. Buck and George I. Forsythe, *High School Recruitment for a Volunteer Army* (Washington, D.C.: Development Alternatives, 1972), 21. Both this survey and the U.S. Army Recruiting Command's "High School Recruiting Plan" (copy in authors' possession) recommended establishing a plan to bring educators (and students) for tours of military installations.

25. Larry Ferlazzo, "Students Are Easy Targets for the Military's Job Training Myths," *FPS: A Magazine of Young People's Liberation*, October–December 1977; "A Decade at a Glance," *All Volunteer*, December 1983.

26. UPI, "Selling Marines Takes Strategy." "Since the high school graduate is the most desired prospect," one army recruiting manual advised, "the high school is where much of the Recruiter's [*sic*] time will be spent." U.S. Army Recruiting Command, *Publicizing Army Recruiting in the Community* (Washington, D.C.: U.S. Department of the Army, Department of Defense, 1976), 23.

27. See J. T. Scepansky, "The Techniques of Modern Recruiting," *Air University Review*, September–October 1968; and Gus C. Lee, *Evaluation of the DoD High School Testing Program* (Alexandria, Va.: Human Resources Research Organization, 1979).

28. Milton H. Maier, *Military Aptitude Testing: The Past Fifty Years* (Alexandria, Va.: Defense Manpower Data Center, 1993), 56; Lee, *Evaluation of the DoD High School Testing*, 3. For comprehensive data on the number of students taking the ASVAB between 1968 and 1978, see Lee, *Evaluation of the DoD High School Testing*, 7.

29. Coumbe and Harford, *U.S. Army Cadet Command*, 303; Martha M. Hamilton, "ROTC: Complete Turnabout," *Washington Post*, June 18, 1979. This evolution in school-military integration suggests that the JROTC was intimately connected to the Pentagon's recruitment needs.

30. Gina Perez, *Citizen, Student, Soldier: Latina/o Youth, JROTC, and the American Dream* (New York: NYU Press, 2015), 56.

31. Carole Aeus, "Fears, Cheers for High School ROTC," *Newsday*, November 14, 1976; Mary Kay Quinlan, "More Nieces Joining Uncle Sam," *Omaha (Neb.) World-Herald*, April 18, 1976. Young women's interest in JROTC fueled the decade's explosive growth in high school military training. Between the school years 1972–73, when the army first admitted female JROTC cadets, and 1975–76, high school girls went from 8 percent to nearly a third of the total enrollment in army JROTC. Quinlan, "More Nieces Joining Uncle Sam."

32. Founded in 1917 as a refuge for conscientious objectors opposed to World War I, the American Friends Service Committee has long been at the forefront of activism for peace, civil rights, freedom of speech, and other causes. Its youth outreach programs date to 1926, when AFSC's Peace Section started a summer program that sent students to speak on the subject of peace. See Mary Hoxie Jones, *Swords into Ploughshares: An Account of the American Friends Service Committee, 1917–1937* (New York: Macmillan, 1937).

33. Fran Donelan to editor, *Baltimore Sun*, November 24, 1979, A15; Karpel, "Teenie Militarists," 45; Phil Ebersole, "Vote Favors Military Training at Smithsburg High," *Daily Mail* (Hagerstown, Md.), February 18, 1971, 12.

34. "High School NJROTC," *All Hands*, September 1969, 10; Karsten, "Anti-ROTC," 119; Joi Jerry Atchison, "Getting a Head Start through NJROTC," *All Hands*, June 1977, 25. NJROTC refers to naval JROTC.

35. Ted Koontz, "U.S. Military Plans Silent Invasion of Schools," *America Report*, May 13, 1974; Gail Purpura, "Junior ROTC—It's 'Selling' the Military," *Courier-Post* (Cherry Hill, N.J.), November 5, 1974; Nicholas von Hoffman, "Pentagon Recruits the Preps," *Chicago Tribune*, September 16, 1975.

36. "Conscious of the Duty to Their Country: High School Junior ROTC Program Grows," LNS Packet 530, June 9, 1973, 3; Ed Hedemann, "WRL Counter-Militarism Project?" *WRL News*, May–June 1974, 6.

37. Between 1969 and 1972, groups like Clergy and Laity Concerned about Vietnam, Women's International League for Peace and Freedom, and National Committee for a Sane Nuclear Policy all experienced membership loss of 10 to 25 percent. Charles DeBenedetti, with Charles Chatfield, *An American Ordeal: The Antiwar Movement of the Vietnam Era* (Syracuse, N.Y.: Syracuse University Press, 1990), 320, 380.

38. "WRL West Annual Report, 1973–74," and "Counter-recruiting Action Outline," 1975, both in GI Press Collection, Wisconsin Historical Society, Madison.

39. Seeley's biographical information is from Central Committee for Conscientious Objectors Annual Report, 1979, box 2, Knolls Action Project Records, M. E. Grenander Department of Special Collections & Archives, Science Library, University at Albany, Albany, N.Y.

40. Bob Seeley, "The Ashes of Victory," *CCCO News Notes* 25, no. 2 (1973): 2. We found most copies of the CCCO publications cited in this book—including *CCCO News Notes*, *Counter Pentagon*, and the *Objector*—in the Alternative Press Collection of the Archives & Special Collections at the Thomas J. Dodd Research Center, University of Connecticut Library, Storrs.

41. Jeremy Mott, "A Hidden Threat," *CCCO News Notes* 25, no. 1 (1973): 4.

42. For descriptions of these campaigns, see Roger Repohl, "Norfolk Catholic High Rejects Navy JROTC," *CCCO News Notes* 25, no. 4 (1973); Ken Berry, "Panel Working to Ban ROTC in High Schools," *Arizona Republic*, September 1, 1973; "Clerics and Pacifists Bid to Kill ROTC in High Schools," *Arizona Republic*, October 17, 1973; Steve Gulick, "JROTC Briefs," *CCCO News Notes* 27, no. 1 (1975).

43. Notable exceptions were Chicago, Dallas, and Atlanta, all of which had long had active JROTC programs in their public schools.

44. Of course, school board members are usually elected in the United States, and it seems likely that elected officials in more conservative rural and suburban communities would not have felt comfortable publicly stating opposition to military programs.

45. Mary Margaret Gren, "Hup-oop-e-four, They Don't Want the Marine Corps," *Washington (D.C.) Star-News*, November 14, 1974; "First Things First," *Washington Star-News*, editorial, November 25, 1974.

46. Susan Miller, "Dare to Struggle, Dare to Win," *Counter Pentagon*, July 1975, 4.

47. "ROTC Cost Factor Stressed at Meeting," *Town & Country*, April 10, 1975, and R. Leslie Chrismer to editor, *Town & Country* (Pennsburg, Pa.), April 3, 1975, both clippings in Local Newspaper Collection, Schwenkfelder Library & Heritage Center, Pennsburg, Pa.

48. Thomas Hylton, "ROTC Program Is Defeated," *Pottstown (Pa.) Mercury*, April 11, 1975; editor's note in Miller, "Dare to Struggle, Dare to Win."

49. Public awareness of the ASVAB was rather limited, probably because critical coverage of

the DoD testing program had appeared only in the house journals of Clergy and Laity Concerned and the Church of the Brethren. See Ted Koontz, "U.S. Military Plans Silent Invasion of High Schools," *America Report*, May 13, 1974, later reprinted as "High School and Military Hard Sell," *Messenger*, August 1974. The high school testing program later merited some discussion in Robert K. Musil, "Operation High School," *Nation*, April 5, 1975.

50. Steve Gulick, "Wolf in Sheep's Clothing," *Counter Pentagon*, November 1975; Steven M. Luxenberg, "Military Admits Free Tests' Dual Use," *Baltimore Sun*, April 5, 1976, A6.

51. ACLU Foundation, *Privacy Report*, January 1976, American Civil Liberties Union of Missouri Records, 1930–2015, series 2: ACLU of Eastern Missouri Files, 1953–1981, subseries VI, box 2, folder 4, Department of Special Collections, Washington University Libraries, St. Louis, Mo.

52. Reports about schools' dropping the program can be found in Task Force on Recruitment and Militarism meeting minutes, January 29, 1976, series III, box 25, Central Committee for Conscientious Objectors Records (hereafter, CCCO Records), Swarthmore College Peace Collection (hereafter SCPC), McCabe Library, Swarthmore College, Swarthmore, Pa. ; "News Shorts," *Counter Pentagon*, February 1976; Lee, "Evaluation of the DoD High School Testing"; Task Force on Recruitment and Militarism retreat report, April 10–11, 1976, series III, box 25, CCCO Records.

53. "Some Ideas and Experiences," *Taking a Stand against War Organizers Newsletter*, March 1976; "Counter Recruiters Counter Recruit," *Counter Pentagon*, May–June 1978.

54. Betty Rademaker, *Why ROTC? Community Response to an Air Force High School ROTC* (Philadelphia: CCCO, n.d.); Richard Malishchak, *Military Training for 14-Year-Olds: The Growth of High School ROTC* (Philadelphia: United Church Press, 1974); John Noller, "Malishchak on JROTC: A Job Well Done," *Counter Pentagon*, April 1974, 9.

55. Steve Gulick, telephone interview by author, August 24, 2011.

56. "Baltimore Conference Report," *Counter Pentagon*, April 1974.

57. Ibid., 1.

58. Ibid., 2.

59. Ibid., 7.

60. Ibid.

61. Army-funded research emphasized the role played by school counselors in navigating the transition to the all-volunteer force: "Gaining the cooperation and support of the guidance counselors is one of the most important single steps in high school recruiting." John M. Buck and George I. Forsythe, *High School Recruitment for a Volunteer Army* (Washington, D.C.: Development Alternatives, 1972), 4.

62. Task Force on Recruitment and Militarism meeting minutes, October 7, 1975, series III, box 25, CCCO Records; Bill Offenloch, "Recruiting and the AGPA," *Catholic Peace Fellowship Bulletin*, summer 1974, 5; John Noller, "Military Dominates APGA Convention," *CCCO News Notes* 26, no. 3 (1974): 7. Because so many APGA delegates complained about the military's overwhelming presence at the 1974 convention, in subsequent years far fewer military recruiters attended. See Steve Gulick, "Military Still Enticing Guidance Counselors," *CCCO News Notes* 27, no. 2 (1975).

63. Among those attending the task force's first meetings in 1975 were organizers affiliated

with the AFSC, Mennonite Central Committee, Catholic Peace Fellowship, National Inter-religious Service Board for Conscientious Objectors, Fellowship of Reconciliation, War Resisters League, and Friends Peace Committee.

64. Task Force on Recruitment and Militarism meeting minutes, December 6, 1976, CCCO Records.

65. Ibid., November 5, 1975; December 6, 1976; and February 21, 1978, series III, box 25, CCCO Records . For more on the 1979 Cincinnati campaign, see agenda for Public Meeting on the Cincinnati Military Academy, January 28, 1979, and Gary Sullivan, "Coalition Plans to Try Blocking Military School," *Cincinnati Enquirer*, January 29, 1979, both in section II, series J, box 3, Fellowship of Reconciliation Records, SCPC.

66. Ann Morrissett Davidon, "The War at Home: An AFSC Report" (unpublished report, American Friends Service Committee, 1976), 23. Copy in authors' possession.

67. As the historian Mitchell K. Hall notes, the Ecumenical Peace Institute (EPI) campaign eschewed antimilitarist ideology while highlighting the cost to school districts of hosting a JROTC unit and questioning the program's educational value. Yet, despite having the advantage of organizing in an extremely liberal area, EPI "failed completely" to reduce the number of JROTC programs proliferating in Northern California. Mitchell K. Hall, *Because of Their Faith: CALCAV and Religious Opposition to the Vietnam War* (New York: Columbia University Press, 1990), 166.

68. The commander was particularly incensed by one brochure, *Join the People Who'll Never Join Today's Military.* Judy Marino, "Off Limits," *Counter Pentagon*, July 1976, 4–5.

69. "Complaint Department," *Counter Pentagon*, December 1976, 8.

70. Sally James, "Veterans Center Organizes Opposition to Draft," *Oregonian* (Portland, Ore.), June 24, 1979.

71. Winfield Falk, "Intelligence Report," Portland Police Department, June 15, 1978, A200-005, City of Portland Archives, Portland, Oregon.

72. "Portland Center Organizes," *CCCO News Notes*, spring 1978, 7–8; "The Counter Recruiters," *Oregon Times* (Portland, Ore.), September 1978, 26; *If You Are Thinking about Enlisting—Part Two—Your Rights and Your Military Lifestyle*, mimeographed brochure found in box 10, Resource Center for Nonviolence Records, SCPC; "I Joined the Navy to See the World," *Portland (Ore.) Scribe*, February 23–March 1, 1978.

73. Peter Sistrom, "Portland's Recruiter Wars," *Willamette Week* (Portland, Ore.), November 6, 1978.

74. Ibid.

75. Bishop Cochran, telephone interview by author, September 24, 2011.

76. "Center to Close," *Oregonian* (Portland, Ore.), October 6, 1979; Bob Gould, telephone interview by author, August 29, 2011.

77. Cochran interview.

78. See, for example, Brian Casserly, "Confronting the U.S. Navy at Bangor, 1973–1982," *Pacific Northwest Quarterly* 95 (2004): 130–139; Roger Peace, *A Call to Conscience: The Anti-Contra War Campaign* (Amherst: University of Massachusetts Press, 2012), 1–6.

79. Christian Smith, *Resisting Reagan: The U.S. Central America Peace Movement* (Chicago: University of Chicago Press, 2010), 176.

80. AP, "Churches Hit Jr. Military Training Bill," *Press and Sun-Bulletin* (Binghamton, N.Y.), March 18 1971; Pennsylvania Council of Churches, "Resolution on Military Training in Secondary Schools," April 11, 1978. We are indebted to Rev. Sandra Struss of the Pennsylvania Council of Churches for her help in obtaining a copy of this resolution.

81. "Keep Military Out," editorial, *Democrat & Chronicle* (Rochester, N.Y.), March 23, 1971; "ROTC Isn't Necessary at High School Level," editorial, *Journal-News* (Nyack, N.Y.), February 27, 1973; Mark Lieberman, "Calls Junior ROTC Bill 'Outrageous,'" *(New York) Daily News*, March 19, 1973.

82. "New JROTC Bill," *Counter Pentagon*, April 1976, 5; Isaac Rehert, "Junior ROTC Revisited," *Baltimore Sun*, October 13, 1979.

Chapter 5. Resisting School Militarism in the Reagan Era

1. Fran Donelan to Seth Kershner, March 24, 2016.

2. Fran Donelan, interview by author, April 5, 2013, Baltimore, Md.

3. See, for example, Brian Casserly, "Confronting the U.S. Navy at Bangor, 1973–1982," *Pacific Northwest Quarterly* 95 (2004): 130–139; and Roger Peace, *A Call to Conscience: The Anti-Contra War Campaign* (Amherst: University of Massachusetts Press, 2012), 1–6. On the thawing of military-civilian relations since Vietnam, see David C. King and Zachary Karabell, *The Generation of Trust: Public Confidence in the U.S. Military since Vietnam* (Washington, D.C.: American Enterprise Institute, 2003); and Christian Appy, *American Reckoning: The Vietnam War and Our National Identity* (New York: Penguin, 2015).

4. Gina Perez, *Citizen, Student, Soldier: Latina/o Youth, JROTC, and the American Dream* (New York: NYU Press, 2015), 33.

5. The next year nine Catholics, including Berrigan and his brother Daniel, who also was a priest, were arrested after burning draft records they had removed from the Catonsville office of the Selective Service.

6. Donelan interview; Kelechi Ajunwa, "It's Our School Too: Youth Activism as Educational Reform, 1951–1979" (PhD diss., Temple University, 2011), 68–70.

7. Christopher A. Bogden, "The Perceived Value of JROTC" (PhD diss., Harvard University, 1984), appendix 2:2, and Russ Robinson, "ROTC Push Rejected in Carroll," *Baltimore Sun*, January 19, 1984.

8. Donelan interview. Crew's time as superintendent coincided with a change in the school district's orientation toward the military. Comparing Donelan's counter-recruitment activities before and after Crew came to power makes the dramatic shift clear. In 1974 Donelan was visiting three high schools in Baltimore every week, a much busier schedule than most counter-recruiters were keeping at that time. By 1976, Crew's second year at the helm, Donelan reported to her colleagues in the Task Force on Recruitment and Militarism, sponsored by the Central Committee for Conscientious Objectors, that she was working more in the surrounding counties and "keeping a low profile in [counter-recruitment] in the Baltimore schools because of a promilitary administrator." Donelan interview; Central Committee for Conscientious Objectors, Task Force on Recruitment and Militarism meeting minutes, January 8, 1976, series III, box 25, Central Committee for Conscientious Objectors Records (hereafter, CCCO

Records), Swarthmore College Peace Collection (hereafter SCPC), McCabe Library, Swarthmore College, Swarthmore, Pa.

9. M. William Salganik, "4 Oppose New City JROTC Unit," *Baltimore Sun*, September 7, 1979. For coverage of the Howard County JROTC debate, see "Howard Peace Activist Scores High School Military Proposal," *Baltimore Sun*, March 1, 1978; Michael Clark, "High School in Columbia to Make a Bid for ROTC," *Baltimore Sun*, October 5, 1978; Michael Clark, "ROTC Program Sought for Columbia School," *Baltimore Sun*, November 15, 1978; *Howard County Times*, editorial, November 22, 1978; Kenneth Walsh to editor, *Howard County Times*, December 6, 1978.

10. Isaac Rehert, "Northwestern Offers Junior ROTC," *Baltimore Sun*, August 11, 1979.

11. Salganik, "4 Oppose New City JROTC Unit." Mitchell served in Congress from 1971 until his retirement in 1986. He founded the Congressional Black Caucus with Democrats Ronald Dellums of California, Shirley Chisholm of New York, and others and served as its chair from 1977 to 1979. Politically progressive and outspoken throughout his career, Mitchell was followed and harassed for years by the Baltimore Police Department's "Red Squad" because of his civil rights activism. See George Derek Musgrove, *Rumor, Repression, and Racial Politics* (Athens: University of Georgia Press, 2012), 58. Donelan relates that she first got to know Mitchell during the Vietnam War, when he allowed her to use his office space for draft counseling sessions. According to Donelan, Mitchell became aware of the JROTC issue through her work with the AFSC. Fran Donelan to Seth Kershner, November 22, 2015.

12. Salganik, "4 Oppose New City JROTC Unit."

13. Laura Scism, "Military in Schools: Fight over ROTC Rekindled," *(Baltimore) News-American*, October 5, 1979.

14. Ibid.

15. Oakleigh Thorne, "The Good, Bad and Ugly of JROTC," *(Baltimore) News-American*, June 18, 1981; Robert Benjamin, "West Point Grad Condemns, Cadet Praises JROTC Program before City School Board," *Baltimore Sun*, June 18, 1981.

16. Thorne, "Good, Bad and Ugly of JROTC"; Benjamin, "West Point Grad Condemns."

17. While sensitive to the race and class dimensions of militarism, counter-recruiters struggled to square their commitment to racial justice with the overwhelming numbers of white activists filling their ranks. Many of the panels and workshops at the inaugural counter-recruiting conference at Stony Run in 1974 (see chapter 4) explored the ways in which counter-recruitment intersected with issues of race and class.

18. Thomas Conrad, Glenn Sheehan, and Stephen Gulick, "Junior ROTC—Expanding," *Counter Pentagon*, February 1975, 4–5; Leslie Pound, "Minority in the Majority," *Dallas Morning News*, December 1, 1981; Baltimore City Public Schools, *Senior High School Desegregation Plan for Baltimore City Public Schools* (Baltimore: BCPS, 1975), table 1, copy in the authors' possession. The accuracy of the schools' statistics is not clear as the district's publications categorized students as either "white" or "non-white." However, at this time the overwhelming majority of the nonwhite students were Black. For more on the history of Baltimore's struggle to integrate its city school system, see Howell Baum, *"Brown" in Baltimore: School Desegregation and the Limits of Liberalism* (Ithaca, N.Y.: Cornell University Press, 2010).

19. Marguerite Vlasits to the editor, *Baltimore Sun*, August 7, 1981.

20. Robert Benjamin, "City Faces JROTC Question: Does Military Belong in School?" *Baltimore Sun*, June 14, 1981.

21. See Lynne M. Woehrle, Patrick G. Coy, and Gregory M. Maney, *Contesting Patriotism: Culture, Power, and Strategy in the Peace Movement* (New York: Rowman & Littlefield, 2008), 118–142; and Lynne M. Woehrle, Patrick G. Coy, and Gregory M. Maney, "The Women's International League for Peace and Freedom and the Challenges of Intersectionality Praxis," *Peace & Change* 41 (2016): 273–301.

22. John T. Warner, "Military Recruiting Programs during the 1980s: Their Success and Policy Issues," *Contemporary Policy Issues* 8, no. 4 (1990): 48; Jack Hart, "High Unemployment Spurs Military Recruiting," *Oregonian* (Portland, Ore.), November 22, 1981; Robb Fulcher, UPI, "Northwest Military Recruitment Up as Economy Slides," *Oregonian*, December 13, 1982; Rolla J. Crick, "Recession Assists Military Recruiters," *Oregonian*, December 30, 1982.

23. Ted Shelsby, "Military Image Becomes Brighter," *Baltimore Sun*, January 2, 1975; Jane Berger, "When Hard Work Doesn't Pay: Gender and the Urban Crisis in Baltimore: 1945–1985" (PhD diss., Ohio State University, 2007), 305, 310; Benjamin, "City Faces."

24. Donelan to Kershner, November 22, 2015; Lacy McCrary, "Military Flavor Gaining Favor in High Schools," *Philadelphia Inquirer*, May 27, 1983.

25. Patrick McGuire, "Ten-Hut! Students Are Doing the Left-Right-Left," *Baltimore Sun*, March 31, 1985.

26. Donelan to Kershner, November 22, 2015.

27. *Baltimore Afro-American*, editorial, October 17, 1964.

28. McGuire, "Ten-Hut!"

29. Appy, *American Reckoning*, 269; Lawrence S. Wittner, *Rebels against War: The American Peace Movement, 1933–1983* (Philadelphia: Temple University Press, 1984), 269.

30. Jerald G. Bachman, "American High School Seniors View the Military: 1976–1982," *Armed Forces & Society* 10 (1983): 88; Wittner, *Rebels against War*, 269.

31. Henry A. Zwartz, "An Empirical Analysis of the Navy Junior Reserve Officer Training Corps" (master's thesis, Naval Postgraduate School, 1987), 18; Arthur T. Coumbe and Lee S. Harford, *U.S. Army Cadet Command: The 10 Year History* (Fort Monroe, Va.: Army Cadet Command, Office of the Command Historian, 1996), 264.

32. Marianne Costantinou, "Kids Rush to Sign Up for JROTC," *Miami Herald*, October 1, 1984; Barbara Miner, UPI, "ROTC Ranks Swelling," *Pacific Stars and Stripes*, August 30, 1983.

33. In 1984 a Pentagon spokesman linked the increasing success of recruiting during the 1980s to Reagan era defense spending. Between FY1979 and FY1983, the army increased its spending on recruitment by two-thirds. By the end of that period the services had spent a combined $996 million for active duty recruitment and employed about fifteen thousand personnel to help recruiters achieve their goals. Randi Henderson, "War Seems Won to Military Recruiters," *Baltimore Sun*, May 23, 1984; "A Decade at a Glance," *All Volunteer*, December 1983.

34. Henderson, "War Seems Won."

35. Osha Gray Davidson, "On Guard," *In These Times*, October 1–7, 1986; "Field File," *All Volunteer*, May 1981; "The Recruit," *Atlanta Constitution*, November 1, 1981; "Field File," *All Volunteer*, December 1981.

36. Ernest Drucker, "Military Recruiting Activity in New York City Public High Schools: Interim Report," unpublished manuscript, June 1985, Acc. 01A-055, box 6, Educators for Social Responsibility Records, SCPC; Elizabeth Sendor, "Here Are the Issues to Weigh When Uncle Sam Wants Your Kids," *American School Board Journal* 169, no. 4 (1982): 28–31. A nationwide survey of counselors also found two-thirds reported positive experiences while working with military recruiters, and many counselors were "lavish in their praise." Kenneth Martin, "Guidance Counselors: A Nationwide Survey," *Recruiter Journal*, December 1985–January 1986.

37. Henderson, "War Seems Won to Military Recruiters"; Jim Garamone, "Military, School Groups Reach Pact on Recruiting," *Navy Times*, September 3, 1984. For the activists' response to "the Pact," see Task Force on Recruitment and Militarism meeting minutes, September 10, 1984, Acc. 95A-036, box 13, CCCO Records.

38. "High School Organizing," special issue of *Objector*, June 6, 1981.

39. Rick Jahnkow, telephone interview by author, March 23, 2011; "Leafletter Arrested," *Draft Notices* (San Diego), November–December 1981.

40. "arrested activists" Diane Carol Blast, "Conscience Comes to the Classroom," *Christian Century*, March 5, 1986.

41. Andrew Skotnicki, telephone interview by author, June 22, 2013; Andrew Skotnicki to Chicago school board, n.d., box 42, Clergy and Laity Concerned, Chicago Branch Records (hereafter Chicago CALC Records), Chicago History Museum, Chicago.

42. "A View from the Village," *All Volunteer*, January 1982

43. Ruth Love to William N. Matthews, January 25, 1983, box 42, Chicago CALC Records.

44. Andrew Skotnicki to Joyce Clark, February 5, 1982, box 42, Chicago CALC Records.

45. Linda Groetzinger to Ruth Love, February 15, 1982, box 42, Chicago CALC Records.

46. Skotnicki interview.

47. Andrew Skotnicki and Marco Pardo, "Equal Access for Peace," *Chicago Tribune*, op-ed, December 19, 1983.

48. Clergy and Laity Concerned v. Chicago Board of Education, 586 F. Supp. 1408 (1984); Rudolph Unger and Marianne Taylor, "City Schools Opened to Antiwar Counselors," *Chicago Tribune*, January 25, 1984.

49. Blast, "Conscience Comes to the Classroom."

50. Davidson, "On Guard"; Marion Malcolm, "Draft Counseling in the Lane County School System," *CALC Report*, March–April 1986; "Chapter News," *CALC Report*, September 1984. For the reaction in New York State, see Andy Mager, "We've Got Our Foot in the Door," *Peace Newsletter* (Syracuse, N.Y.), September 1984, and Upstate Resistance meeting minutes, April 19, 1986, series 7, box 1, Knolls Action Project Records, M. E. Grenander Department of Special Collections and Archives, Science Library, University at Albany, Albany, New York. Two other relevant legal rulings from the 1980s are *Searcey v. Crim*, 692 F. Supp. 1363 (1988), which found that Atlanta activists could present information critical of the military, and *San Diego Committee against Registration and the Draft v. Grossmont Union High School*, 790 F.2d 1471 (9th Cir. 1986).

51. Henderson, "War Seems Won to Military Recruiters"; Susan G. Foster, "Plan to Expand Junior ROTC Program Provokes Debate," *Education Week*, November 3, 1982; "Community Organizing and High School Outreach," *Objector*, January 1989.

52. The two campaigns began in 1979 and 1983. For more on the 1979 campaign, see "Public Meeting on the Cincinnati Military Academy," meeting agenda, January 28, 1979, and Gary Sullivan, "Coalition Plans to Try Blocking Military School," *Cincinnati Enquirer*, January 29, 1979, copies of both in section II, series J, box 3, Fellowship of Reconciliation Papers, SCPC. For more on the 1983 campaign, see "Public Military High School Struck Down in Cincinnati," *Objector*, October 15, 1983, 4–5.

53. "Community Organizing and High School Outreach," *Objector*, January 1989, 8.

54. Maggie Carter, "Project Rooted in Community," *Objector*, April 15, 1986, 5.

55. Susan Stern, "Toeing the Military Line: The Other Side," *Oakland Tribune*, October 20, 1985; Ann Wrixon, "Youth-Run Program," *Objector*, April 15, 1986.

56. "Peace and Justice Youth Outreach Project," undated pamphlet, Acc. 95A-036, box 21, CCCO Records.

57. "CCCO 1986 Annual Report," copy in box 2, Knolls Action Project Records.

58. *Real War Stories*, no. 1 (Forestville, Calif.: Eclipse Comics, 1987), inside back cover. We are grateful to Rick Jahnkow for providing us with a copy of this comic book.

59. Rick Jahnkow, telephone interview by author, January 12, 2013.

60. Task Force on Recruitment and Militarism meeting minutes, May 14, 1984, Acc. 95A-036, box 13, CCCO Records; Glen Anderson, "Community Acts to Out JROTC from Local High School," *Objector*, September 1986.

61. Amy Beegle, "Conflicting Perspectives on Patriotism within Music Education in the United States during Wartime," in Alexandra Kertz-Welzel and David G. Hebert, eds., *Patriotism and Nationalism in Music Education* (Burlington, Vt.: Ashgate), 132. For more on the history of veterans' organizations, see Wallace Evans Davies, *Patriotism on Parade: The Story of Veterans' and Hereditary Organizations in America, 1783–1900* (Cambridge, Mass.: Harvard University Press, 1955).

62. Rob Pfeiffer, telephone interview by author, February 15, 2013. Peace-and-justice book covers were a common counter-recruiting tactic. See, for example, David Falls, "Book Covers for Peace," *Objector*, April 15, 1986, 10; "San Diego Counter-Militarism," *National Campaign to Demilitarize Our Schools Newsletter* 1 (winter 1992): 3; Rick Jahnkow, "San Diego Developments," *National Campaign to Demilitarize Our Schools Newsletter* 1 (spring 1994): 3. However, relatively few groups involved youth in the design of book covers. For an example of one such contest, organized by the Eugene-Springfield, Oregon, chapter of the Fellowship of Reconciliation, see "News of Local Groups," *Fellowship* 57 (June 1991): 22.

63. Pfeiffer interview.

64. "Veterans: An Important Voice," *Objector*, December 1983; "The Day the Helicopter Came to School," brochure published by Veterans Education Project, Amherst, Mass., Acc.: 02A-041, box 12, CCCO Records..

65. Gillam Kerley, "School Board Curbs Recruitment," *Objector*, April 15, 1986, 3–4; Madison VVAW, "VVAW: 9, Recruiters: 0," *Veteran* 16 (February–March 1986): 15.

66. The nuclear freeze movement proposed a bilateral suspension of the testing, production, and future deployment of nuclear arms, as well as the steady reduction of existing arsenals. After the movement officially began in Washington, D.C., in March 1981, it caught on quickly as city councils, state legislatures, and other official bodies in forty-three states passed resolu-

tions approving the freeze. Volunteers established local freeze chapters in two-thirds of the country's congressional districts, and nearly one million demonstrators gathered in New York's Central Park in June 1982 to support the proposal—the largest U.S. demonstration of any kind before or since. See James Carroll, *House of War: The Pentagon and the Disastrous Rise of American Power* (New York: Houghton Mifflin Harcourt, 2007), 386–397.

67. Miner, "ROTC Ranks Swelling."

68. *News-American*, editorial, October 7, 1979; *Dallas Morning News*, editorial, December 2, 1981.

69. David Clark Scott, "ROTC Marches Back onto Campuses," *Christian Science Monitor*, March 11, 1981; Mel Evans, "JROTC: More Than Spit and Polish," *Omaha (Neb.) World-Herald*, January 9, 1985.

70. Robin Young Roe, "More Joining Junior ROTC," *New York Times*, October 11, 1981.

71. Evans, "JROTC: More Than Spit and Polish."

72. Nicholas von Hoffman, "Pentagon Recruits the Preps," *Chicago Tribune*, September 16, 1975.

73. Coumbe and Harford, *U.S. Army Cadet Command*, 269.

74. Stephen Gulick, telephone interview by author, August 24, 2011.

Chapter 6. A Resurgent National Movement

1. Lawrence Wittner, *Toward Nuclear Abolition: A History of the World Nuclear Disarmament Movement, 1971–Present* (Stanford. Calif.: Stanford University Press, 2003), 3:406.

2. Rick Jahnkow, "The Peace Movement Needs to Shift Its Emphasis," *Draft Notices* (San Diego, Calif.) 10, no. 6 (1989): 1.

3. Rick Jahnkow, "Youth and Alternatives as Part of a Larger Anti-militarism Movement," *Objector*, July 1988, 11. By 1990 counter-recruitment leaders were describing TFORM as, variously, "in limbo" and "on hiatus." National Campaign to Demilitarize Our Schools, meeting minutes, July 25, 1990, and May 6, 1991, copy in authors' possession, courtesy of Rick Jahnkow.

4. Gary Wolf to Rick Jahnkow, December 28, 1989, copy in authors' possession.

5. National Campaign to Demilitarize Our Schools, meeting minutes, February 16, 1990, copy in authors' possession.

6. Undated draft (probably spring 1990) of campaign proposal circulated to NCDOS planners, copy in authors' possession.

7. National Campaign to Demilitarize Our Schools, "Proposal Adopted in 1990 by the Founding Organizations of NCDOS," n.d., copy in authors' possession.

8. "Toting the Casualties of War," *Business Week*, February 6, 2003, https://www.bloomberg.com/news/articles/2003-02-05/toting-the-casualties-of-war. Walter LaFeber, the distinguished scholar of international relations, accepts an estimate of more than 100,000 total Iraqi losses. See his *America, Russia, and the Cold War, 1945–2006*, 10th ed. (New York: McGraw-Hill, 2008).

9. Keith Matyi, "Operation Desert Care," *Recruiter Journal*, December 1990.

10. Debra Viadero, "Teachers Tackle Today's 'Most Important Issue': Persian Gulf," *Education Week*, January 16, 1991.

11. Howard Lisnoff, "A Storm of War, A Whisper of Peace," *CCCO News Notes*, spring 1991, 7.

12. Viadero, "Teachers Tackle."

13. Rick Jahnkow, "School Campaign Taking Shape," *NCDOS Newsletter*, winter 1992; National Campaign to Demilitarize Our Schools, meeting minutes, October 25, 1991, copy in authors' possession; Delaware Valley Students and Youth Act for Peace and Justice, "Countering Military Recruitment," *Education for the People*, October 1991, box 2, Social Change Periodicals Collection, Special Collections and University Archives, University of Massachusetts Amherst Libraries.

14. Bob Henschen, telephone interview by author, August 7, 2012; Bob Henschen, "Houston Activists Gain Equal Access to Classrooms," *NCDOS Newsletter*, summer 1996.

15. "California School Boards Hinder Military Recruiters," *Objector*, March–April 1991.

16. Alan Morrell, "Schools Urged to Ban Military," *Democrat & Chronicle* (Rochester, N.Y.), December 4, 1991.

17. Bob Lonsberry, "Battle over Recruiter Ban Is a Waste," opinion column, *Democrat & Chronicle* (Rochester, N.Y.), March 11, 1994; Sam Diener, "Rochester Victory in Counter-recruitment," *NCDOS Newsletter*, winter 1992, 5.

18. Morrell, "Schools Urged to Ban Military."

19. "JROTC Units Stopped by Community Protest," CCCO press release, July 7, 1995, Acc. 02A-41, box 10 Central Committee for Conscientious Objectors Records (hereafter CCCO Records), Swarthmore College Peace Collection (hereafter SCPC), McCabe Library, Swarthmore College, Swarthmore, Pa.; Political-Military Studies Project on the JROTC, Center for Strategic and International Studies (hereafter CSIS), *Junior Reserve Officers' Training Corps: Contributing to America's Communities* (Washington, D.C.: CSIS, 1999), 22; National Campaign to Demilitarize Our Schools, meeting minutes, July 31, 1993, copy in authors' possession.

20. Katherine van Wormer, "Challenging a Creeping Military Presence," *Friends Journal*, June 1994, 19; "San Jose State Faculty Kick ROTC Off Campus," *NCDOS Newsletter*, summer 1992; Kathy Russell, "Keeping ROTC off Campus through a Faculty Referendum Process," presentation at meeting of Central New York Peace Studies Association, Cortland, N.Y., November 13, 2010, copy in authors' possession; Lee Duemer, "The History of the Reserve Officer Training Corps among the Association of American Universities from 1982 to 1992: Review of Institutional Responses to ROTC Policy Regarding Homosexuals," *Education Policy Analysis Archives* 5, no. 9 (1997).

21. See, for example, Patrick Novotny, "The Post-Cold War Era, the Persian Gulf War, and the Peace and Justice Movement in the 1990s," *Social Justice* 26, no. 3 (1999): 190–203.

22. Central Committee for Conscientious Objectors, *1992–1993 Youth & Militarism Directory* (Philadelphia: CCCO, 1991), 23; Jahnkow, "School Campaign Taking Shape," *NCDOS Newsletter*, winter 1992, 2.

23. Harold Jordan, interview by author, March 7, 2012, Philadelphia; Harold Jordan to Ann Wrixon, June 3, 1986, Acc. 02a-41, box 5, CCCO Records.

24. National Campaign to Demilitarize Our Schools, meeting minutes, July 25, 1990, copy in authors' possession.

25. The Gallup "Confidence in Institutions" survey recorded that, in February 1991, 85 percent of respondents had "quite a lot/a great deal" of confidence in the military.

26. Colin L. Powell, with Joseph E. Persico, *My American Journey* (New York: Random House, 1996), 555–556; John W. Corbett and Arthur T. Coumbe, "JROTC: Recent Trends and Developments," *Military Review* 81, no. 1 (2001): 40.

27. Sam Nunn, *Domestic Missions for the Armed Forces* (Carlisle Barracks, Pa.: Strategic Studies Institute, U.S. Army War College, 1993), 5. See also Helen Dewar, "Nunn Urges Military Shift," *Washington Post*, June 24, 1992.

28. Lesley Bartlett and Catherine Lutz, "Disciplining Social Difference: Some Cultural Politics of Military Training in Public High Schools," *Urban Review* 30 (1998): 125.

29. Ibid., 119–136.

30. Ross Collin, "On the March: Social and Political Contexts of the Expansion of the Junior Reserve Officers' Training Corps," *Educational Policy* 22, no. 3 (2008): 457–482.

31. Jon Marcus, AP, "Revived Junior ROTC Programs Prove a Hit in High Schools," *Philadelphia Inquirer*, November 29, 1996.

32. Jonathan S. Landay, "Parents Protest Military's Role in the Classroom," *Christian Science Monitor*, October 5, 1995; Corbett and Coumbe, "JROTC: Recent Trends and Developments," 41; CSIS Political-Military Studies Project on the JROTC, *Junior Reserve Officers' Training Corps*, 4.

33. Corbett and Coumbe, "JROTC: Recent Trends and Developments," 40; Political-Military Studies Project on the JROTC, *Junior Reserve Officers' Training Corps*, 45.

34. CSIS Political-Military Studies Project on the JROTC, *Junior Reserve Officers' Training Corps*, 29; Marcus, "Revived Junior ROTC Programs"; Millicent Lawton, "Coalition of Peace Groups Seeks to Rid Schools of Military Influences," *Education Week*, February 5, 1992, 5.

35. Harold Jordan, telephone interview by author, February 24, 2011; Lehigh Pocono Committee of Concern, Youth and Militarism Working Group, meeting minutes, April 22, 1993, copy in authors' possession; Judy Rohrer, "Bethlehem Activists Prevent JROTC Invasion," *Objector* 13 (September 1993).

36. Eugene J. Carroll Jr., "JROTC: Who Needs It?" *New York Times*, June 26, 1993; Walter Winfield Jr. to editor, *New York Times*, August 18, 1993.

37. Harold Jordan, telephone interview by author, February 17, 2011. For more on the struggle to keep JROTC out of Seattle, see Scott Harding and Seth Kershner, *Counter-recruitment and the Campaign to Demilitarize Public Schools* (New York: Palgrave Macmillan, 2015), 73–74.

38. "JROTC Units Stopped by Community Protest," CCCO press release, July 7, 1995, Acc. 02A-41, box 10, CCCO Records; NCDOS meeting minutes, October 24, 1992, copy in authors' possession.

39. Unless otherwise noted, all quotes in this section are drawn from our telephone interviews of Harold Jordan (February 17, 2011) and Catherine Lutz (February 7, 2011). Lutz is one of the foremost scholars of U.S. militarism. Perhaps best known for her award-winning book, *Homefront: A Military City and the American Twentieth Century* (Boston: Beacon, 2002), she has also written about the topic in other publications. See, for example, Catherine Lutz, "Warmaking as the American Way of Life," 45–61, in Hugh Gusterson and Catherine Besteman, eds., *The Insecure American: How We Got Here and What We Should Do about It* (Berkeley: University of California Press, 2009).

40. Catherine Lutz and Lesley Bartlett, *Making Soldiers in the Public Schools: An Analysis of*

the Army JROTC Curriculum (Philadelphia: AFSC, 1995), 16. For more about the discussion of curriculum, see pp. 19 to 29.

41. Arthur T. Coumbe, *History of the U.S. Army Cadet Command: Second Ten Years, 1996–2006* (Fort Monroe, Va.: U.S. Army Cadet Command, 2008), 324–325.

42. Bruce Orvis and Beth Asch, *Military Recruiting: Trends, Outlook, and Implications* (Santa Monica, Calif.: RAND, 2001), 41; Coumbe, *History of the U.S. Army Cadet Command*, 308.

43. Orvis and Asch, *Military Recruiting*, 35; "The Changing Recruiting Environment," *Recruiter Journal*, February 1994, 24.

44. A sympathetic discussion of Hutchinson's claims appears in Bruce D. Callander, "The Recruiters and the Schools," *Air Force Magazine*, October 2001. For a more critical take on how a military recruiting mandate found its way into an omnibus education bill, see Brian Lagotte, "Children in the Ranks: The Militarization of Educational Policy" (PhD diss., University of Wisconsin, Madison, 2012), 63–88.

45. See Henry Giroux, *The Abandoned Generation: Democracy beyond the Culture of Fear* (New York: Palgrave Macmillan, 2003); and Diane Ravitch, *The Death and Life of the Great American School System: How Testing and Choice Are Undermining Education* (New York: Basic Books, 2016.)

46. Brian Lagotte, "Turf Wars: School Administrators and Military Recruiting," *Educational Policy* 28, no. 4 (2012): 547–577; U.S. Army Recruiting Command, *School Recruiting Program Handbook* (Fort Knox, Ky.: U.S. Army Recruiting Command, 2006), 1; Harding and Kershner, "'A Borderline Issue.'"

47. Yvette Richardson, interview by author, May 14, 2012, Fort Worth, Tex.

48. Ibid.

49. Adam McGlynn and Jessica Lavariega-Monforti, "The Poverty Draft? Exploring the Role of Socioeconomic Status in U.S. Military Recruitment of Hispanic Students," paper presented at the annual meeting of the American Political Science Association, September 2–5, 2010, Washington, D.C.

50. Richardson interview.

51. Stuart Tannock, "Is 'Opting Out' Really an Answer? Schools, Militarism, and the Counter-recruitment Movement in Post–September 11 United States at War," *Social Justice* 32 (2005): 163.

52. Michael Gillespie, "Counter-recruitment Meeting in Des Moines," *Washington Report on Middle East Affairs*, August 2005, 60; Janine Schwab, interview by author, March 8, 2012, Philadelphia; Alexander Cockburn, "Whatever Happened to the Anti-War Movement?" *New Left Review* 46 (July–August 2007): 38.

53. Lizette Alvarez, "Army Giving More Waivers in Recruiting," *New York Times*, February 14, 2007.

54. Seth Kershner and Scott Harding, "Addressing the Militarization of Youth," *Peace Review* 26, no. 2 (2014): 252.

55. Bree Hancock, interview by author, May 13, 2012, Fort Worth, Tex.

56. Rick Jahnkow, "San Diego Students Give Pink Slip to High School Military Program," *Draft Notices*, April–June 2012.

57. Scott Harding and Seth Kershner, "Students against Militarism: Youth Organizing in the Counter-recruitment Movement," 257–273, in Julie Gorlewski and Bradley Porfilio, eds., *Left behind in the Race to the Top: Realities of Education Reform* (Charlotte, N.C.: Information Age).

58. Scott Harding and Seth Kershner, "Just Say No: Organizing against Militarism in Public Schools," *Journal of Sociology & Social Welfare* 38, no. 2 (2011): 79–110.

59. Jill Tucker, "School Board Votes to Dump JROTC Program," *San Francisco Chronicle*, November 15, 2006; Carl T. Hall, "San Francisco Torpedoes JROTC," *U.S. Naval Institute Proceedings* 133 (March 2007): 56–60; Lauren Smiley, "JROTC under Fire in S.F. Schools," *San Francisco Weekly*, April 8, 2009.

60. Smiley, "JROTC under Fire in S.F. Schools,"; Tucker, "School Board Votes to Dump JROTC."

61. Harding and Kershner, *Counter-recruitment and the Campaign to Demilitarize Public Schools*, 73–74.

62. Corbett and Coumbe, "JROTC: Recent Trends and Developments," 40.

63. One example was an exchange in the Yahoo! counter-recruitment forum in June 2014 between Rick Jahnkow and Sam Diener, who had led anti-JROTC campaigns as a CCCO organizer in the 1990s.

64. In all three cases scholars have demonstrated how campaign strategies centered on child protection and human rights have pushed moral narratives to the margins. See Rachel Waltner Goossen, "Disarming the Toy Store and Reloading the Shopping Cart: Resistance to Violent Consumer Culture," *Peace & Change* 38 (2013): 330–354; Neil S. Forkey, "High Anxiety in St. Lawrence County: Citizen Action and U.S. Military Flights, 1989–1992," *New York History* 99, no. 34 (2018): 440–463; Katherine McCaffrey, "Environmental Struggle after the Cold War: New Forms of Resistance to the U.S. military in Vieques, Puerto Rico," 218–242, in Catherine Lutz, ed., *The Bases of Empire: The Global Struggle against U.S. Military Posts* (New York: NYU Press, 2009); and Charles C. Moskos and John Whiteclay Chambers II, eds., *The New Conscientious Objection: From Sacred to Secular Resistance* (New York: Oxford University Press, 1993).

65. We are indebted to Marian Mollin, whose comments at the 2011 Peace History Conference reminded us of the role moral discourse plays in the peace movement.

Conclusion

1. Charles A. Goldman et al., *Geographic and Demographic Representativeness of the Junior Reserve Officers' Training Corps* (Santa Monica, Calif.: RAND, 2017), 77–79.

2. Jennifer Villaume, "March 2 Success Goes Mobile in Mississippi," *Recruiter Journal* (November 2011): 12.

3. See annual reports available online under "Resources" at DoD's website for STARBASE, which bills itself as "a Department of Defense youth program," https://dodstarbase.org.

4. Supportive statements from the office of Senator Sanders regularly appear in the newsletter of the Vermont STARBASE program. See, for example, the fall 2010 newsletter, https://starbasevt.org/wp-content/uploads/2016/01/Starbase_Vermont_Fall_2010.pdf.

5. Numerous studies have documented the rise of U.S. militarism after 9/11. See, for example, Andrew J. Bacevich, *Washington Rules: America's Path to Permanent War* (New York: Metropolitan, 2010); and Catherine Lutz, "Warmaking as the American Way of Life," 45–61, in Hugh Gusterson and Catherine Besteman, eds., *The Insecure American: How We Got Here and What We Should Do about It* (Berkeley: University of California Press, 2010). For one of the first anthologies of such writings, see Roberto J. González, Hugh Gusterson, and Gustaaf Houtman, eds., *Militarization: A Reader* (Durham, N.C.: Duke University Press, 2019).

6. Rick Jahnkow, telephone interview by author, June 29, 2021.

7. Eliot A. Cohen, "Bring ROTC Back to Elite Campuses," op-ed, *Washington Post*, December 21, 2010.

8. Barack Obama, "Transcript: Obama's State of the Union Address," January 25, 2011, text as released by the White House, https://www.npr.org/2011/01/26/133224933/transcript-obamas-state-of-union-address.

9. For discussion of the successful San Marcos struggle, see Linda Pershing, "At CSU San Marcos, Resistance to ROTC Succeeds," *Draft Notices* July–September 2009. A critical examination of the CUNY campaign appears in Zoltán Glück et al., "Organizing against Empire: Struggles over the Militarization of CUNY," *Berkeley Journal of Sociology* 58 (2014), http://berkeleyjournal.org/2014/10/organizing-against-empire-struggles-over-the-militarization-of-cuny/. We are indebted to John Lawrence, professor of psychology at the College of Staten Island, for his insights about the CUNY anti-ROTC campaign.

BIBLIOGRAPHY

Manuscript Collections

ALBANY, N.Y.

*M. E. Grenander Department of Special
Collections & Archives, University at Albany*

Knolls Action Project Records

New York State Archives

New York State Police Bureau of Criminal Investigation Reports, Non-Criminal Investigations
Files, New York State Troopers Files

AMHERST, MASS.

*Robert S. Cox Special Collections and University Archives
Research Center, University of Massachusetts Amherst Libraries*

Social Change Periodicals Collection

CHICAGO

Chicago History Museum

Clergy and Laity Concerned, Chicago Branch Records

NEW HAVEN, CONN.

Special Collections, Yale Divinity School Library

George A. Coe Papers

PENNSBURG, PA.

Schwenkfelder Library & Heritage Center

Local Newspaper Collection

PORTLAND, ORE.

City of Portland Archives

Police Historical/Archival Investigative Records

PRINCETON, N.J.

Seeley G. Mudd Manuscript Library, Princeton University

American Civil Liberties Union Records

STORRS, CONN.

*Archives & Special Collections at the Thomas J. Dodd
Research Center, University of Connecticut Library*

Alternative Press Collection
Walter Landauer Papers

SWARTHMORE, PA.

Swarthmore College Peace Collection

Central Committee for Conscientious Objectors Records
Committee on Militarism in Education Records
Educators for Social Responsibility Records
Fellowship of Reconciliation (U.S.) Records
John Nevin Sayre Papers
Resource Center for Nonviolence Records
Women's International League for Peace and Freedom Records

Frequently Cited Newspapers and Periodicals

All Hands
All Volunteer (later renamed *Recruiter Journal*)
Arizona Republic
Baltimore Sun
CCCO News Notes
Christian Century
Counter Pentagon
Democrat & Chronicle (Rochester, N.Y.)
Education Week
NCDOS Newsletter
New York Times
Objector
Oregonian (Portland, Ore.)
Washington Post

Interviews

Cochran, Bishop. Telephone interview, September 24, 2011.

Donelan, Frances. Interview, April 5, 2013, Baltimore, Maryland.

Gould, Bob. Telephone interview, August 29, 2011.

Gulick, Stephen. Telephone interview, August 24, 2011.

Hancock, Bree. Interview, May 13, 2012, Fort Worth, Texas.

Henschen, Bob. Telephone interview, August 7, 2012.

Jahnkow, Rick. Telephone interview, March 23, 2011.

Jahnkow, Rick. Telephone interview, January 12, 2013.

Jahnkow, Rick. Telephone interview, June 29, 2021.

Jordan, Harold. Telephone interview, February 17, 2011.

Jordan, Harold. Telephone interview, February 24, 2011.

Jordan, Harold. Interview, March 7, 2012, Philadelphia.

Lutz, Catherine. Telephone interview, February 7, 2011.

Pfeiffer, Rob. Telephone interview, February 15, 2013.

Richardson, Yvette. Interview, May 14, 2012, Fort Worth, Texas.

Schwab, Janine. Interview, March 8, 2012, Philadelphia.

Skotnicki, Andrew. Telephone interview, June 22, 2013.

Selected Books, Articles, Dissertations, and Reports

Abrams, Ray. *Preachers Present Arms: A Study of the War-time Attitudes and Activities of the Churches and the Clergy in the United States, 1914–1918*. Philadelphia: University of Pennsylvania Press, 1933.

Allen, Devere. *The Fight for Peace*. 2 vols. New York: Macmillan, 1931. Reprint, New York: Garland, 1971.

Appy, Christian. *American Reckoning: The Vietnam War and Our National Identity*. New York: Penguin, 2015.

———. *Working-Class War: American Combat Soldiers and Vietnam*. Chapel Hill: University of North Carolina Press, 2000.

Bachman, Jerald G. "American High School Seniors View the Military: 1976–1982." *Armed Forces & Society* 10, no. 1 (1983): 86–104.

Bailey, Beth. *America's Army: Making the All-Volunteer Force*. Cambridge, Mass.: Harvard University Press, 2009.

Barthell, Daniel. "The Committee on Militarism in Education, 1925–1940." PhD diss., University of Illinois, 1972.

Bartlett, Lesley, and Catherine Lutz. "Disciplining Social Difference: Some Cultural Politics of Military Training in Public High Schools." *Urban Review* 30, no. 2 (1998): 119–136.

Bennett, Scott H. *Radical Pacifism: The War Resisters League and Gandhian Nonviolence in America, 1915–1963*. Syracuse, N.Y.: Syracuse University Press, 2003.

———. "Radical Pacifism and the General Strike against War: Jessie Wallace Hughan, the

Founding of the War Resisters League, and the Socialist Origins of Secular Radical Pacifism in America." *Peace & Change* 26, no. 3 (2001): 352–373.

Boeckel, Florence Brewer. *Between War and Peace: A Handbook for Peace Workers*. New York: Macmillan, 1928.

Bolt, Ernest C. *Ballots before Bullets: The War Referendum Approach to Peace in America, 1914–1941*. Charlottesville: University of Virginia Press, 1977.

Boyer, William H. *Education for Annihilation*. Honolulu: Hogarth Press, 1972.

Brock, Peter. *Pacifism in the United States: From the Colonial Era to the First World War*. Princeton, N.J.: Princeton University Press, 1968.

Brock, Peter, and Nigel Young. *Pacifism in the Twentieth Century*. Syracuse, N.Y.: Syracuse University Press, 1999.

Brumberg, Stephan F. "New York City Schools March off to War: The Nature and Extent of Participation of the City Schools in the Great War, April 1917–June 1918." *Urban Education* 24, no. 4 (1990): 440–475.

Buck, John M., and George I. Forsythe. *High School Recruitment for a Volunteer Army*. Washington, D.C.: Development Alternatives, 1972.

Casserly, Brian. "Confronting the U.S. Navy at Bangor, 1973–1982." *Pacific Northwest Quarterly* 95 (2004): 130–139.

Chambers, John Whiteclay II. *The Eagle and the Dove: The American Peace Movement and United States Foreign Policy, 1900–1922*. Syracuse, N.Y.: Syracuse University Press, 1991.

Chaney, Louis H. "Military Training in the Secondary Schools." Master's thesis, Butler University, 1940.

Chatfield, Charles. *For Peace and Justice: Pacifism in America, 1914–1941*. Knoxville: University of Tennessee Press, 1971.

Clifford, John Gary. *The Citizen Soldiers: The Plattsburg Training Camp Movement, 1913–1920*. Lexington: University Press of Kentucky, 1972.

Cloward, Richard A., and Frances Fox Piven. *Poor People's Movements: Why They Succeed, How They Fail*. New York: Vintage, 1979.

Cohen, Robert. *When the Old Left Was Young: Student Radicals and America's First Mass Student Movement, 1929–1941*. New York: Oxford University Press, 1993.

Cooney, Robert, and Helen Michalowski, eds. *The Power of the People: Active Nonviolence in the United States*. Philadelphia: New Society, 1987.

Cortright, David. *Peace: A History of Movement and Ideas*. New York: Cambridge University Press, 2008.

Coumbe, Arthur T. *History of the U.S. Army Cadet Command: Second Ten Years, 1996–2006*. Fort Monroe, Va.: U.S. Army Cadet Command, 2008.

Cox, Marcus S. *Segregated Soldiers: Military Training at Historically Black Colleges in the Jim Crow South*. Baton Rouge: Louisiana State University Press, 2013.

Craig, John M. *Lucia Ames Mead (1856–1936) and the American Peace Movement*. Lewiston, N.Y.: Edwin Mellen Press, 1990.

Curran, Thomas F. *Soldiers of Peace: Civil War Pacifism and the Postwar Radical Peace Movement*. New York: Fordham University Press, 2003.

Curti, Merle. *Peace or War: The American Struggle, 1636–1936*. New York: W. W. Norton, 1936.

Davis, Allen F. *American Heroine: The Life and Legend of Jane Addams*. New York: Oxford University Press, 1973.

DeBenedetti, Charles. "Educators and Armaments in Cold War America." *Peace & Change* 34, no. 4 (2009): 425–440.

———. *The Origins of the Modern American Peace Movement, 1915–1929*. Millwood, N.Y.: KTOPress, 1978.

———. *The Peace Reform in American History*. Bloomington: Indiana University Press, 1980.

DeBenedetti, Charles, with Charles Chatfield. *An American Ordeal: The Antiwar Movement of the Vietnam Era*. Syracuse, N.Y.: Syracuse University Press, 1990.

Downs, Donald, and Ilia Murtazashvili. *Arms and the University: Military Presence and the Civic Education of Non-military Students*. New York: Cambridge University Press, 2012.

Eagan, Eileen. *Class, Culture, and the Classroom: The Student Peace Movement of the 1930s*. Philadelphia: Temple University Press, 1981.

Ekirch, Arthur A. Jr. *The Civilian and the Military*. New York: Oxford University Press, 1956.

Enloe, Cynthia. "The Recruiter and the Sceptic: A Critical Feminist Approach to Military Studies." *Critical Military Studies* 1, no. 1 (2015): 3–10.

Fosdick, Harry Emerson. *The Present Crisis*. New York: Association Press, 1918.

Foster, Carrie A. *The Women and the Warriors: The U.S. Section of the Women's International League for Peace and Freedom, 1915–1946*. Syracuse, N.Y.: Syracuse University Press, 1996.

Fox, Richard Wightman. *Reinhold Niebuhr: A Biography*. New York: Harper & Row, 1987.

Friesen, Matthew C. "Framing Symbols and Space: Counter-recruitment and Resistance to the U.S. Military in Public Education." *Sociological Forum* 29, no. 1 (2014): 75–97.

Giroux, Henry. *The Abandoned Generation: Democracy beyond the Culture of Fear*. New York: Palgrave Macmillan, 2003.

Goldman, Charles A., Jonathan Schweig, Maya Buenaventura, and Cameron Wright. *Geographic and Demographic Representativeness of the Junior Reserve Officers' Training Corps*. Santa Monica, Calif.: RAND, 2017.

Goossen, Rachel Waltner. *Women against the Good War: Conscientious Objection and Gender on the American Home Front, 1941–1947*. Chapel Hill: University of North Carolina Press, 1997.

Gronowicz, Anthony, ed. *Oswald Garrison Villard: The Dilemma of the Absolute Pacifist in Two World Wars*. New York: Garland, 1983.

Hall, Mitchell K. *Because of Their Faith: CALCAV and Religious Opposition to the Vietnam War*. New York: Columbia University Press, 1990.

Harding, Scott, and Seth Kershner. "'A Borderline Issue': Are There Child Soldiers in the United States?" *Journal of Human Rights* 17, no. 3 (2018): 322–339.

———. *Counter-recruitment and the Campaign to Demilitarize Public Schools*. New York: Palgrave Macmillan, 2015.

Hershberger, Guy. *War, Peace, and Nonresistance*. Harrisonburg, Va.: Herald Press, 1944.

Howlett, Charles F., and Audrey Cohan. *John Dewey: America's Peace-Minded Educator*. Carbondale: Southern Illinois University Press, 2016.

Howlett, Charles F., and Robbie Lieberman. *A History of the American Peace Movement from Colonial Times to the Present*. Lewiston, N.Y.: Edwin Mellen Press, 2008.

Howlett, Charles F., and Glen Zeitzer. *The American Peace Movement: History and Historiography*. Washington, D.C.: American Historical Association, 1985.

Hughan, Jessie Wallace. *Three Decades of War Resistance*. New York: War Resisters League, 1942.

Huntington, Samuel P. *The Soldier and the State: American Civil-Military Relations*. Cambridge, Mass.: Harvard University Press, 1957.

Jones, Mary Hoxie. *Swords into Ploughshares: An Account of the American Friends Service Committee, 1917–1937*. New York: Macmillan, 1937.

Kazin, Michael. *War against War: The American Fight for Peace, 1914–1918*. New York: Simon & Schuster, 2017.

Kennedy, David M. *Over Here: The First World War and American Society*. New York: Oxford University Press, 1980.

Kershner, Seth, and Scott Harding. "Addressing the Militarization of Youth." *Peace Review* 26, no. 2 (2014): 250–257.

Kirk, Robert. *Earning Their Stripes: The Mobilization of American Children in the Second World War*. New York: Peter Lang, 1994.

Klapper, Paul. *The Teaching of History*. New York: D. Appleton, 1926.

Kleidman, Robert. *Organizing for Peace: Neutrality, the Test Ban, and the Freeze*. Syracuse, N.Y.: Syracuse University Press, 1993.

Knight, Louise W. *Citizen: Jane Addams and the Struggle for Democracy*. Chicago: University of Chicago Press, 2005.

Kosek, Joseph Kip. *Acts of Conscience: Christian Nonviolence and Modern American Democracy*. New York: Columbia University Press, 2009.

Lagotte, Brian W. "Children in the Ranks: The Militarization of Educational Policy." PhD diss., University of Wisconsin—Madison, 2012.

Lee, Gus C. *Evaluation of the DoD High School Testing Program*. Alexandria, Va.: Human Resources Research Organization, 1979.

Levine, Daniel. *Jane Addams and the Liberal Tradition*. Madison: Wisconsin Historical Society Press, 1971.

Lewis, Penny. *Hardhats, Hippies, and Hawks: The Vietnam Antiwar Movement as Myth and Memory*. Ithaca, N.Y.: Cornell University Press, 2013.

Lovell, J. P., and P. S. Kronenberg, eds. *New Civil and Military Relations*. New Brunswick, N.J.: Transaction, 1974.

Lutz, Catherine. *Homefront: A Military City and the American Twentieth Century*. Boston: Beacon, 2001.

Lutz, Catherine, and Lesley Bartlett. *Making Soldiers in the Public Schools: An Analysis of the Army JROTC Curriculum*. Philadelphia: American Friends Service Committee, 1995.

Maar, Henry Richard, III. "The Lost Years: The American Peace Movement, From Vietnam to Nuclear Freeze." *Peace & Change* 44, no. 3 (2019): 386–411.

Marchand, C. Roland. *The American Peace Movement and Social Reform. 1898–1918*. Princeton, N.J.: Princeton University Press, 1972.

Mead, Lucia Ames. *Swords into Ploughshares*. New York: G. P. Putnam's Sons, 1912.

Miller, Cheryl. *Underserved: A Case Study of ROTC in New York City*. Washington, D.C.: American Enterprise Institute, 2011.

Mollin, Marian. *Radical Pacifism in Modern America*. Philadelphia: University of Pennsylvania Press, 2006.

Moore, Emma Moore, and Andrew Swick. *Leveraging ROTC to Span the Civil-Military Gap*. Washington, D.C.: Center for a New American Security, 2018.

Moskos, Charles C., and John Whiteclay Chambers II, eds. *The New Conscientious Objection: From Sacred to Secular Resistance*. New York: Oxford University Press, 1993.

Neiburg, Michael S. *Making Citizen Soldiers: ROTC and the Ideology of American Military Service*. Cambridge, Mass.: Harvard University Press, 2000.

Orvis, Bruce, and Beth Asch. *Military Recruiting: Trends, Outlook, and Implications*. Santa Monica, Calif.: RAND, 2001.

Paige, John Charles. "The American University and the Student Peace Movement." Master's thesis, Oklahoma State University, 1973.

Pema, Elda, and Stephen Mehay. "Career Effects of Occupation-Related Vocational Education: Evidence from the Military's Internal Labor Market." *Economics of Education Review* 31, no. 5 (2012): 680–693.

Penn, Alan. *Targeting Schools: Drill, Militarism, and Imperialism*. London: Woburn Press, 1999.

Perez, Gina. *Citizen, Student, Soldier: Latina/o Youth, JROTC, and the American Dream*. New York: NYU Press, 2015.

Peterson, H. C., and Gilbert Fite. *Opponents of War, 1917–1918*. Seattle: University of Washington Press, 1957.

Rodin, Doris G. "Opposition to the Establishment of Military Training in Civil Schools and Colleges in the United States, 1919–1941." Master's thesis, American University, 1959.

Schaffer, Ronald. "The War Department's Defense of ROTC." *Wisconsin Magazine of History* 53, no. 2 (winter 1969–70): 108–120.

Schott, Linda. *Reconstructing Women's Thoughts: The Women's International League for Peace and Freedom before World War II*. Stanford, Calif.: Stanford University Press, 1997.

Schrecker, Ellen. *The Lost Promise: American Universities in the 1960s*. Chicago: University of Chicago Press, 2021.

———. *No Ivory Tower: McCarthyism and the University*. New York: Oxford University Press, 1986.

Smith, Christian. *Resisting Reagan: The U.S. Central America Peace Movement*. Chicago: University of Chicago Press, 2010.

Stomfay-Stitz, Aline M. *Peace Education in America, 1828–1989: Sourcebook for Education and Research*. Metuchen, N.J.: Scarecrow Press, 1993.

Talbert, Roy. *Negative Intelligence: The Army and the American Left, 1917–1941*. Jackson: University Press of Mississippi, 1991.

Thomas, William H. *Unsafe for Democracy: World War I and the U.S. Justice Department's Covert Campaign to Suppress Dissent*. Madison: University of Wisconsin Press, 2009.

Tracy, James. *Direction Action: Radical Pacifism from the Union Eight to the Chicago Seven*. Chicago: University of Chicago Press, 1996.

U.S. Army Recruiting Command. *Recruiter Handbook*. USAREC Manual no. 3-01. Fort Knox, Ky.: USAREC, 2011.

Wallis, Jill. *Valiant for Peace: A History of the Fellowship of Reconciliation, 1914–1989*. London: Fellowship of Reconciliation, 1991.

Wechsler, James A. *Revolt on the Campus*. New York: Macmillan, 1935.

Wells, Tom. *The War Within: America's Battle over Vietnam*. Berkeley: University of California Press, 1994.

Wittner, Lawrence. *Rebels against War: The American Peace Movement, 1933–1983*. Philadelphia: Temple University Press, 1984.

———. *Toward Nuclear Abolition: A History of the World Nuclear Disarmament Movement, 1971–Present*. Vol. 3. Stanford, Calif.: Stanford University Press, 2003.

Zaroulis, Nancy, and Gerald Sullivan. *Who Spoke Up? American Protest against the War in Vietnam, 1963–1975*. New York: Holt, Rinehart, & Winston, 1984.

Zeigler, Valerie H. *The Advocates of Peace in Antebellum America*. Bloomington: Indiana University Press, 1992.

Zwartz, Henry A. "An Empirical Analysis of the Navy Junior Reserve Officer Training Corps." Master's thesis, Naval Postgraduate School, 1987.

INDEX